WHAT IS A BOOK?

JOSEPH A. DANE

What Is a Book?

• • •

The Study of Early Printed Books

University of Notre Dame Press

Notre Dame, Indiana

Library of Congress Cataloging-in-Publication Data

Dane, Joseph A.
  What is a book? : the study of early printed books / Joseph A. Dane.
       pages   cm
  Includes bibliographical references and index.
  ISBN-13: 978-0-268-02609-7 (pbk.)
  ISBN-10: 0-268-02609-2 (pbk.)
  1. Bibliography—Methodology.   2. Incunabula—Bibliography—
Methodology.   3. Early printed books—Bibliography—Methodology.
4. English literature—Bibliography—Methodology.   5. Bibliography, Critical.
6. Editions.   7. Books—History—1450–1600.   8. Books—History—17th
century.   9. Books—History—18th century.   10. Printing—History.   I. Title.
  Z1001.D227   2012
  002.09—dc23
                              2012001191

∞ *The paper in this book meets the guidelines for permanence and durability of
the Committee on Production Guidelines for Book Longevity of the Council
on Library Resources.*

To Sid

CONTENTS

· · ·

PART I
ELEMENTS OF MATERIAL BOOKS

PART II
HISTORY OF BOOKS AND HISTORIES OF
BOOK-COPIES

ABBREVIATIONS

· · ·

BMC British Museum Catalogue. *Catalogue of Books Printed in the XVth Century Now in the British Museum,* 13 vols. (1908; London: British Museum, 1963–).

BSB-Ink *Bayerische Staatsbibliothek Inkunabelkatalog,* 7 vols. (Wiesbaden: Ludwig Reichert Verlag, 1988–), http://www.bsb-muenchen.de/inkunabeln.181.0.html.

CIBN Bibliothèque Nationale, *Catalogue des Incunables,* 2 vols. (Paris: Bibliothèque Nationale, 1981–2006).

ECCO Eighteenth Century Collections Online, infotrac.galegroup .com (db = ECCO).

EEBO Early English Books Online, eebo.chadwyck.com.

ESTC English Short Title Catalogue, 1473–1800 (London, British Library), estc.bl.uk.

Goff Frederick R. Goff, *Incunabula in American Libraries: A Third Census of Fifteenth-Century Books Recorded in North American Collections* (New York: Bibliographical Society of America, 1964).

GW *Gesamtkatalog der Wiegendrucke,* 10 vols. (Stuttgart: Hiersemann, 1928–), http://www.gesamtkatalogderwiegendrucke.de/.

Hain Ludwig Hain, *Repertorium Bibliographicum,* 4 vols. (Stuttgart: Cotta, 1826–38).

HEHL Henry E. Huntington Library, San Marino, California.

ISTC Incunabula Short Title Catalogue, www.bl.uk/catalogues/istc/.

STC A. W. Pollard and G. R. Redgrave, *A Short-Title Catalogue of Books Printed in England, Scotland, and Ireland, and of English Books Printed Abroad, 1475–1640* (1926); 2nd ed. 3 vols., revised and enlarged by W. A. Jackson, F. S. Ferguson, and Katharine F. Pantzer (London: Bibliographical Society, 1976–91).

VGT   *Veröffentlichungen der Gesellschaft für Typenkunde des XV. Jahr-hunderts,* 32 vols. (Halle: 1907–39).

Wing   Donald Wing, *A Short Title Catalogue of Books Printed in En-gland, Scotland, Ireland, Wales, and British America and of English Books Printed in Other Countries, 1641–1700,* 3 vols. (1945–51); 2nd ed. 4 vols. (New York: Modern Language Association, 1972–98).

ILLUSTRATIONS

* * *

Unattributed photos are from personal copies.

ACKNOWLEDGMENTS

• • •

This book took a lot longer than it should have, but I'm generally grateful for those things that still do. There are a number of people who deserve my thanks: these include Percival Everett, Chris Freeman, Alice Gambrell, Alexandra Gillespie, the Greens, Barbara Hanrahan, Kermit Hummel, John Ladley, Katie Lehman, Paul Needham, Michael Peterson and Michaeline Mulvey, Sandra Prior, Sandra Stover, the staffs of the Huntington Library, the William Andrews Clark Library, the Library of Congress, Doheny Library of the University of Southern California, and Bowdoin College Library. Others are there when you need them most, and I thank especially Linda Carpenter, Sidney Evans, Paulina Kewes, Seth Lerer, Laura Scavuzzo-Wheeler, and Scott Staples. It is difficult to imagine how life could have been without them. Finally, what I owe to Jaenet Guggenheim, can, since April 5, 2011, never be expressed or known.

FIGURE I.1. Shakespeare editions. Photo courtesy of the William Andrews Clark Memorial Library, University of California, Los Angeles.

Introduction

Lear: Do's any heere know me?
This is not *Lear:*
Do's *Lear* walke thus? Speake thus? Where are his eies?
Either his Notion weakens, his Discernings
Are Lethargied. Ha! Waking? 'Tis not so?
Who is it that can tell me who I am?

Lear's words seem prescient. Who is Lear among those Lears shown in figure I.1? There are video versions on DVD and on tape; paintings; hundreds of text versions with their thousands of notes. When we enter a library, we find the versions that I will be most concerned with below. But limiting the notion of Lear to these books does little to clarify who or what Lear is. There is the Lear of the 1623 First Folio. There is another Lear in the 1608 quarto, who says something quite different from what he says in the Folio passage, quoted above, and even seems to say it in prose, which by a strange convention of modern typesetting I can quote without respecting the line endings of the original:

Lear: Doth any here know mee? why this is not *Lear,* doth *Lear* walke thus? speake thus? where are his eyes, either his notion, weaknes, or his discernings are lethergie, sleeping, or wakeing; ha! sure tis not so, who is it that can tell me who I am?

There are the Lears in the eighteenth-century editions of Alexander Pope, Lewis Theobald, William Warburton, Samuel Johnson, and, more recently, in the editions of Michael Warren. Some of the more recent Lears result from the late twentieth-century view that the very assumption of a single play behind all the various versions entitled *King*

Lear is erroneous; there are actually two plays, or three.[1] Yet this multiplicity of Lears is itself a simplification. It is not quite correct to say that figure I.1 above shows *the* First Folio, or *the* Theobald edition of Lear, or *the* quarto, nor that my quotations come from *the* First Folio or *the* quarto. Rather, what the illustration shows is the copy of the First Folio at the William Andrews Clark Memorial Library in Los Angeles, one that is not quite the same as other copies, my own copy of the second Theobald edition, and facsimile copies of the early quartos; the quotations are taken from an online facsimile of the 1608 quarto at the Huntington Library in San Marino and the Norton facsimile of the First Folio, whose texts may not be identical to that in other copies of the same book.[2] Any of these can be used to read something we loosely describe as *King Lear*, just as any copy of the First Folio can be used to discover things about what we call *the* First Folio of Shakespeare. But the particularity of these objects is very stubborn, and the more we look at the material objects in this photo, the less easy it is to make the comforting, sweeping generalizations that might convince the theatrical Lear that we know, even if he does not, "who he is."

This book is written as an introduction to the kinds of questions these Lears raise: what is a book? what is a book-copy? And who is it that can tell just what these things are? I am thus especially concerned with the language and methods of thinking that make such problems and their solutions possible. What are the methods scholars of books use in studying material books, and what are the implications of these methods on our understanding of what books are and do? My premise is that one does not need to be a specialist in book history, book collecting, or literary scholarship to consider the practical issues posed by physical books, any more than one needs to be a specialist in Elizabethan drama in order to deal intelligently with a play by Shakespeare.

An Introduction to Introductions

My subject here can be defined as the study of material books. My discussion in the following chapters is more closely focused than that, or more eccentrically focused than that, since physical books cannot, I think, be usefully studied in the abstract. The chapters below constitute an introduction to the study of material books as I have experienced them, complete with obsessions and moments of inattention. The conventional field I deal with is books printed during the hand press period, that is, a period in western printing history ending in the early nineteenth century. But I cannot claim to cover that field in the ordinary sense of academic coverage. Most of the examples I discuss come from fields and subfields I know best. These are roughly early English books to 1640 (STC books), eighteenth-century English books related to the reception of English medieval texts, and incunabula (books printed in the fifteenth century). And most of the problems I discuss are those that have caught my attention in the past: press variation, the notion of ideal copy, the peculiarities of facsimile reproduction, the uses and limitations of electronic resources. That this array of examples and even issues does not define a seamless field or corpus of information is something I acknowledge; I do not see how a scholar can or would want to construct a field of study in any other way.

To write a standard introduction to a field is to advance implicitly a set of dubious assumptions, key among them that there are effectively two areas, two levels of competence, two sets of material. The first consists of introductory material: basic knowledge, a set of procedures, terminology, etc. The second is the practical application of such knowledge in the field. You learn what a collation formula is so that you can subsequently use one to describe or catalogue books you find in a library. You learn how to use a database so that you can do your own bibliographical work. The writer of the introduction is assumed to be familiar with all facts and procedures that define or characterize the field.[3]

My objection to this assumption should be implicit in the above sentences. No one has the knowledge of any field in the humanities required to write a comprehensive introduction to that field. Nor will anyone but the most focused of specialists learn introductory material A or introductory procedure B in order to perform professional task C. Rather the reverse: most of us simply perform task C, adopting whatever language and procedures we need in order to make that task interesting. For the most part, we ignore all else. That is how we introduce ourselves to a field. Introductory language is thus bound up with the most abstruse of scholarly problems, and the most complex of problems is inseparable from the most basic terminology: you cannot operate on either of these levels without involving yourself in the other.

The present book is introductory; but it does not shield the introductory student or non-specialist from what bibliographers find the most interesting problems in their field. Many of the examples and issues here are those I have written about elsewhere—cataloguing conventions, early Chaucer folios, fifteenth-century books. I assumed, studying these things, I would be writing for specialists, but I never thought that the things I was interested in were the province of specialists alone. There were many things that made material books interesting to me then and they are still the things that make books interesting to me now.

Bibliography

A technical term used to indicate the field I have outlined here is *bibliography*. The term, however, is not well defined either in a general or in a technical sense; it has ordinary meanings that have little bearing on the field (e.g., "works cited" lists), and even scholars of material books do not agree on what should be included within the technical definition. Bibliography is associated with what is now called *book history*, itself a conglomerate of fields of study and interest. Book collecting, librarianship, printing history, editorial history, literary history and criticism—all, in certain contexts, can be imagined as legitimate parts of bibliography since all are embodied in physical books. Most scholars would consider studies within these fields bibliographical to the extent that they focus primarily on material books rather than on the texts within those books, the distribution of those books, their social impact, or the history of reading practices.

I look at a material book: it is evidence of all kinds of things, all kinds of histories. There are innumerable points of interest and countless polemics in which I could engage. Bibliographers often focus on problems that seem overly scrupulous: the differences in typefaces on a single page, the tipped-in intrusive engraving in an otherwise pristine book, an anomaly in paper structure. Such bibliographical details or facts can be amusing, but they are not necessarily interesting in and of themselves. What interests me is the use and especially the misuse of such detail, how our handling of what we consider facts reveals flaws and rifts in our basic approach to any problem involving evidence. How do we get at the histories and polemics that the details we find suggest, or how have I gotten at them myself? If those who catalogue books for libraries cannot establish conventions for describing two copies of the Gutenberg Bible so that the nature of those two copies can be compared, there is probably something wrong: either with the book or with the assumptions we bring to it. Which is it? If the physical evidence of early printed books does not support some fundamental cultural myth (say, the idea of the rise of humanism), something is wrong there too: is it in the evidence itself? or the way we discuss it?

Physical books constitute evidence, and material evidence is not something that should merely support our grander abstract notions and narratives (Fred is a murderer, and my job as an investigator is to find the evidence to convict him); evidence is something that challenges those narratives (maybe Fred, murderous though he is thought to be, didn't commit this murder; maybe there was no murder at all).

Each physical book provides evidence of some sort, facts of some sort, and presents problems of some kind. It does not matter whether this is a monumental book such as the Gutenberg Bible or a run-of-the-mill book, maybe a late edition of an unread seventeenth-century English play, maybe a book on your local library shelf. If monumental books happen to have received more attention in book history, that is because, well, *they have received more attention in book history.* Most of the information in these books is accessible to anyone. Serious work in the field of book history and bibliography consequently does not require a mastery of technical language, nor does it require a long or even brief apprenticeship under a mentor. The basic method of bibliography is simple and could be summed up as follows: the organization of readily perceived details of material books and a common-sense explanation of anomalies related to them. One of the greatest and most influential of late nineteenth-century bibliographers, Henry Bradshaw, stated that methodology directly: "arrange your facts rigorously and get them plainly before you, and let them speak for themselves, which they will always do."[4]

Whether Bradshaw's facts actually will speak for themselves (and the conventional answer today is that they will not), there is no inscrutable mystery to any of this. And although professional bibliographers and experienced scholars may grumble, first-rate work can be done and is being done by beginning students in the field and by the rankest of amateurs. Certainly, if you examine a thousand books, you ought to be in a better position to examine the thousand-and-first book; what you say about this book ought to be more interesting than what you said about the first book in this series. But there is no guarantee of that, and plenty of evidence to the contrary. What experts in this or any other field tend to say and think becomes more and more predictable as their presumed expertise deepens, and an overly schooled way of perceiving and defining books may obscure as many interesting details of book history as it illuminates. One of the reasons I am writing this present book rather than searching out anomalies in the vaults of rare book libraries is the unnerving feeling I have as I pick up a rare book that I know exactly what I will say about it before I even look at it.

Bibliography and Technical Language

In order to deal with books bibliographically, you must communicate with others who have dealt with those books. And this requires some understanding of the conventional language of book history and bibliography as well as the pitfalls and limiting assumptions of such language. Some of the language is basic: folio, format, flyleaves (I will present that in chapter 1). To learn what such terms mean is both useful and easy. Some is abstruse, and, however precise, its utility is far from clear: for all but students of technology, the names of the individual parts of the hand press are probably not necessary, and though some introductions to bibliography present that language as basic, I will skip over most of it here. In addition, some of the most important and interesting terms are problematic and the meaning of these terms far from settled. Even in an ideal bibliographical world, it is almost impossible to define "typeface," and in the real world, even the best scholars err by describing leaves as pages or by reversing that seeming shibboleth, *cancellandum/cancellans* (the difference between a leaf that has been cancelled and the leaf that replaces it).

Such technical language serves various functions. Technical distinctions can be heuristic, in that they help us discover things that are *there* in the book itself; an anomaly in a collation formula might mark a history of revision or censorship in that text. Others are descriptive and can help us communicate what we find in books to others. It is useless for me to argue about *my* copy of the First Folio of Shakespeare (1623) if you think I am talking about something you should find in *your* copy of the Second Folio (1634).

In certain contexts, such distinctions need to be respected; yet in most discussions of books, many of these distinctions will be tentative and their boundaries porous. Ordinary historical readers evaluate a number of book features (size, shape, page format, color of the type) in a somewhat impressionistic manner; they do not organize their perceptions systematically. Impressions thus are an essential part of book history in a way that they might not be in, say, physics. And if there is a split between technical language and the experience of such untutored readers, either historical ones whom we study or modern ones who study with us, that is due to the inadequacy of technical language to describe the basic reality of such a reader confronting a particular book.

There is thus no absolute canon of technical language used in book history or bibliography; "diverse men they spoke diversely" and different bibliographers and book historians will make use of varying terminology and conventions. Furthermore, the real world is itself imperfect, its features often self-contradictory and its history unknown; it does not conform to and sometimes stubbornly resists even the most careful distinctions defined by our technical terminology. The language I introduce here is only what is required to discuss particular issues and to understand other scholars when they discuss the same things.

Books and Book-Copies

The most basic term used here is *book* and this is also the most difficult. As used here, it will always be limited to its most ordinary senses. As more studies are written about books or "the book," more typographical conventions are used to describe it ("the book," "the Book," "Book," etc.). Thus, in Lucien Febvre and H.-J. Martin's influential, but now quite dated, *The Coming of the Book,* it is nearly impossible to know exactly what the subject matter might be in any paragraph, as "le livre," "des livres," and "Le Livre," permit an often bewildering passage from workmen to typography to European economic history to philosophies of reading. "The Book" is simultaneously a thing, a force, an event, a history.[5]

Exciting as these definitional leaps may be, I am taking a much more narrow definition of what the book is. A *book*, as understood here, is always something that exists in immediate and direct relation to a material *book-copy,* and the distinction between the book and the book-copy is defined here as basic to any study of material books. A *book-copy* is always a material object that exists in time and space and carries with it its own unique history. It is what you are holding as you read this sentence. The word or term *book,* in this context, is a technical term; the word *book* refers to some abstract concept that allows us to speak of a number of book-copies as a unit, as essentially identical. The book known as "The Shakespeare First Folio of 1623" includes all extant two hundred plus copies of that book as well as the hundreds we assume to have vanished. A book in this sense (that is, when contrasted with a book-copy) can be described, but it cannot be held, seen, or sensed. The book-copy you are now reading is unique; but the book you are reading is the same one I am now inscribing to one of my friends.

Some fields of book history deal primarily with the abstraction of the book (for example, the textual history of Shakespeare); other fields within book history deal almost exclusively with book-copies, not books (for example, the study of book ownership, or what is called *provenance*). Descriptions, even casual ones, of a printed book will generally include two types of details: those pertaining to the abstract book of which this particular book is a representative (it has a title page reading "The Works of Shakespeare") and those which are *copy-specific* (this copy has an ownership stamp of a local library). The difference is crucial but not always entirely straightforward. Imagine, for example, a lithograph by Edvard Munch. Conventionally, each copy is a member of a series, and may be numbered. *The* lithograph is thus the totality of this series and may finally refer to the plate used by Munch to produce each individual copy. *The* lithograph is both all of the real lithographs and none of them.

Now most examples in the real world likely include a frame; perhaps all of them do. But an art historian discussing the lithograph or illustrating it in an article would not include the frame; to do so would imply that the topic was not *the* work of art but rather what art historians might call the material support of *this* copy. Even in the case of a unique painting, a similar argument applies. To include a frame within an illustration implies that the topic of discussion is not *the* painting (which exists from its moment of completion until the present) but rather the state of the painting when joined to that frame.

If you were to go further and imagine a group of art collectors who are concerned more with the frames of these prints than with the prints themselves and who occasionally consider the lithograph absolutely inseparable from the frame in which it is found, you would be approaching the ordinary situation we find in book history. Here, the abstract notion (*book*) blurs much more easily into the notion of a particular object (*book-copy*); and the libraries and collectors who control such objects place considerable value on each aspect. Most of us, whether we are scholars, librarians, or even book thieves, find it hard to imagine the book at all apart from its embodiment in book-copies. I should emphasize that there is no moral distinction between those persons concerned with frames and bindings, those concerned with the book or the lithograph plate, and those concerned with the text in the book or Munch's art. Shakespeare's First Folio can provoke useful discussion of Shakespeare's poetry, printing history, and the aesthetics of binding. But considerable confusion can arise when the various groups have to communicate and often mistakenly think they are talking about the same thing.

Books, Book-Copies, Edition

We can create any number of abstract categories of books: folios, books about fish, books bound by Grolier. All are legitimate; but not all are significant from a bibliographical point of view: "books printed by Aldus Manutius" is an interesting bibliographical category, as is "books about medicine"; "books of the great poets" would generally not be of bibliographical interest, although it might well be of cultural or literary interest; "books with the word *the* in the title" is, by contrast, likely to be of interest to no one, although it is certainly as real or legitimate as any of the other categories or series.

The most important of these units or categories for bibliographers and students of printing history is the *edition*. For early printed books, the term *edition* refers to those book-copies produced by a single setting of type at a printing house that were considered by their printers textually and economically interchangeable. Other terms used for this are *print-run* and *impression,* although these terms often refer to the individual sheet or book part. In most cases, when a scholar uses the word *book* in a bibliographical context, this is the unit referred to—the edition. It is the project foreseen and realized by a printer that results in individual book-copies sold and distributed as interchangeable units. To speak of such a book as "the 1602 Chaucer" or "the Gutenberg Bible" in a bibliographical sense is to speak of these interchangeable book-copies, not of the beautifully or pitifully bound book-copy in a rare book room.

A bibliographical edition can include identifiable subgroups: some copies might be printed on vellum, some on paper. But within these subgroups each book-copy is regarded as interchangeable with any other of that subgroup. Copy-specific features (peculiarities of inking? type of binding? owner's marks? missing pages? added pages?)—such things are accidents or contingencies, in some cases accidents of production, in others, accidents of later reception and history.[6]

Printing is distinguished from other methods of textual dissemination such as manuscript production precisely in what is implied by and the contradictions contained within such terms as *repeatable, identical, representative,* or, the term used above, *interchangeable.* Two book-copies of the same book from the same edition (for example, the Huntington Library and the Clark Library copies of the Shakespeare First Folio) are the same in ways that two copies of a text written out by a scribe or transmitted over the internet are not. Considered strictly as books, that is, as members of an edition, these two book-copies are not merely similar; they are identical. At the same time (and this is what makes the practical study of material books particularly interesting) the uniqueness of any physical object cannot be suppressed; in the face of that interchangeability constituted by the historical edition, the uniqueness of individual book-copies of the same book inevitably asserts itself.

The difference between these things—the book and its representative book-copies—can be thought of as a function of the institution of printing. But it is equally valid to consider this difference constituted by the intellectual assumptions of the scholar or observer. Compare figures 6.3 and 6.4 in chapter six with those in my conclusion, figures C.1 and C.2. Figures 6.3 and 6.4 are the work of professionals. Figure 6.4 I ordered from the Huntington Library photo department. I shot figure 6.3 (a page of the 1528 *Regimen sanitatis Salerni*), as I have before, from a professionally produced facsimile in F. S. Isaac's *English and Scottish Printing Types* of 1930.[7] Although figure 6.4 is from a book-copy at the Huntington, and Isaac's facsimile from a copy at the British

Library (I think), stripped of their bindings, the implication is that *any other copy of these editions could have provided the same picture;* Isaac does not even identify the source of his facsimiles. The implication of the figures in my conclusion is different: my figure C.2 is not the title page of the 1602 Chaucer but the title page of *this particular copy,* and this book-copy has a history different from the history of any other book-copy in the edition. Who is this "Henry Mellor" who once owned this book?

In the context of what we call a book, book-copies are essentially the same. When we talk about the *book,* abstract bibliographical considerations take precedence over those of physics: certain real differences (the different molecules that constitute the different leaves) are irrelevant. A scholar thus might legitimately use my figure C.2 to represent not this copy but a unit of the book: "the title page of the entire edition." But as soon as that scholar highlights or otherwise indicates the binding and the ownership marks, things change; the salient features of the 1602 Chaucer shown in my conclusion become copy-specific: they belong to the book-copy and not to the book.

There are many cases where the basic distinction made here will not be made explicit in our language. We can certainly speak of holding a book, even though we know we are really holding a book-copy. And there are doubtless many other expressions in bibliography and book history where the same thing holds: it is pointless to object to the phrase "turn the page" even though bibliographically what we turn is a "leaf." As long as the use of terminology is clear or useful, only the professional bibliographers need worry about whether it is correct.

The Hand Press Period

My emphasis is on early printed books, particularly books printed in English and books of interest to English readers. The conventional cut-off date for histories of this kind is "around 1800." In printing histories, the date marks the end of what is known as the hand press period, although production of books by the hand press continued much longer. An enumerative bibliographer might view this date as the final date included in the ESTC (the English Short Title Catalogue). A cliché that one often reads in book histories is that a printer working in the eighteenth century would feel quite at home if teleported to Caxton's press; and it is perhaps as useful to pretend to believe in this as it is to point out its obvious absurdities.[8]

The first decades of the nineteenth century see the development of lithography, the iron press, and stereotyping, a process that permits the reprinting of identical copies of earlier books without having to store bulky trays of standing type.[9] These technological developments strain the bounds of traditional bibliographical language—language in large part designed to discuss books printed in the sixteenth and seventeenth centuries.

Such technology remains important to early book history, and the 1800 cut-off pertains only to the definition of the basic subject matter. Early printed books and early printed book-copies are enmeshed in the conventions of the modern book trade, nationalistic histories, and the often obscure conventions of bibliographical description and cataloguing developed in the last two centuries. It would be impossible to discuss seventeenth-century editions intelligently without some awareness of the twentieth-century cataloguing conventions that define them; in the twenty-first century, we need to have some basic understanding of electronic media as well. It would be equally naïve to suppose that the fifteenth-century books one studies are pristine and have not been subject to all the sophistications and sophistries of nineteenth- and twentieth-century technologies of copying and forgery.

Organization

I have organized my chapters around familiar issues in bibliography. Part one deals with basic procedures of printing and the basic parts of the physical book—size, paper, type, illustration. Part two deals with what can be imagined as the history of book-copies—cataloguing conventions, provenance, electronic media. Some of the chapters are reasonably straightforward, meaning, they can be understood simply by examining physical books; these include my discussion of the bibliographical language of basic book parts, such as binding, leaves, quires, format. Others are more complex, for example, chapter 11 on ideal copy, the bibliographical notion that is basic to the concepts of book reproduction and distribution, basic also to printing history in general.

I discuss this concept in a later chapter not because it is less essential to printing history than others but rather because it is less easily understood.

Although I have tried to organize these chapters such that they can be read in sequence, it is not always useful to move from simple to complex, to compartmentalize topics, or to hold off discussion of something interesting and difficult because more preliminaries seem required as its logical foundation. I thus bring up material where I feel it should be discussed, and I will occasionally follow the bibliographical implications of that material even though this does not fit some perfectly articulated map of the field. It does not make sense to me to discuss the cataloguing of Donatus fragments in chapter 11, their function as binding strips in chapter 10, and the implications for early literacy somewhere else.

You will thus not need to master any of the information in, say, chapter 5 on typography or even the terminology in chapter 2 to understand my discussion of provenance or my critique of electronic resources in later chapters. A reader who finds nothing of interest in any chapter here should move as quickly as possible to the next one. With one or two exceptions, each chapter contains an application of the language and principles that chapter presents. These are not selected because they are the central problems associated with the topic defined in that chapter but because I have had some special interest in them or experience with them.

There is only one general bibliographical rule or principle I have imagined that I have enough confidence in to pass on. You should examine a physical book under a single assumption, and you do not need any introduction to do this: never leave a library without knowing more than you knew going into it, and never close a book without knowing more than you did before opening it.

• • •

PART ONE

Elements of
Material Books

. . .

CHAPTER ONE

Terminology

I. Basic Terminology

The basic terminology associated with printed books and their physical structure should pose less difficulty than it does. Only for the most complex of bibliographical problems is precise bibliographical language required, and for most cases of book description ordinary language will be sufficient.[1] Readers of the following chapter are thus invited to move on to other chapters of this book as soon as the utility of the distinctions made here is not apparent to them.

There are several basic forms in which those things we call books can be found. A book can exist electronically; it can be written on a scroll, either continuously or in a series of pages, or it can exist as what we now consider a conventional book—a *codex*. It can be handwritten, printed, and may or may not contain a text. Book history, as understood in the West, is the study with primary emphasis on one of these forms: the printed, textual codex. The codex is a book assembled as a series of leaves, generally bound on one side; it is likely the form of the one you are reading now. Constructing a book in this fashion requires particular conventions of printing and folding and an easily intelligible means of guiding a reader through the text. Many of the physical and visual elements of a book are direct functions of these considerations.

A book has material elements, textual ones, formal and structural elements. Yet what we define as a basic element of a book depends on the intellectual context in which we are describing that book; readers of poetry would not analyze the material and visual elements on a page the same way as would a physicist, nor would they define the same elements as the most significant. And not all the elements we might identify in a book are bibliographical or of interest to bibliographers. Because what we call a book is a nexus of various histories and fields, it is impractical to insist on a strict hierarchy of such levels, for example, from material to abstract. How we finally organize the elements we see or define in a book will depend always on what questions we wish to ask of that book.

The illustration of a single page might show one set of elements: type style and size; number and width of columns; running heads; rules; page or folio numbers; catchwords; signatures (fig. 1.1). The illustration of a book opened to its first leaf might reveal another set of elements: board; pastedown; flyleaf; ownership marks; bookplate (fig. 1.2). One way to look at these elements is in relation to the basic distinction between a book (the idealized product of a printing press—the engraving in figure 1.1) and a book-copy (the individual material book and its history—the damage to the title page in figure 1.2).

What distinguishes a printed book from a manuscript is not the mere fact that it is printed but that it is one of a series: the book-copy we hold, while unique, can be thought of as repeatable. To the printer who printed it, it was interchangeable with any other copy produced during that print-run. Thus, we speak of the 1623 *edition* of Shakespeare, by which we mean the products of a particular printing project of Shakespeare in this particular shop (Jaggard's) at this particular time (1623); this is what we mean by the *book,* the idealized, abstract version of any of the various *book-copies* of the 1623 Shakespeare that we might hold and read.

Some of the most important bibliographical elements we will identify on a page are those that will be the same throughout the edition (the running heads, page numbers, signatures); these are elements of the book. Others might be unique to a book-copy (the ownership mark, a badly inked running head or line of text). We should thus be aware of how anything we see in a book relates to other copies of this book or edition or even to copies of other editions: is what we see unique to this book-copy? or is it part of a series? and what series? Even the handwritten ownership mark may be a part of a series, for example, the collection of books owned by that individual owner (see chapter 9 on provenance). In a bibliographical sense, the typography of this page will be

If to be fad is to be wife;
I do moft heartily defpife
Whatever SOCRATES has faid,
Or TULLY writ, or WANLEY read.

Dear DRIFT, to fet our Matters right,
Remove thefe Papers from my Sight;
Burn MAT's DES-CART', and ARISTOTLE:
Here, JONATHAN, Your Mafter's Bottle.

FIGURE 1.1. Matthew Prior, *Poems on Several Occasions* (London, 1718), 381.

in.l.ci.q.C.de dist.pig.

Contractus dolosus stricti iuris nõ põt rescindi p
actionem de dolo glo.in.l.si maior in
ver.põt.C.de dolo.

℩ Lõtractus dolo psonete factus valz glo.z aleg.in.l. elegan
ter de dolo z bal.in.l.multum ut.col.C.si qo altcri vel sibi idem
de dolo tutoris nisi po prcipet sm aleg.ibi.

℩ Lõtractus dolosus valet in pudiciuz dolosi lz impugnari
possit rõne forme. Bal.in.l.transactione in.ij.no.C. de transa.
vide bar.in.l.in cause la.ij.si sian pn.ff.de mino.z.j.c.v.pe.

℩ Lõtractus dolosus vel furtiuus vel cladestinus in pudi
ciũ fisci nõ valz.l.pe.z ibi bal.C.de re.ven.

℩ Lõtractus dolosus est ipso iure nullius
vbi qiq̇ y aleg.ff.de dolo.qõ vez nisi iesus e
.§.si qo colludctcz ibi doc.de act.emp.z bal
cui.z gmo.rei ven.z ideo sm bar.in.d.§.si q
sum agere qtra lesum z petere qp declaret n
Bar.i.l.si quos.C.de decur.lib.z.z aleg.in.
vbi plene glo.doc.z bal.z aleg.in.l.an.l.mrti
pac.z bal.in.l.i.in.ii.col.v.sed bic qro.C.pl
cit valere qtractuz silatum si po altera velit r
sm glo.qp dicit sin.in.l.vnio.ff.de ritu nup.z
.l.elegater z infra ver.dolus d.i.v.v.

℩ Lõtractus dolosus iuramcto firmatus
bibitus a lege.z rũc absolutio nõ reqrit.secun
ver.iuramctuz seruãduz.v.ii.z melius in v.

Contractus

menticulosus q in carcere celebraf.l. q
in carcere.ff.qo me.cau.

℩ Lõtractus in carcere celebratus regulariter nõ valz. d.l. q
i i carcere qõ verũ est cũ eo q ipsuz secit carcerari inuile secus i
uiste sm bart.in.l.q neqz.§.solutũ.ii. de ver.sig.z in.d.l.q in car
cere. Jtc verũ nisi in sui vtilitatc factus sit qp valz sm bal.in ru
bri.C.de re.ven.in ver.itc reqrit qp ule. Jtc veruz nisi Jctus sit
iuitus qp valet sm bal.in tracta.sima.ya.col.z in.l.i.in.i coin.ad
fi.v.reuoco igit in dubiũ.C.si qo alt.testa.pbi.de boc tñ arri.vi
de bar.in.d.l.q in carcere.vbi et dicit qsuetudinc esse qp de carce
re cxtrabat qui vult qtrahere.sed nibil referre cx quo reinetur
sub costodia dũ ctrabit vide ibi ang.z aleg.z p bal.in.l.i.C. de
cõfcf.z L amfr.an.z qn qtra v. sessioncoz.col.de pba.z ang.
in.l.ne no carcerez.v.ij.pz et pdictio.C.de cxac.z trib.lib.z. z
ã.ver.carceracius.v.lruu. Jte nisi fiat ab eo q redimif ab hostt
bus a quo valz facta pmissio in carcere.sm ang.fin.in.l. nemo
carcerc.C.de cxac.tribu.l.z.z aleg.in.d.l.q in carcere.

℩ Lõtractus cũ tyrãno an valeat bal.in ant.decernimus vl.
col.v.venio ad tertiũ de fa.fan.ccc.qp fic.z bar.in tracta.de tyrã
no.vii.q.pn.z.z Jctus d.i.ver.glv.

℩ Lõtractus inter med.cuz z infirmũ nõ vz no.in.l. medicus

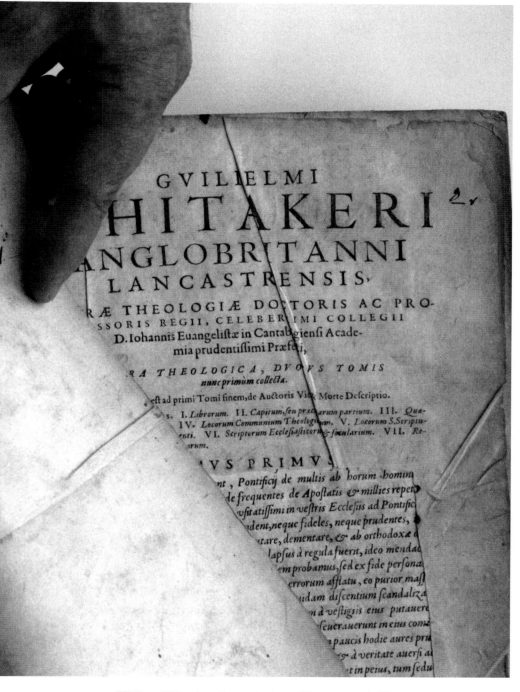

FIGURE I.2. William Whitaker, *Opera theologica* (Geneva, 1610). Photo courtesy of the George J. Mitchell Department of Special Collections & Archives, Bowdoin College Library, Brunswick, Maine.

identical to the typography of the page in any other book-copy from this edition; handwritten corrections and marks of ownership (for example, the ownership marks in fig. C.1 or the bookplate in fig. 1.2 above) are matters of provenance—they are associated with this book-copy, not with the edition.

II. Elements of the Page: Page Format and Typography

The most obvious features of a book are elements related to the text, that is, elements of page format and typography. These include such matters as the size of the text block, number of columns, and type style and size. The illustrated page in figure 1.3 shows a folio in two columns, printed in gothic type. Useful measurements might include the text block: 162 × 272 mm; including the running heads and marginalia gives a measurement of 176 × 284 mm. Another is the measurement for twenty lines of type measured from the bottom of line 1 to the bottom of line 21—here 94 mm (see chapter 6). Margin size might also be noteworthy. Has the book been cut down for binding? Have any annotations been trimmed? Was the book owned, read, and used before being rebound in its present binding?

As we move through the book, we will see a series of other details, and as we look at these, we can see that some are associated with those who wrote the book, others with those who printed it, still others with those who owned the book-copy. Most books have indications of title, author, and printer. In a modern book, this information is on the title page or on the verso of the title page. In an early book, this information is at the end in a *colophon:* "Venitijs in officina Lucę Antonij Iuntę Florentini Anno. M.D.XLVII. Mense Iulio" (fig. 1.4). Title pages are detachable from a book in a way that a colophon printed with the text is not. In those cases where the information on the title page conflicts with what is in the colophon, the colophon takes precedence. The title pages of some early books may have been printed in quantity and thus doubled as advertising flyers, telling viewers where they could buy the book. Many sixteenth-century English books contain the bookseller's address on the title page: "Wyllyam Bonham, dwellynge at the sygne of the kynges armes in Pauls Churchyarde" (Chaucer, *Works*, 1542).

Alas (qd. she) out of this regioun,
I wofull wretch and infortuned wight,
And borne in cursed constellatioun,
More gon, and thus departen fro my knight,
Wo worth alas, that ilke daies light,
On which I saw him first with open twaine,
That causeth me, and I him all this paine.

Therewith the teares from her eyen two
Doune fell, as shoure in Aprill swithe,
Her white breast she bet, and for the wo,
After the death she cried a thousand sithe,
Sens he that wont her wo was for to lithe,
She mote forgone, for which disauenture
She held her selfe a forlost creature.

She saied, how shall he doen and I also,
How should I liue, if that I from him twin,
O dere heart eke that I loue so,
Who shall that sorow slaen, that ye ben in?
O Calcas father, thine be all this sin:
O mother mine, that cleped wert Argiue,
Wo worth that day that thou me bare on liue.

To what fine should I liue & sorowen thus,
How should a fish withouten water dure?
What is Creseide worth from Troilus?
How should a plant or liues creature
Liue withouten his kind noriture,
For which full oft a by word here I sey,
That rootlesse mote greene soone dey.

I shal doen thus, sens neither sword ne dart
Dare I none handle, for the cruelte,
That ilke day that I fro you depart,
If sorow of that nill nat my bane be,
Then shall no meat ne drinke come in me,
Till I my soule out of my brest unsheath,
And thus my seluen woll I doen to death.

And Troilus, my clothes euerychone
Shull blacke ben, in tokening hart swete,
That I am as out of this world agone,
That wont was you to set in quiete,
And of mine ordre aye, till death me mete,
The obseruaunce euer in your absence,
Shall sorow ben, complaint, and abstinence.

Mine hart, and eke the woful ghost therein
Bequeath I with your spirit to complaine
Eternally, for they shall neuer twin.
For though in yearth twinned be we twaine,
Yet in the field of pitie, out of paine,
That hight Elisos, shall ben ifere,
As Orpheus and Eurudice his fere.

Thus heart mine, for Intenior alas
I soone shall be chaunged, as I wene,

But how shull ye doen in this sorowfull caas,
How shall your tender hart this sustene?
But hart mine, forget this sorow and tene,
And me also, for soothly for to sey,
So ye well fare, I rechche not to dey.

How might it euer redde ben or isong
The plaint that she made in her distresse,
I not, but as for me my little tong
If I discriuen would her heauinesse,
It should make her sorow seeme lesse
Than that it was, and childishly deface
Her high complaint, and therfore I it pace.

Pandare, which that sent from Troilus
Was unto Creseide, as ye haue heard deuise,
That for the best it was accorded thus,
And he full glad to doen him that seruise,
Unto Creseide in a full secret wise,
There as she lay in tourment and in rage,
Came her to tell all holly his message.

And fond that she her seluen gan to greete
Full pitously, for with her salt teares,
Her breast and face ibathed was full wete,
Her mightie tresses of her sonnish heares,
Unbroiden, hangen all about her eares,
Which paue him very signe of martire
Of death, which that her hart gan desire.

When she him saw, she gan for sorow anon
Her tearie face atwixt her armes hide,
For which this Pandare is so wo bigon,
That in the hous he might unneth abide,
As he that felt sorow on euery side,
For if Creseide had erst complained sore,
Tho gan she plaine a thousand times more.

And in her aspre plaint, thus she seide:
Pandare first of toies mo than two,
Was cause, causing unto me Creseide,
That now transmued ben in cruell wo,
Whether shall I say to you welcome or no?
That alderfirst me brought unto seruise
Of loue alas, that endeth in such wise.

Endeth then loue in wo? Ye or men lieth,
And all worldly blisse, as thinketh me.
The end of blisse aye sorow it occupieth,
And who troweth not that it so be,
Let him upon me wofull wretch see,
That my selfe hate, and aye my birth curse,
Feeling alway, fro wicke I go to worse.

Who so me seeth, he seeth sorow all atonis,
Paine, tourment, plaint, wo, and distresse,
Out of my woful body harme there none is,
As langour, anguish, cruell bitternesse,

FIGURE 1.3. Geoffrey Chaucer, *Works* (London, 1602), fol. 170.

quia operatio earum eft nobis incognita. Ex hoc fequiſ
ꝙ omnis noſtra cognitio quam habemus de formis ſub
ſtantialibus eſtꝑer operationem,ſiue per alia accidentia
& figuras, & ideo diſcernimus inter hominem mortuũ
& viuum non autem diſcernimus ita bene inter carnem
viuam & mortuam, quia operatio eius non eſt cognita
& figura videtur eſſe eadem:Cuius autem operatio eſt in
cognita illud non cognoſcitur niſi per figurã ſicut anti-
quorum mortuorum corpora quę ſunt redacta in cinere
non cognoſcimus niſi per aliquam figuram.Concludit
igitur ꝙ homiomera.i.corpora quę habēt partes eius ra
tionis cum toto: ſicut caro,neruus,piliː fiunt tanquã ab
agente.ſ.inſtrumentalitːà caliditate & frigiditate per mo
tum factum ab ipſis:tanquam ex materia fiunt ex humi
do & ſicco:& differunt inter ſe ꝑ prædeterminatas paſ-
ſiones.ſ.duritie,mollitie,tractione,comminutione &c.
& ex hac oportet ea cognoſcere quale ſit vnumquodꝗ
ex talibus prędominatis poſtquam forma ſubſtantialis

eſt nobis incognita.Sed corpora diſſimilium partium
vt facies, manus, non differunt per tales qualitates niſi
ratione eorũ ex quibus cõponuntur ſicut fialę vel archę
non eſt cauſa calidum vel frigidum niſi inquantum ſunt
cauſa argēti vel ligni ex quibus talia componuntur.ſed
differunt formis naturalibus exiſtentibus in eis,ſicut ar-
tificialia differunt formis artis:licet materia eorũ vt me-
talla differant paſſionibus iſtis. Deinde epilogat dicens
ꝙ iſto modo cognoſcimus quid ſint homiomera. quia
tunc cognoſcimus aliquid cũ cognoſcimus cauſam na-
turalem eius vel formalem,& melius cum cognoſcimus
vtranꝗ.Maxime autem cognoſcimus aliquid cum cognoſcimus omnes eius cauſas quia perfecta cognitio ha
betur de rebus per omnes cauſas earum. Cum autem co
gnoſcimus homogenea quæ ſunt partes aliorum con-
ſiderandũ erit de alijs vt de animalibus & plantis ouæ
conſtituuntur ex his partibus.

Laus Deo.

REGISTRVM.

✳ ✳✳ a b c d e f g h i k l m

Vnaquęꝗ harum literarum tres reponit
chartas,m excepta quæ duas.

Venetijs in officina Lucę Antonij Iuntę Florentini
Anno.M.D.X L V I I. Menſe Iulio.

FIGURE 1.4. Colophon and register. Thomas Aquinas, *In Meteora Aristotelis
commentaria* (Venice: Giunta, 1547). Photo courtesy of the George J. Mitchell
Department of Special Collections & Archives, Bowdoin College Library,
Brunswick, Maine.

Associated only with the printer of the book are purely visual details such as illustrations and ornaments. Some of these details are integral parts of the printed page (e.g., ornaments, tail and head pieces, borders), that is, they were printed at the same time as the text. Others, such as engravings, involved a different printing process and, in most cases, were *tipped in,* or added to a book after it was printed (see chapter 4).

Eighteenth-century books often are printed with instructions regarding the engravings to be inserted. Occasionally, these additions are unique to individual copies. Laurence Sterne's *Tristram Shandy* calls for a marbled page, and each copy of most early editions includes a piece of marbled paper pasted onto the appropriate leaf. Since marbled paper was handmade in individual sheets, every sheet of marbled paper is visually unique, and so too is every copy of *Tristram Shandy* that employs such paper.

Other details can only be understood within the context of a series of editions. Figure 1.3 from the 1602 Chaucer shows in the margin a number of pointing fists, sometimes called *manicules.*[2] These are the printer's version of highlighting marks made by readers in early printed books and in medieval manuscripts, emphasizing passages they found of importance or interest. In early printing, manicules became conventional; the fists printed on the page in figure 1.3 may be pointing out passages of significance; but they may also be purely ornamental. The first fist in the left column seems to suggest that the line is an autonomous piece of wisdom or sententiae: "How should a fish withouten water dure?" [How can a fish live without water?] The reason for marking the second line in that same stanza is less clear: "That rootless more greene soone dey." The line marked in the second column contains such an egregious printing error that it is almost unintelligible. The earlier editions of Chaucer from which these were copied show instead of these manicules a virtually random series of ornamental marginalia.

III. Binding Elements

For books printed before the nineteenth century, binding elements must be considered as part of individual book-copies, not as part of the book. Until the nineteenth century, most bindings were built by hand onto individual copies of the book; even so-called trade bindings (commercial bindings put on multiple copies of the same book prior to sale) were handmade. In general, a binding of any book that has passed through the book trade is not part of the book itself. In this sense, bindings are comparable to the frames of paintings: structures in which nearly all paintings are found but which are rarely, until the twentieth century, considered part of the paintings they support.

The basic parts of bindings are the board, the cover of the board, and the cords to which the leaves of the book are sewn (see figs. 5.1 and 8.1). Many books include extra leaves between the board and the leaves of the book. A leaf pasted to the board is a *pastedown* (in fig. 1.5, the pastedown has been lifted from the board; see also fig. 1.2 above); a leaf that is not pasted to the board is a *flyleaf* (in fig. 1.5, this is the blank leaf preceding the text). The endleaves of any book are thus of two kinds: those that are part of the edition and included in what is sometimes called the *book block* (i.e., leaves of the book proper, which may include blanks) and those added in the process of binding. Strictly speaking, only the additional leaves can be called *endleaves* or *endpapers,* since a blank leaf that is part of the print-run is not an endpaper but rather "leaf x" of the book. The origin of endpapers is often worth noting: are they from the original printer? the owner? or the bindery? Since they often come from earlier books or manuscripts, the nature of that source is often worth investigating even if it has no apparent relation to the book in which it appears (see chapter 10).

Ownership and Provenance

Marks of ownership and provenance can occur anywhere within the book, but the most important marks are either on or implied by the binding, or else on the initial leaves of the book. An ownership mark that appears on the endpapers must have been added during or after the current binding was put on the book (the binding date provides what is called a *terminus post quem*—a "limit after which" the owner signed the book); an ownership mark on the printed pages of the book has as a *terminus post quem* the printing date. These marks may be a simple owner's signature; there may be dates, indications of prices, even shelfmarks of libraries. There may be a series of owners, with some names erased. Owners may have provided printed bookplates. A bookplate and li-

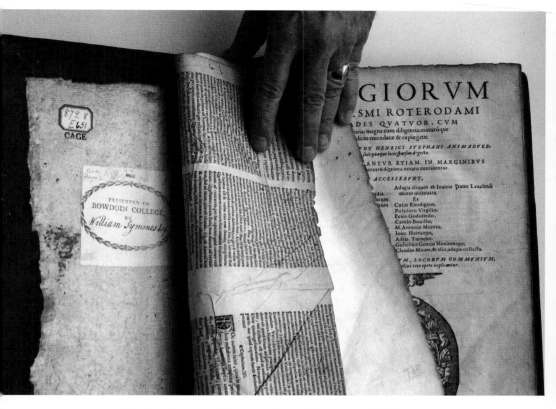

FIGURE 1.5. Binding elements. Erasmus, *Adagia* (Geneva, 1612). Photo courtesy of the George J. Mitchell Department of Special Collections & Archives, Bowdoin College Library, Brunswick, Maine.

brary shelfmark are shown in figure 1.2; ownership names can be seen in various examples here (see figs. C.1 and C.2 in the conclusion).

IV. Book Structure

For bibliographers, the most important elements are those that pertain to book structure, that is, how the book is put together. A codex consists of a number of leaves. A *leaf* has two surfaces and each of these surfaces is called a *page.* A leaf therefore has two pages, which are identified as *recto,* the side that appears on the right when a book is opened, and (oddly) *verso,* the reverse side of that page, or the page that appears on the left when a book is opened. The leaves of a book are formed of a larger *sheet* of paper. For basic types of books, these full-size sheets from the papermaker are folded in predictable ways to produce the variously sized leaves of different books. All the leaves produced by the folding of a single sheet of paper and bound as a unit are considered *conjugates*, that is, the leaf is physically conjoined with other leaves of the same original sheet.

Paper is manufactured in large sheets of standard sizes. If the initial sheet of paper is folded once to form two leaves, the book that results is a *folio.* In many bibliographical studies, especially those of the nineteenth century, the word *bifolium* is used to describe the sheet so folded as to produce two leaves. If the sheet is folded twice, the book will be a *quarto:* each sheet will be folded so as to produce four leaves. If it is folded again, the book is an *octavo:* each sheet will be folded so as to produce eight leaves. *Format* is the technical term used to describe these various foldings.[3] Figure 1.6 illustrates the relation of these basic sizes when books are put together from sheets of the same size. More complex foldings exist, but for most purposes, these are sufficient, and even in the book trade, the term *duodecimo* is used indifferently to refer to any book smaller than an octavo.[4] Note that the actual size of a book is not only a function of folding but also of the size of the initial sheet. Thus, a fifteenth-century folio is often smaller than an eighteenth-century quarto, since the initial sheets of paper used for such books were often smaller than those used in the eighteenth century.

Complicating this matter are cases where the printer begins not with full sheets but with half sheets cut from full sheets. A printer could then fold these half sheets once and produce a book of what structurally are folio quires. This is a common type of fifteenth-century book. Some bibliographers refer to such books as quartos, since each leaf is one quarter of a full sheet of paper, although others might describe them just as accurately as folios in half sheets.[5]

The shape of a conventionally folded book is a function of the shape of the original sheet. The standard shape of paper used in book making has resulted in different shapes for different book formats. For example, folios are the same shape as octavos. Quartos are more square and duplicate the shape of the initial sheet (see fig. 1.6 above). Mathematically, there is one shape of paper that will produce folios,

ETEORA
NTARIA

s solertissime lector Aristo-
duplici interpretatione,
expositore diuo Tho-
commentaria nunc
dhuc illustriora
eunt.

issime castigato.

FIGURE 1.6. Three format sizes. Photo courtesy of the George J. Mitchell Department of Special Collections & Archives, Bowdoin College Library, Brunswick, Maine.

quartos, and octavos of exactly the same shape: A4 paper, or paper of the shape $1 \times \sqrt{2}$. Although this principle was known as early as the fifteenth century, neither printers nor papermakers have followed it.

A book that has been much trimmed from this original shape in order to be bound or rebound is less desirable to a collector than one that has not had the margins trimmed. A book with little trimming is called *uncut*, although this term is often misused and misunderstood; less ambiguously, such a book could be called *untrimmed*. A book that has not even had the folds of sheets cut so that the leaves can be turned individually is *unopened*. The easiest way to determine whether a book has been trimmed is to compare it with other copies of the same book. Alternatively, one can examine the paper to determine whether it bears all the qualities of a complete sheet, including the deckled edge (see chapter 2).

Quire Structure and Printed Indications of Structure

The printed marks on a page relating to book structure are several: page or folio number, catchwords, quire marks. All refer to the way the sheet was folded and the way the folded sheets were put together.

Early books can be *paginated* (numbered by the page) or more commonly *foliated* (numbered by the leaf), and such numbering can be in roman or arabic. Until the eighteenth century, both pagination and foliation were inconsistently and often inaccurately used: numbers were not strictly sequential, and printers were not scrupulous about their accuracy. Thus, to refer to a page or leaf of an early book can be ambiguous: "page 231" might well precede "page 70"; there might be two leaves marked "folio 85." Bibliographers thus refer to specific locations within a book in terms of physical book structure.

Each book is constructed as a series of *quires,* or *gatherings* (the terms are synonymous). For a folio, a gathering might consist of one sheet or as many as five sheets (rarely more), all folded together; each quire thus has between two and ten leaves (= four to twenty pages). The most common quire size for folios is three to five sheets. Phrases such as "folio in 6s," "folio in 8s" mean "folio in six leaves per quire," "folio in eight leaves per quire." The early Latinate phrases are "quaternion" (a quire of four bifolia, or eight leaves), "quinternion" (a quire of five

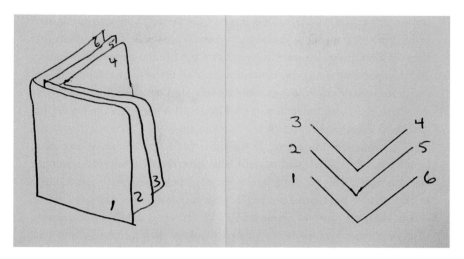

FIGURE 1.7. Folio in 6s.

bifolia, or ten leaves). In a structure of a folio in 6s, leaf 1 is conjugate with leaf 6, leaf 2 with leaf 5, leaf 3 with leaf 4 (fig. 1.7). A folio in 10s would be a folio whose gatherings contained five sheets, that is, ten folios or leaves, and twenty pages. Leaf 1 of each quire would be conjugate with leaf 10; leaf 2 with leaf 9 and so on. Books, especially those in folio, are often constructed of quires of inconsistent size: gatherings alternating 8s and 6s for example, or, at the end of the book, gatherings of whatever size is necessary to accommodate the final section of text.

Each leaf has a real or implied *signature,* or *quire mark,* identifying the quire and the position of the leaf within that quire. In fifteenth-century printed books, these are not always printed, although in books of the sixteenth and seventeenth centuries, they nearly always are. Signatures function as guides for whoever might handle the book prior to binding; this could be a worker at press, a bookseller, initial owner, or binder. Each sheet needs to be identified as to where it fits in the book, but not every leaf of each sheet needs to be identified. The mark A1 means "quire A, sheet 1"; A2 means "quire A, sheet 2." Printers print as many signatures on each sheet as will make the placement of that sheet unambiguous. In a folio quire in 6s, the outer two sheets need only one signature mark. The interior sheet will generally have two signatures (A3 and A4) to let the binder know this is the innermost sheet of that quire; without the mark A4, the binder would have no way of knowing how many sheets were intended to be in that quire. Thus, the first quire of a folio in 10s would likely be marked as follows: A1 A2 A3 A4 A5 | A6, with four unmarked leaves following (the leaves conjugate with A4, A3, A2, and A1).

The most common type of quarto is bound as one sheet per quire (= four leaves); these quartos generally have three signature marks per sheet, and a reader flipping through such a book will find: A1, A2, A3, blank, B1, B2, B3, blank, etc. If all quartos consisted of quires of single sheets, only the first of these signs (A1, B1, etc.) would be necessary, since a quick experiment with a folded sheet of paper will show that there is no way of misfolding a sheet correctly signed "A1." But quartos can also consist of quires of two sheets (= eight leaves); binders seeing signature marks A1, A2, and A3 on a single sheet thus know that they are dealing with a conventional quarto in single-sheet quires.

Early Italian printers generally included a guide to such structure on the last page or pages of a book, called a *register.* Sometimes the register contains a list of quires or a statement (figure 1.4 above lists the signature for each quire followed by: "Each one of these quires has three bifolia [= six leaves] except for m which has two"), and sometimes it includes a systematic table listing the initial words of each sheet in each quire. Nearly any early Italian book will provide an example.

Formulae of Collation

The way the printed sheets of a book are folded and put together is called its *collation;* bibliographers in turn have a number of conventions for describing a book's collation, called *collation formulae.*[6] The rules for writing such formulae can be extremely complex, but the formulae themselves are generally far easier to interpret than to construct:

fol. A^6 B^6 C^6 . . . P^6 = a book constructed in folio, with quires of six leaves signed A–P.

$4°$ $(A–S)^4$ = a book constructed in quarto, with quires of four leaves signed A–S.

Quires are generally lettered, skipping certain letters (*j* and *v* were re-garded until the eighteenth century as the same letters as *i* and *u* respec-tively; *w* is not generally used). Bibliographers nearly always use arabic when referring to the numbering within a quire, although printers might use roman or arabic for this purpose. If there are more quires than letters in the alphabet, printers generally repeat the alphabetic se-quence with doubled letters. Printers might use uppercase letters for this second sequence, AA, BB, CC, or uppercase and lowercase, Aa, Bb, Cc . . . (see fig. 1.1, indicating E1 of the fifth alphabetical sequence of quires). Sometimes printers use common abbreviation symbols (par-ticularly -*rum*) to extend the alphabet.

There are various ways of noting the collation details: *inferred* sig-natures (those quires not marked with a printer's mark or whose signa-tures have been trimmed) are often put in brackets in collation formulae, although not all libraries and bibliographers follow this logical conven-tion. Printers frequently printed the main text before the preliminaries, which might include a title page, table of contents, even an introduc-tion. The text block of these books will start with a new quire, usually signed A1 or B1. Early books whose main text begins in mid-quire are very likely to be page-for-page reprints of other printed books.

Printers use various nonalphabetical signs for preliminaries, but bibliographers will generally indicate them with the Greek letter π, re-gardless of the signature mark used by the printer.[7] The second or third alphabetical series of quires can also be indicated in various ways: some bibliographers repeat exactly what the printer uses (Aa or AA, etc.; see example in fig. 1.1 above); more commonly, they adopt the convention that was rarely if ever used in historical printing: a bibliographer's 2A, 2B, etc. refer to any second signature set the printer might have marked as Aa or AA, Bb or BB (the quire in figure 1.1 would be identified as 5E). Thus (A–Z)⁴ 2(A–D)⁴ would mean a book in quires of four leaves consisting of twenty-eight quires (A, B, C . . . Z, Aa, Bb, Cc, Dd).

Since page and folio numbers can be unreliable in early books, scholars often refer to passages in a book by its signature marks. To refer to particular lines of a book, one might write, say, A8v, meaning the verso of the eighth leaf of quire A. Only apparently more complex is, say, 3A9v.8, meaning "the signature Aaa, that is, the first quire of the third series of alphabetical quires, leaf 9 verso, line 8." Other scholars might identify the same line as AAA9v.8. For books printed in two columns, some scholars indicate the column by a or b, resulting in such seemingly Byzantine references as, say, 3B7v.b.13. In figure 1.1, the quire is 5E, the leaf is 5E1 (it is the first leaf of the quire), and the page is 5E1r; in figure 1.3, the page would be identified as 2G2r.

Modern rules for book description have replaced this type of collation formulae with a statement concerning the sequence of leaves or sequence of pages. These are easier to interpret but give no indication of the quire structure of the book. Here, for example, is the Huntington Library collation for Shakespeare's First Folio:

> [18], 303, [1], 46, 49–100, [2], 69–232, [2], 79–80, [26], 98, [2], 109–156, 257–993 [i.e. 399], [1], p. (fol.)

The meaning of this formula is more straightforward than it appears: the arabic numbers refer to pages ("p."). (Roman numerals in a collation formula conventionally refer to leaves.) I begin from the left: "There are 18 unnumbered pages, followed by 303 pages numbered in sequence; that is followed by one unnumbered page, and a page numbered 46. There follows a sequence of coherently paginated pages numbered 49–100, then two unnumbered pages. That is followed by a sequence of pages numbered 69–232 . . . ; there is a sequence numbered 257–399, but the last page is incorrectly numbered 993; the last page is followed by a blank page. The whole book is in folio. Many formulae also provide the actual number of leaves or pages in the book. I think that such information is contained in the above formula, but it is not easy to extract.

Catchwords

Another printed indication of book structure is the *catchword*, shown above in figures 1.1 ("SOLO") and 1.3 ("Annoy,"). Like foliation and signatures, catchwords originated in medieval manuscripts, where they functioned not for the reader but for the binder or the person who constructed the physical manuscript. In many manuscripts, each quire has a single catchword at the bottom right of the last page, indicating the word that begins the following quire. The manuscript book would have been put together according to these catchwords, or, at least, the catchwords would have provided a way of proofreading the final structure.

In a book with systematic and intelligible signature marks, such catchwords are superfluous. Thus, in early books, they seem almost ornamental and appear erratically. They might be located at the end of a quire or at the end of a folio. In the early sixteenth century, catchwords often compete with what are conventionally called *catchtitles,* that is, abbreviated titles in the lower margin that appear either once per quire or on each initial folio of a bifolium. These occur regularly in certain book genres (e.g., in yearbooks and, in particular, Latin grammars by Whittinton). Catchtitles are still found in modern German books (the German term for them is *Normen*).

In eighteenth-century English books, catchwords become conventional; the English printer Jacob Tonson includes a catchword on each printed page. The easiest interpretation is that the catchword becomes an aid to the reader, or simply a printing banality readers expected to see. But this may not be correct. In a popular book of the late eighteenth century, Thomas Warton's three-volume *History of English Poetry* (1774–81), a typical page consists of text, quoted material, and notes, often themselves full of quoted material (see fig. 5.3). The catchword usually belongs to the main text; when a footnote runs over to the next page, however, the catchword belongs to the run-over footnote, and there is no catchword for the text. I suppose a contemporary reader might have been cheered by this somehow. But it took me the better part of an hour to determine the conventions governing the catchwords in this book, and it is hard to see how casual readers would make use of them. It is more likely they served as aids to the typesetters who constructed these pages.

Unsigned, Unfoliated Books

Most books printed from the sixteenth to eighteenth centuries are easily described by the above conventions of book structure, but fifteenth-century books, created before these printing conventions became settled, sometimes pose problems. Many books printed in the fifteenth century have no signature marks at all; this suggests that these books were folded and collated very carefully at the printing shop rather than delivered as loose sheets to a binder. Some bibliographers refer to the structure of these books without noting whether signatures are printed or inferred. Libraries, furthermore, have their own cataloguing conventions for describing such books, and for books without printed signatures, it is sometimes impossible to cite a page or leaf in such a way as to ensure that someone with access to a copy in another library can find that page. The most notorious example of this problem in early printed books is the Gutenberg Bible; the collation formulae used even in standard catalogues are so various that one cannot confidently locate a page referred to through one collation formula in any other copy. For books bound too tightly to reveal quire structure, only a careful study of paper can reveal the patterns of conjugacy that demonstrate the original book structure. Blessedly, for nearly all fifteenth-century books, the determination of quire structure has already been done by owners and their librarians.

Conclusion

The book elements described in this chapter could be arranged in a number of schemes and hierarchies, but defining such things presupposes what is important about any individual book and about books in general. And what is important about any book or book-copy depends entirely on the interests of the person examining it.

As a Chaucerian, I might construct a hierarchy beginning with material elements (paper), moving on to elements of visual format, then to matters of book construction (quire structure) and its relation to the organization of the text; I might finally consider textual features that show how that printed text relates to Chaucer's text. How do the economics of paper and printing contribute to the organization of the text? and how does all this, in turn, help us to understand the way Chaucer might have been received and understood during, say, the seventeenth century? How does the institution of printing determine our own modern view of Chaucer?

But this is purely a reflection of my own Chaucerian interests, and I might be interested in entirely different questions. What are the trade routes for paper? How does a major printing project deploy its materials? I might in this case place at the summit of my concerns the chain and wire lines of the paper, which would determine stocks of paper. Is there any difference between the paper stocks used in this book project and in other book projects by the same printer? and did the printer buy large uniform stocks of paper to be used for projects involving folio editions of major authors? In this case, authorial matters are merely a preliminary concern; they are of interest only in determining how much paper a printer might have foreseen necessary for a particular printing project.

Anyone who looks at a book will bring different concerns, and many of these depend on circumstances that have little to do with the book immediately at hand. If I am studying my copy of the 1602 Chaucer, I would consider immediately the crassly practical question of availability and accessibility of evidence. Do I have multiple copies of this edition available to me? Or am I better equipped with copies of other Chaucer editions? Do I have large resources of seventeenth-century English printed books? Am I interested in Chaucer? his editors? those who owned Chaucer? or those who read Chaucer? And, as I finally discovered with this very book-copy, will any of my decisions prove to be the right ones?

· · ·

CHAPTER TWO

The Matter of Size

The most readily perceivable piece of evidence about a book-copy and paradoxically the first thing eliminated in an electronic copy of that book or any edition of its text is its sheer mass. This mass is a direct function of two factors: the size of the paper and the number of leaves or sheets used in the book. The impact of size on a reader is immediate and requires no bibliographical expertise to judge. Size is a factor in all aspects of book production and reception: it indicates the cost of producing and distributing a title; it affects the way books are and can be read; and it also affects the way books are collected. The size of books in some cases defines for us the material basis of what we consider book history to be.

Size and Production

The cost of printing a book is generally considered a direct reflection of the cost of the materials to produce it. Most estimates of production costs of early books suggest that paper alone accounts for at least a third of the total expense of any unbound book.[1] The more efficient the production the greater a percentage of the production costs are in materials. In a letter to Pope Sixtus IV, included as a preface to a 1470 edition of Jerome, Giovanni Andrea Bussi claims that printing makes it possible for even a poor student to buy books, since the contemporary printed book costs little more than the price of the blank paper or parchment used in earlier manuscripts. But a corollary of this enthusiastic observation is that material costs became more significant in printing than they had been in early manuscript production.[2] That is, material costs constituted a greater percentage of the total cost of the book.

Given the high material costs, early book publishers could not afford to produce more books than they expected to sell. Printing excess copies meant more than simply tying up investment; it also meant taking on the warehousing costs that would otherwise be borne by paper manufacturers—costs for which there would be no compensation. Large, expensive editions could not have been expected to sell quickly: evidence from the final dissolution of Koberger's firm in 1509 shows that of the German and Latin copies of the massive *Nuremberg Chronicle* the firm printed in 1493, some 517 remained unsold and housed in various distribution points, including 236 copies in Milan and 111 in Breslau.[3] The sheer size of books would have intensified all these production difficulties: large books require more raw materials than small ones; they require more space to warehouse; they are more expensive to transport.[4]

Size and Reading

Early printers were capable of producing books in various sizes or formats, and the difference between a folio format and a smaller format often involves the purpose and function of a book. A large folio cannot be easily moved: it is something to be consulted in a specific location. If it is read, it cannot be read casually. It must be studied, and special equipment such as a lectern or table is sometimes necessary. A smaller book, by contrast, is portable; and many, but not all, are utilitarian. Examples include grammar books. Such books are small; they are generally quartos. Some, like the Donatus *Ars Minor*, contain nothing but paradigms of Latin verbs and nouns. They are thus not intended to be read in any ordinary sense: they are intended to be used in reading something else. Grammar books were a staple of early printing, and most copies were, as book historians often claim, "read to death" (see further chapter 10).

Liturgical books provide a good example of the various functions of different book sizes (see fig. 2.1).[5] The antiphonal is designed for a choir; a missal is read by a priest while standing at an altar. Both need

FIGURE 2.1. Antiphonal; missal; book of hours. Photo courtesy of the George J. Mitchell Department of Special Collections & Archives, Bowdoin College Library, Brunswick, Maine.

to be large enough to be read at a distance. A breviary (not shown in the illustration) is a reference book and can be printed in any convenient size or format. The smaller book of hours is a private book of prayers designed for portability.

The conclusions one would draw from the relation of size to function can quickly be supported by other material and visual elements: Is the book ornamented or does it contain only text? What material is it printed on, vellum or paper? If vellum, does it seem that the vellum is chosen for durability? or luxury?

For secular books, size might be a matter of pure luxury. In the case of liturgical books, size is a matter of function, not economics, and size can be mapped directly onto genre. But no general rule can be applied to books of all genres. One of the largest books found in libraries today is Audubon's 1827–38 *Birds of America* (a "double elephant folio"); this is a work of art, and in the library where I have easiest access to it, it is available for viewing only in a glass case. It stands in sharp contrast to several miniature books found in the same library, for example, Hawthorne's "David Swan: A Fantasy," produced by Tamazunchale Press in 1984, a book only two inches high (the Audubon is over thirty-nine inches high). Yet these books, somewhat oddly, are in the same genre. No one reads or uses them: both are primarily objects of display.

Secular Books in Multiple Format

The same title can of course be published in different forms. The "large paper" six-volume folio edition of Pope's *Iliad* of 1715–20 dwarfs the duodecimo edition, also in six volumes, printed by Lintot in 1720–21. The nearly unmanageable folio volume could hardly have been used for ordinary reading. It is a display volume, a monumental testament to the monumental nature of the text and authors involved (Homer and Pope).[6] For Shakespeare, all Complete Works editions of the seventeenth century were produced in folio; in the eighteenth century, smaller, multivolume editions of Shakespeare's complete works are common, with editions produced by many of the major men-of-letters: Pope, Rowe, Theobald, Warburton, and Johnson. All of these are quarto or octavo. Chaucer editions go through a similar process. All Chaucer Complete Works from 1532–1687 are in folio, as is the edition of 1721, the first printed in roman type. The earliest printed version of Dryden's translations of Chaucer is also in folio (*Fables*, 1700). But the many editions, translations, and modernizations that follow in the eighteenth century are all in quarto or octavo.

Anything we can say about the reception of Chaucer, that is, how he was read and evaluated historically, needs to be discussed in terms of these physical changes, even if the conclusions we draw may be contestable. Do we say that the shift in sizes is a function of reading habits? or an indication that Chaucer is now being read as a classic rather than simply being displayed on the shelves as one? Has Chaucer become a standard author? one appropriate for multi-volume collections such as Bell's *Poets of Great Britain?* Has the class of readers who either read or simply displayed their Chaucer been extended to include ordinary readers, that is, those who could afford to buy and house small books but not large ones?[7]

Size and Survival

The way size affects production and use of books can be imagined by anyone who thinks about these books. Somewhat less obvious is the way this sheer mass of particular books has affected the definition of what we think historical books are. Book evidence is always mediated, even if that evidence is actual material books rather than catalogues and scholarly discussions of these books.

The "raw evidence" of early books is now housed on library shelves, where physical space is limited. Large books require more of this limited and consequently expensive space, a fact that makes them both more visible than other books and paradoxically less accessible. The Huntington Library in San Marino, California, owns a number of enormous Italian legal books printed in the fifteenth century: some are classified "LF" (= large folio, as opposed to an ordinary folio, classified as F); the largest of these are classified by the Huntington as "F3." These books were a common product of fifteenth-century Italian presses. They were never much valued by early book collectors and most remain in their original bindings since they were not considered worth the cost of rebinding. Size, in this case, is (or was) inversely related to value.

In the British Library, there are relatively few of these large Italian legal books compared to the numbers produced, and size is one of the reasons for this.[8] Its collection of incunables was amassed in the nineteenth century, and many were bought from the large stocks of books that came available with the closing of monasteries in Germany, also the source for nearly half the incunables now at the Huntington.[9] When the British Library (known then as the British Museum) was buying books, those not directly related to classical or vernacular literature or to the early history of printing were considered run-of-the-mill. Such books in the nineteenth century were quite cheap, so much so that transporting them became a significant percentage of their overall cost. It made more economic sense at the time to import ordinary folios (thus saving on these transportation costs) than large oversized folios from Italy. By contrast, when the Huntington began building its collection in the early twentieth century, the price of incunables had risen considerably, enough so that transportation costs were a negligible percentage of total costs: a book costing several thousand dollars can be moved cheaply in terms of its value; a book costing one hundred dollars cannot. The Huntington bought what was available, regardless of size, and if you study early books at the Huntington, the large Italian legal books ought to constitute a large percentage of what you see.

But they don't. Size, which has little bearing on what the Huntington bought, turns out to be a major factor in what you can actually study.

At the Huntington, you can call ordinary folios from the shelves with great efficiency. You can compare them, study them, check for variants. But if you decide to study early editions of Gratian, in LF or F3, you will soon hit a wall. These books are heavy, often awkwardly shelved; the F3s were once housed on a narrow balcony, and some book runners were physically unable to bring them down. If you call up such a book at the Huntington, or at any library that owns them, you will soon make the acquaintance of the people who have to bring them to you, and once you do, you will think very hard before asking for numerous examples.

If you have the temerity or the indifference to human suffering to get such a book to your desk, and if the library has multiple copies of the same book (most do not), it is almost physically impossible to get two copies together to compare them. I can put a facsimile of the Caxton *Canterbury Tales* on my desk and compare it with a real copy in any library that happens to have one. I can do this also with copies of early Terence editions. But I have never attempted this simple task with a Huntington F3. To do so would require two oversized book stands or lecterns. I would have to stand rather than sit. And certain ordinary procedures of collation (having both books in view at the same time) are physically impossible given the constraints of the human eye. Ordinary information available for most material books is not available for these; for some scholarly purposes, they effectively do not exist.

Relations of Size to Cost: A Practical Experiment

How much "book" does it take to publish a given text? The following is an experiment that can be conducted in any library or by judicious use of many online or printed catalogues. The question is a simple one: Is a large book more expensive than a small book? Is it cheaper to print a text in quarto format than to print that same text in folio?

In the earliest days of book production, the economics seem simple: books were sold by the sheet, and their cost was a direct function of the number of sheets required for each book. It seems completely obvious that a text printed in a large format should be more expensive than the same text printed in small format. However, the evidence suggests this is not necessarily the case.

Let us take an example of a classical text. When I first began to consider the problem of cost in relation to size, I used an edition of Pliny's *Epistles*, not because this is a particularly interesting text but because a local library happened to have multiple early copies. The four copies produced the following results:

Edition	Format	Number of Leaves or Pages	Number of Sheets
1478	folio	92 leaves	46
1518 (Aldine)	octavo	338 (525) leaves	42 (66)
1600 (Etienne)	quarto	646 (979) pages	81 (122)
1722 (Tonson)	12mo	298 (360) pages	13 (15)

On the face of it, there appears to be no consistent relation between format and material cost. The quarto from 1600 requires double the sheets of the Aldine octavo, but the Aldine requires nearly the same number of sheets as the earlier 1478 folio. The parenthetical figures indicating supplemental text point to another problem: what constitutes the text of Pliny in these editions is not really comparable. All but the fifteenth-century edition are printed with other texts such as the Panegyric of Trajan, and the fifteenth-century text of the Letters is not the same as that in later editions. The 1600 quarto includes extensive commentary. Increasing the number of editions examined here does not help; I have done that, and all these problems remain.

I then turned to Chaucer, whose textual tradition is more familiar to me and one I have used as an example earlier in this chapter. Surely the change from large folio editions to smaller portable editions in the eighteenth century must have been driven by economies of material. I compared Tyrwhitt's five-volume octavo edition of the *Canterbury Tales* with the text in one of the earlier blackletter folios. I included the preliminary leaves of the folio along with those used to print the *Canterbury Tales:*

Edition	Format	Number of Leaves or Pages	Number of Sheets
1602 (CT portion with prelims.)	folio	108 (128) leaves	64 sheets
1774–78	octavo	1664 pages	104 sheets

The octavo edition seems more expensive! But that cannot be right. If we eliminate the preliminary leaves, along with notes and glossary of both editions, and consider only the text portions of the Tales themselves (this requires eliminating two of the five volumes of Tyrwhitt), we get almost identical figures: 56 sheets for the Tyrwhitt. There seems no difference in cost, despite the format. One can manipulate these figures to make what appears to be a more rational case: the first edition by Caxton (1478), in folio, required 187 sheets; the 1798 reprint of Tyrwhitt's edition in large quarto required 163 sheets. But even these figures hardly prove what seems to be the obvious argument: that the larger format is more expensive than the smaller one. There are too many other factors involved: typeface, page layout, amount of annotation, margin size. As I extended this study to other texts, I found these variables impossible to eliminate.[10]

Size may well matter. But there is no obvious way one can quantify exactly how it matters. Its value and function can only be determined by considering its place in the larger complex of what constitutes each book and book-copy.

CHAPTER THREE

. . .

Materials

Ink, Paper

I. Ink

The late seventeenth-century manual of printing by Joseph Moxon, *Mechanick Exercises on the Whole Art of Printing*, is a basic source for information on the workings of the early press (see further chapter 4). Moxon includes detailed descriptions of such processes as typecasting, implying that these were within the province of the printer, but does not include sections on either paper manufacture or ink manufacture. The "Inck-Maker," according to Moxon, is simply one of those Workmen (like letter-cutters, typecasters, compositors, and correctors) subservient to the Master Printer as the Body is to the Soul. According to Moxon, early printers did not bother with the details of ink-making, and neither should we:

> the process of making Inck being as well laborious to the Body, as noysom and ungrateful to the Sence, and by several odd accidents dangerous of Firing the Place it is made in, Our English Master-Printers do generally discharge themselves of that trouble.[1]

Today, systematic study of ink cannot be conducted without the use of sophisticated equipment. Even then, the results are often ambiguous and can reflect the interests of those commissioning the tests.[2] For this reason, ink does not receive a great deal of attention in ordinary biblio-graphical studies. Nonetheless, certain gross features of ink are easily discernible, and these are often a direct function of the printing or writing process.

Ink used in ancient writing is carbon based, and its color comes from lamp black. Such ink sits on the surface of the writing material and thus can be erased simply by scraping it away. In the Middle Ages, the most common ink material was "iron gall" made from gall nuts (containing tannic acid). The iron gall was mixed with iron salt, which turned black when oxidized. The process of oxidation continues after the ink is used, and these once black inks now appear brown.[3] Printing ink is blackened with lamp black, as was ancient ink, but such ink is oil based. It is thick, much like the ink used in ballpoint pens, and because it is unaffected by oxidation, its color does not fade: the ink in a fifteenth-century book is as dark today as it was when printed; or so we think. All these ink types had been developed before the advent of printing, and their qualities in terms of writing, ease of erasure, block-printing, engraving, etc. were well known to early printers.

The differences in these inks can be of bibliographical interest. Any book with early handwritten annotations will reveal them. The ink from printers is black; the ink from a pen is usually brownish, the result of the oxidation of iron content. Some fifteenth-century blockbooks were printed with two kinds of ink on the same page; the difference in color is now apparent, as it likely was not when these books were printed.[4] Annotations by early owners can occur in pencil, ink, or crayon; those in ink will have a brownish hue similar to writing seen in manuscripts. Traces of printing ink also appear in manuscripts, al-though these manuscripts are extremely rare. An otherwise clean manu-script containing ink smudges darker than the ink used in the writing of the manuscript is likely to have been in a printer's shop, perhaps used as a copytext for a printed edition.[5]

The characteristics of these inks are also important in book restora-tion and correction. A restorer can easily enough match a color of ink. What will be less easy is matching the chemical composition closely enough so that the color changes of each ink over time will be the same. Corrections in manuscripts and printed books as well as relative dates of annotations can sometimes be indicated by differences in ink colors that originally might have matched.

II. Paper

In contrast to ink, paper can be studied visually in fairly sophisticated ways, and no special equipment is required: a ruler and a light source are all that is needed.

Perhaps for this reason, the subject of paper is now increasingly included within bibliographical studies. Differences in paper stocks of any book are easily seen and recorded, and these can in turn be mapped onto the textual structure of the book.

Until the late nineteenth century, the basic material for papermaking was linen rags, beaten to a pulp, and mixed with water. This mixture was poured into a handheld *paper mold* to form individual sheets. A paper mold consists of a rectangular wooden frame supporting a wire screen of horizontal and vertical wires. Wires are closely strung in one direction (the long way). The marks left by these wires on a sheet of paper are called *wire lines* or *laid lines*. Across these, supporting them, are a series of wires placed roughly one to three centimeters apart, forming *chain lines;* in many frames, an extra chain, called a *tranchefile,* will be placed closer to its neighboring chain at the edge of the frame. These chains can be attached to the wires by stitches that also leave visible marks in the finished paper.

Any paper made in such a hand mold will reveal these wire and chain lines when held against a light (see fig. 3.1a–c below), and if it has not been cut or trimmed, it will also reveal the ragged *deckle edge* characteristic of paper made in a hand mold. Most handmade European paper will also have a *watermark,* an image formed from wire sewn on one side of the mold in such a way that it will appear in the middle of one of the leaves of a sheet folded as a folio. Watermarks are medieval in origin, but at least in early paper, the various bulls' heads, pots, grapes, and hands have no symbolic meaning. Some paper contains a countermark: a mark sewn into the side of the mold opposite the watermark; like the watermark, this will appear in the middle of one of the two conjugate folio leaves of a sheet folded in folio.

Most paper produced up through the eighteenth century will show wire and chain lines characteristic of a particular mold, and most will also contain watermarks. In the eighteenth century, a method of papermaking new to the West was developed for what is called *wove paper;*

the molds are made of fine wire woven together as in cloth. The paper made by this process has a random pattern of fibers, with no visible chain or wire marks.[6] By the mid-nineteenth century, paper begins to be mass produced in papermaking machines; and such paper (what one paper historian calls "anonymous") begins to lose the individual and identifying characteristics of earlier mold-based paper.[7]

After a sheet of paper forms in the mold, it is turned out onto felt to dry. Any paper made in a paper mold will thus have two distinct sides, the mold side (the side of the sheet that was in contact with the wires of the paper mold) and the felt side (the side in contact with the felt). The differences are often characterized by paper historians as "rough" and "smooth," and other more abstract and colorful terms are used to describe this difference as well, for example, "aggressive texture." These qualities are not ones my eyes consistently see. Nonetheless, the two sides of most handmade paper can be easily determined with what bibliographers call a *raking light,* which is nothing more than a drugstore flashlight that you shine across the paper. The physical indentations of the chain lines on the mold side will be clearly visible on most handmade paper. This is not information a bibliographer normally needs to know, but it can be useful in determining book structure: a leaf cannot be conjugate with another leaf unless the mold and felt sides match.

Although the most common material for papermaking was linen fibers from rags, paper can be made with almost any base material. Due to rag shortages in the nineteenth century, experiments were conducted with various materials, including horse manure. Even the wrappings of mummies will do, and there is a persistent claim among paper historians that mummy paper was actually manufactured in midcentury America, although no physical fragment of such paper has survived.[8] The use of rags for papermaking has important implications on the book trade; it is one factor that helped urbanize the production of book making. The major source of the raw material for paper was used linen, that is, the underwear from human beings, who are more concentrated in urban than in rural areas. Since running water was also essential in the production process, paper mills had to be located along rivers. In England, where the primary source of clothing was wool, paper was imported, and the first English papermaker seems to be John Tate, who operated a paper mill for a few years in the late fifteenth century. That there were fewer printers in England in the fifteenth century may have as much to do with what the English were wearing as what they were reading.[9]

III. Paper and Book Structure

Traditionally, bibliographers describe book size in terms of paper. The basic paper unit is the *sheet,* the unit produced by the papermaker in the paper mold. Sheets come in various traditional sizes, and some bibliographers include the initial sheet size in their descriptions of books. Conventionally, bibliographers are most concerned with what happens with the sheet in constructing the book. To be sewn into a book, the sheet has to be folded; one fold produces a folio; two folds produce an octavo; three produce a quarto (discussed in chapter 2). This is the book *format.*

The folding of the sheet can be related to many material features of the original sheet of paper. In a leaf of a folio, the chain lines will be vertical, and the watermark will appear in the middle of one of those folio leaves. In a quarto, each leaf will have horizontal chain lines; the watermark will appear in the gutter of one of the pairs of leaves that make up that sheet. Fold it again, into an octavo, and the chain lines will be horizontal; the watermark will appear at the crossing of the two folds (top left of a recto leaf); parts of it may be visible on as many as four of the eight leaves in the quire. The location of the watermark on smaller formats (12mo, 16mo) will of course depend on the way the sheets are folded and printed. Some formats involve cutting the sheet before folding, and a common example found in most rare book libraries is the 12mo format characteristic of small editions of the classics printed by Elzevier in the seventeenth century; the twelve-leaf quires in a typical Elzevier edition are formed by cutting the printed sheet into units of eight and four leaves.[10]

Understanding these formats involves visualizing the relation of the sheet surfaces (the basic units of printing) to leaves and pages of the printed book quires. The easiest way to do this in most formats is simply to construct a model sheet: draw the chain lines and a watermark and begin folding it. Even complex formats involving cutting of the sheet can be understood this way. Knowing where to find a water-mark and how the chain lines will appear in particular formats should be second nature to bibliographers, but when studying paper, I keep a model of a full sheet marked with chain lines discretely folded up on my desk at all times.

Standard bibliographical descriptions do not consistently identify the size of the initial sheet nor the size of the sheet from which the quires of a book are made; nor do they always state explicitly whether the printer starts with full sheets or half sheets. The size and nature of the initial sheet will be determining factors in the size and appearance of the finished book. A folio constructed using as a basic unit a half sheet rather than a full sheet, for example, will be squarish in shape, like a quarto, and the chain lines on each page will be horizontal, as they are in conventional quartos, rather than vertical, as they are in conventional folios.

The terminology describing paper size is often bewildering, but few of what Dard Hunter estimated as the 240 sizes of paper are in common use at any one time.[11] For early printed books, the most com-mon terminology is based on paper made in Bologna in the fourteenth century. Four sizes are distinguished:

> imperialle 74 × 50 cm = imperial
> realle 61.5 × 44.5 cm = royal
> meçane 51.5 × 34.5 cm = median
> reçute 45 × 31.5 cm = chancery

A chancery sheet is one-half the size of a royal sheet; a median sheet one half the size of an imperial sheet. The most common size for ordi-nary books is the chancery.[12] These sizes are still the basis of sizes named and used in later printing. Gaskell's table of common types used in the seventeenth and eighteenth centuries is as follows (I give the di-mensions listed for late eighteenth-century English examples):

> super royal (imperial) 70 × 49 cm
> royal (lombard) 61 × 49 cm
> medium (carré) 57 × 44.5 cm
> demy 56 × 44.5 cm

crown (post) 49.5 × 39 cm
foolscap 42.5 × 34.5 cm
pot 39.9 × 31.5 cm[13]

Additional sizes are variants of these: pinched post, demy double, etc.; the meaning of others is obvious: for example, "double elephant" (the size used in the Audubon *Birds of America* noted in chapter 2). Since most bound books have been trimmed in some way, the size of the initial sheet is not always apparent in any given book-copy.

As early as the fifteenth century, certain books were printed on two types of material: some copies of the Gutenberg Bible are printed on paper, others, more luxurious, on vellum. The two are typographically identical and thus considered part of the same edition. A similar distinction applies to those books printed in the eighteenth century designated by their printers as "large paper" copies. These are typographically identical to ordinary copies but printed on larger paper. In the nineteenth century, William Morris also printed certain editions on both paper and vellum.

IV. Watermarks

Since each paper mold is physically unique, the paper used in the leaves of any book-copy should in theory be identifiable. The combination of chain lines, wire lines, and perhaps watermark should distinguish the physical paper mold, and this might well suffice to locate a manufacturer and to provide a date for any sheet of paper in an early book. Until recently, the most picturesque feature of paper—its watermark—was seen as a kind of fingerprint permitting identification of that paper stock. But too few bibliographers studied paper evidence and compilations of watermarks to build up a solid methodology for the use of such evidence; others, particularly Anglo-American bibliographers, simply dismissed the evidence from watermarks entirely.[14]

Watermarks have been noted as early as the eighteenth century. Joseph Ames included woodcuts of watermarks used in Caxton books in his 1749 *Typographical Antiquities* but suggested no use for them; they "may be observed by the curious." A century later, a more serious study of paper appeared in Samuel L. Sotheby, *Papermarks*, volume 3 of his

Principia Typographica (London, 1858).[15] Sotheby included reproductions of watermarks used in many early printed books including blockbooks. These provide a limited corpus of material; paper used in a given early book-copy could be identified as the same recorded in Sotheby.

The most important attempt at a comprehensive catalogue of watermarks is C. M. Briquet's four-volume *Filigranes* (1907), containing several thousand hand-drawn watermarks organized according to what the mark represents, each taken from a piece of paper dated from external evidence; most are from dated manuscripts.[16] Theoretically, you could compare the "bull's head" in a leaf from a book you were studying to the dozens and dozens of bull's head watermarks reproduced in Briquet. You would then follow Briquet's notes on the origins of that paper and perhaps say "something" about the origin and date of the paper. But whether you could say "something reliable" about the origin and date of that paper is a different question. Scholars often seem to assume that to describe a watermark as "similar" to a watermark in Briquet means that the paper is also "nearly" of the same date and perhaps of the same origin. But this is not necessarily the case. What matters is identity, not similarity. Allan Stevenson claims in the introduction to the 1968 re-edition of Briquet that one's chances of actually matching a watermark in any given sheet of paper with one in Briquet are 5 percent.

Briquet's illustrations are hand drawn and not all contain the same details: some indicate the position of the watermark in relation to chain lines; others include the wires used to sew the watermark onto the mold. Briquet's method was to give one example of each watermark. But individual watermarks vary over their history, since the wire that forms them can move in relation to the more stable pattern of wire and chain lines.

A more extensive compilation is based on the research of Gerhard Piccard, published in some seventeen "Findbücher" and now available online.[17] These volumes reproduce watermarks in Piccard's collection in the Hauptstaatsarchiv Stuttgart. The catalogue is organized, like Briquet's, by object; this means, amusingly enough, that you must learn the German word for, say, "griffon," and have the wherewithal to associate it with the French word in Briquet. Even with this extensive collection, it is rare for an average researcher to find information of bibliographical note that could not be had otherwise; for example, this is a fifteenth-century book printed unremarkably on fifteenth-century Italian paper.

Numerous other projects exist online as well; these are either in progress, and thus incomplete, or limited to a small, definable corpus of material.[18] As long as the corpus of evidence is manageable, that is, relatively small and well defined, and the question to be answered well focused, watermark identification is not difficult. If you can reasonably assume that a match for a watermark in a book is available in a given corpus of recorded watermarks, finding that match will be almost mechanical. An example might be the watermarks in early blockbooks. Each blockbook edition was printed with a mix of paper stocks, but the number of these stocks is limited. The watermarks in the blockbook collection of the Bibliothèque Nationale have all been recorded in beta-radiography and published in volume 1 of the library's catalogue of fifteenth-century books; in my experience, these reproductions are sufficient to identify the paper in any other example of these books. Since many individual blockbooks have been sophisticated by modern restorers, such evidence is often crucial in reconstructing their original structure.[19]

Watermarks and the Identification of Paper Stocks

The notions of similarity and identity do not function the same way in all areas of bibliographical description. When dealing with such things as layout or typography, we might consider even vague similarity significant: for example, small octavo books printed in italic type in the early sixteenth century by Aldus Manutius's Aldine Press are similar in appearance. Such similarity was deliberate and a mark of genre: octavo books were "texts of the classics," and their appearance was part of a marketing strategy. Printers at Lyons produced imitations of these books and Aldus himself considered them forgeries. As another example, an English printer of the late seventeenth century prints a large book in blackletter because that printer wants it identified as a Bible: it is similar to other Bibles, and that similarity is in this particular case a mark of genre (see chapter 6). In such cases, similarity is part of what might be called the "received function" of the book. The notion of similarity in a watermark, however, is of a completely different order;

neither the watermark nor the structure of the paper (chain lines and wire lines) was intended to be perceived by the ordinary reader except in the most general way.

To understand the difficulties of defining or identifying a paper stock by means of a watermark, let us return to the fingerprint analogy. Your finger is going to produce a variant of the same identifiable fingerprint no matter what doorknob it touches or when it does so ("same" here means a product of the same source). But the physical wire mark that made a bull's head impression is not going to make the same bull's head impression after hundreds of sheets of paper since some of the essential character of that wire mark may have changed—it has bent into a new shape; it has slipped on the chains. Furthermore, a different mold altogether could have a very similar watermark. A now classic study by Allan Stevenson showed that early papermaking molds were constructed in what were intended as interchangeable pairs; thus watermarks are not really singular, but "twins."[20]

Watermark identification is plagued by vagaries of description: what does it mean to say that watermark X is "similar to" or "like" watermark Y? An eighteenth-century papermaker could create a watermark "similar to" a fifteenth-century one, although blessedly, they seem not to have done this. That similarity, of course, would mean nothing in relation to the general differences in the paper. Two watermarks similar in appearance are not necessarily closer in time or culture than two watermarks that are dissimilar. As with fingerprints, the only claim of value is the claim of absolute identity. A forensic scientist does not say "Suspect's prints are 'similar' to those of the perpetrator"; the only judgment the expert is asked to make is whether the suspect's prints *are* those of the perpetrator. It may not really mean much to say "this mark is similar to Mark #3216 in Briquet," as some scholars suppose, any more than it means anything to say my thumbprint is similar to the thumbprint of George Washington or Jack the Ripper.

Allan Stevenson

The use of watermarks as a means of identifying a stock of paper encountered serious bibliographical resistance in the twentieth century, particularly by the German incunabulist Konrad Haebler and also among many Anglo-American bibliographers.[21] By midcentury, more sophisticated methods of treating paper evidence were developed by Allan Stevenson. If, for example, a printer used the same stock of paper to print a book or series of books, it might be possible to trace minute and regular changes in the shape of a watermark through comparison of the impressions it made on individual sheets of paper. If two undated books appear to be printed with the same paper, it might be possible to determine which is later, since minute modifications in the appearance of a single watermark might reveal a regular pattern of deterioration. This is tedious, time-consuming work, and it requires access to many copies of the same book as well as an eye for minutia. Furthermore, the only books that anyone would bother examining from this standpoint are monumental books, such as books by Caxton or the earliest printed books from Mainz. Such books are not lying around in readily accessible heaps in a local library. Yet Stevenson showed what could be done in this area; it was not necessary to date any particular paper in an absolute sense but only in relation to other paper that could be classified as from the same stock. Stevenson was able to chart regular changes in particular watermarks from particular molds and thus date the paper in one book or edition relative to the paper used in other editions.[22]

V. Use of Paper Evidence

Most researchers will not be able to use paper evidence to make fine distinctions in dating a book or manuscript. If you have a seventeenth-century English quarto and try to match the watermark in Briquet, there is a chance that you will find something similar; but in so doing, you will only confirm that the seventeenth-century quarto is printed on paper that is roughly contemporary or slightly earlier than the date given on the title page. If the paper does not seem contemporary, or you identify the watermark with a Briquet example that is much earlier, there are likely problems in your notion of what constitutes "identity."

Paper evidence will be of more general bibliographical utility in identifying the structure of a book and its quires. It is a fairly easy matter to determine conjugacy of individual leaves (which leaves were made from the same sheet of paper). It is easy to identify different stocks of paper in a book, and if multiple copies of the same book are available, it is also fairly easy to see how these stocks of paper are used, that is, whether they are used randomly or there is a clear relation between paper stock and book part: did the printer print the various sections of a book in a particular order? were the preliminaries printed last? was a particular quire reprinted after the entire book was printed? The information is not definitive in terms of dating a book or even identifying its paper. But it is at least useful for describing parts of a book or book-copy in relation to other parts of that book's print-run or that particular book-copy.

Paper structure and watermarks can be recorded in a number of ways. Watermarks can be copied freehand or as tracings. They can also be copied, perhaps more accurately, by "rubbings," although few libraries will permit this. To create a rubbing, sandwich the printed page between a hard smooth surface (a plastic clipboard works fine) and a sheet of ordinary copy paper. Rub over the copy paper with a soft pencil. A relatively clear picture of the watermark should appear, along with a usable image of the chain and wire lines. It goes without saying that this cannot be done in a rare book room without asking permission; in many libraries, it is not worthwhile asking for such permission.

A more expensive way of recording watermarks and paper structure is by beta-radiography, whereby a photographic plate is exposed to a radiographic sheet through the paper, resulting in a photograph of the leaf's chain lines, wire lines, and watermark. This is prohibitively expensive as well as time-consuming. A much more efficient way of recording paper structure is by backlighting a leaf and photographing it with a standard digital camera. The advantages of beta-radiography and even rubbings are two: (1) the text printed on the page does not interfere with the final image (at least in theory), and (2) the images are produced by contact with the leaf and thus perfectly reproduce its size and shape (by contrast, an image produced by photography will necessarily be distorted by the ordinary functioning of a camera lens placed at less than infinite distance). But images can be easily manipulated, for better or for worse, and any advantage a contact image might have over a digital photograph is lost as soon as that contact image is itself reproduced in a publication. Again, special permission is required for any kind of photography in rare book libraries.[23] See figure 3.1a–c showing the same watermark reproduced by (a) rubbing, (b) tracing, (c) back-lit photography. Watermarks should all be pictured from the same side

FIGURE 3.1a–c.
Watermarks
(a) rubbing;
(b) tracing;
(c) backlit.

that is, the mold side or the felt side; but there is no strict bibliographical convention for this, and those watermarks intended to be seen from
the felt side (for example, they contain a readable number or letter) are
generally reproduced that way in bibliographical descriptions whatever
the conventions used for other marks.

The problems of reproducing an image of a watermark may be easier to avoid than to solve. The purpose of recording details of paper
structure is to identify the paper stock—the product of a particular
paper mold or set of molds. To do this, a number of paper historians
have redirected attention away from watermarks toward wire and chain
lines, since these are both more stable and can be accurately described
without recourse to expensive beta-radiography.

One way to record the defining features of paper structure is simply
to measure the distances between chain lines. A detailed and systematic
method for recording such information is given by David Vander Meulen; this method involves measuring the distance between chain lines in
millimeters, noting in the formula the position of the watermark. A description of a paper stock or sheet of paper might in Vander Meulen's
system look like this:

(%) (9) | 30 | 29.5 | 37.5 | 31 | 28 | 29 | 28.5 | 29 | (29) | 29.5 | 30 | 38.5
| 4.5 [24.5 | 26] 4 | 29 | 28 | 19.5 | 20 | (13) (%)

This formula is less formidable than it appears: a vertical line indicates
a chain line and the following number the distance in millimeters to the
next chain line; % means deckle edge; a parenthetical number is an es-
timation (for the gutter, or the greatest width when the paper has been
trimmed between chain lines); the brackets indicate the widest points
of the watermark.[24] A formula like this enables any other researcher to
identify the paper from the numerical series without recourse to matching watermarks visually.

There are many variants of this method. I set the ruler at 0 for the
first chain line, and my own simplified series for the sheet described
above would read 0, 30, 59, 97, 128, 156 . . . . If I have the patience, I can
add to this the number of wire lines per some arbitrary unit as the inch
or centimeter. In any given book, such formulae are generally sufficient
to distinguish stocks of paper or to answer a question such as "is this

paper from the same stock?" For a single leaf, this method should provide the evidence to answer the question "is this leaf possibly conjugate
with another leaf in the quire?" In a book constructed with handmade
paper, paper stocks reveal themselves through chain and wire lines far
more readily than they do through differences in watermarks. Bulls'
heads, pots, hands: these are common; molds with chain lines intersect-
ing a ruler at -5, 0, 18, 36, 55 mm . . . are much less so.

Paying attention to the chain and wire lines will also quickly reveal
large historical differences in the structure of paper. The best way to
understand changes in paper manufacture is to spend time looking at
books from the fifteenth to the nineteenth century, and then looking at
more books from the fifteenth to the nineteenth century. The growing
regularity in the construction of paper in books from the later periods
will be soon apparent, along with the increasing fineness of the chain
and wire lines. It will not take much experience to determine whether
an endpaper in a fifteenth-century book bound in an eighteenth-
century binding is contemporary with the printed book or the binding;
and an afternoon spent doing this will be much more efficiently and
enjoyably spent than trying to match the watermark of the suspicious
paper with an image in Briquet.

Ambiguities in the Term Paper Stock

The most basic term in studying the relation of paper to book structure
or to printing history is *paper stock*. This is the principle of identity involved in paper and thus fundamental in the same sense that the term
edition is fundamental to the discussion of printing projects. Like the
term *edition,* this term can have multiple and legitimate meanings even
in a bibliographical context.

From the manufacturing standpoint, there is a legitimate sense in
which *stock* would mean "the sum-total of sheets produced by the same
mold or set of molds." The meaning here would be the same general
meaning that applies to a printer for the term *print-run* of an individual
sheet (see chapter 11 on ideal copy). The papermaker intended to make
one kind of paper and did so, using two separate molds. The printer
regarded the products from these two molds as interchangeable. The
material evidence (the various sheets of paper produced from these

molds) would thus be defined in terms of the apparent or idealized intentions of the papermaker.

A printer, however, would not define stock this way. A stock for the printer might be "the sum-total of paper purchased for a particular project" or even "the sum-total available for a particular project," and this would be purchased not from a papermaker but from a distributor, who might define stock entirely differently as "what could be gathered together from one or more papermakers and sold as a unit to a printer."

During the hand press period, paper was sold and distributed in bales, and it is not certain how clean or uniform such bales were as they moved from papermaker to distributor to printer. Because paper was expensive (paper costs are estimated as constituting over 30 percent of the total cost of an early printed book), no one in this process could afford to store unlimited quantities. Furthermore, something comparable to a warehouse could and must have belonged to everyone involved in paper distribution: the papermaker, the distributor, and the printer; in these warehouses, was paper stored rationally? and was it used according to some principle such as "first (or last) in, first out"? No one involved in early papermaking and distribution necessarily defines or treats paper stock in a way convenient for a bibliographer, that is, as "a run of paper produced by the same molds"—something determined by what could be called the internal evidence of the paper itself. Nonetheless, this seems the only reasonable definition for a bibliographer to use. If there is external evidence that two identifiable bibliographical stocks are part of the same economic stock, that is easy enough to note.

Paper Stock and Book-Copy Irregularities

The first and most important principle of paper evidence is that any paper evidence gathered from a single book-copy is copy-specific. Not until multiple copies of the same book have been examined can any statements be made about the relation of paper to an edition. The earlier the edition, the more important this principle is.

Irregularities in paper use appear on many levels. When we examine an early book, watermarks will occur at particular places depending on the folding (the format) of the book. In any folio gathering, half the leaves will show a watermark, and this watermark will appear in the center of one of the two leaves of each bifolium; the conjugate leaf will generally appear blank; in some cases, it may have a countermark. In addition, wherever the watermark appears (on the right or left hand side of the sheet), it could be right-side up, or upside down, that is, you could be facing the mold side or the felt side. Thus in any book, the sheets in a folio, quarto, or octavo can be oriented in one of four ways. The easiest way to understand this is by constructing a model of a sheet of paper with a watermark, then folding it for one of these formats.

Examining the watermarks of any printed folio will soon reveal what appears to be a random orientation of sheets. The first leaf of a quire might show the watermark right-side up. The first leaf of the next quire might have the watermark upside down; it might have no watermark (the watermark appears on the conjugate leaf). A second copy from the same edition will show a similarly random orientation of sheets, one with no discernible relation to the orientation of individual sheets in the first copy. I have examined many single book-copies and multiple copies of the same book checking such evidence in all its tedious detail, and I cannot remember seeing one with a systematic orientation of sheets. Such random orientation of paper applies to folios, quartos, or octavos. The paper obviously came off the mold systematically, that is, the papermaker did not remove paper from the mold capriciously, nor mischievously gather it in heaps with mold sides and felt sides opposed. Somewhere between the papermaker and the end of the printing process, sheets of paper were turned and inverted at random, even within a presumably stable paper stock.

In addition, rarely do I find a large early printed book produced in what could be described as the same paper stock throughout; nor do two copies of the same book necessarily show the same relation of paper stock to text; and never is the paper systematically oriented with respect to book structure. Randomness is built in to the material basis of book production. If we have before us two copies of the 1623 edition of Shakespeare, we speak loosely of having two copies of the same book. A library with the goal of collecting a complete set of early Shakespeare editions would only want one of them. But many of their material and even their textual features will doubtless differ. As we will see in later chapters, there will be differences involving marks of ownership, details of binding, accidents of press, even deliberate corrections. And these differences begin with the very materials from which those books are constructed, that is, from the very molecules that form the paper on up through the manufacturing and distribution process. The principle or force of individuality is built in to the materials from which the book is made, seemingly defying what seems to be the very *raison d'être* of printing—the production of identical and interchangeable copies of the same text.

Applications

Paper evidence can be of value in the study of monumental books and run-of-the-mill books. In many cases, the use of paper evidence will be negative. It is possible to determine, say, that leaf 6 is not conjugate with leaf 1 of a particular book, or that bifolium 1.6 of a folio in 6s is "not of the same apparent stock" as bifolium 2.5. In a case of a book-copy showing multiple stocks of paper, the uses of these stocks can be charted against such textual features as chapter divisions, book parts (preliminaries vs. text), even differences in typography. Is the apparently single book in fact two books? or a combination of different editions and issues? Do other copies show the same patterns of paper distribution and book parts? Do the patterns of paper stocks indicate the sequence in which the various book parts were printed?

In some cases, paper evidence can provide positive results. Caxton's *Recuyell of the Historyes of Troye* (1474) is the first book printed in English. Of the more than twenty copies of this book, one has an engraving on the opening leaf, leaf 1 of a quire of ten leaves. This engraving shows what appears to be Caxton presenting a copy of the book to his patron; it is often reprinted in modern Caxton studies, but until recently, the evidence of its authenticity was never articulated. The best bibliographers of the nineteenth century, certain as they were that Caxton volumes did not contain engravings, did not even note the existence of this engraving, assuming it was tipped in at a later date. Even those who eventually argued for its authenticity used paper evidence in such a vague way, referring thirdhand to its structure, that the evidence was unusable and the arguments consequently unassailable.

Yet the paper evidence is neither difficult nor ambiguous. The leaf has been repaired in the early nineteenth century, as have many leaves in valuable early books. The engraving itself has been trimmed, placed in a frame, and both frame and engraving pasted onto tissue backing. There are thus three different papers involved: the paper on which the engraving is printed, the paper of the frame added in the nineteenth century, and the backing tissue. The only paper of bibliographical significance is the paper on which the engraving is printed. To determine the possible authenticity of the leaf requires only measuring the chain lines and comparing the basic structure of that paper with what would be the conjugate in an ordinary book (leaf 10). They match.[25]

A final case concerns book restoration. The nature of endleaves, pastedowns, and even questionable book repairs can often be determined by paper evidence. Nineteenth-century restorers often used early paper to effect repairs, and even tried to match the chain lines of the frame with the chain lines of the framed leaf. In many cases, this was a purely aesthetic matter, not an attempt at fraud, since the frame is completely obvious.

There are cases, however, where the intentions of the restorer are not so clear. Book dealers have routinely completed early books for clients, sometimes by handwritten leaves or partial leaves, sometimes by lithograph or Xerox copies of missing leaves, and sometimes by tipping in missing leaves from other book-copies. Restorations made with modern paper will be obvious from the paper evidence. The most ingenious of these completions will involve the use of early paper, sometimes contemporary with the book to be restored. Blank paper for this purpose was once readily available. The notion of bibliographical "completeness" did not mean "containing all blank leaves" until late in the twentieth century; thus the blank leaves of even valuable books could be removed and used for printing up leaves missing from other books.[26] Nineteenth-century copies are usually lithographs, and thus easily detectable. Twentieth-century forgeries using such early paper can pose more difficulties (see chapter 12, section II).

CHAPTER FOUR

• • •

Mechanics of the Press

Variation

One of the strangest experiences a student of literature once had was confronting the opening sections of Ronald McKerrow's *Introduction to Bibliography for Literary Students* and the detailed description of the parts and operations of the seventeenth-century press: coffin, frisket, winter, carriage, points, and perfecting. There might be a reason to learn all these things, but McKerrow does not always make clear what those reasons are. You can do a lot of driving without understanding the intricacies of a fuel-injection engine; but you do need to know the consequences of applying a brake or turning a wheel counterclockwise.

Press mechanics interest me in the same way that paper interests me. Both are a source of variation. The basic procedures at press systematically violate what seems to be the *raison d'être* of printing: rather than creating multiple copies of the same thing, printing produces a sometimes messy array of individual things. To McKerrow, we study the press in order to eliminate its pernicious effect on the literary text: by determining what words in Shakespeare's text were due to actions in the press room, we might be closer (theoretically) to what Shakespeare wrote. Modern bibliographers are more apt to see that the actions of the press are productive of the very instabilities that we now find most interesting about literary texts.

I. Mechanics of the Press: Joseph Moxon, *Mechanick Exercises*

For the mechanics of early printing and book production, modern scholars rely to a large extent on Joseph Moxon, *Mechanick Exercises on the Whole Art of Printing* (1683–84). This text was a basic source for other printing manuals written in the nineteenth century and has been reprinted in the twentieth century.[1] Moxon provides a detailed, book-length description of all the operations at a printing press: materials used by printers (secs. 2–9); the physical press (secs. 10–11); letter-cutting and typefounding (secs. 12–17); "The Compositers Trade" (sec. 22); "The Correcter and his Office" (sec. 23); "The Press-mans Trade" (sec. 24); "The Office of the Warehouse Keeper" (sec. 25). McKerrow relied heavily on Moxon for his 1927 *Introduction to Bibliography,* and much of Moxon's language as well as his assumptions have established themselves through McKerrow in bibliographical studies.

Moxon's descriptions seem to be applicable to the workings of the press at least until the development of the iron press in the early nineteenth century; and many scholars assume often silently that even fifteenth-century printing followed procedures similar to those described in Moxon's manual. In the sketch below, I focus on the press operations that produce the variation and anomalies found in actual books.

Copytext, Typesetting, and Imposition

The basic production of a book begins with a *copytext*—the physical text from which the typesetter sets type. That text may or may not be edited; it may or may not come directly from the author; it can be a manuscript or an earlier printed edition. Moxon describes the preparation of the copytext as part of the work of the compositor (sec. 22).[2] From Moxon's description, it seems clear that the goal of a printer is generally not the production of what modern editors might consider an accurate or reliable text but rather the production of a printed text that appears, to its users, error-free.

Typesetting, as described by Moxon, involves several physical processes. Type is held in a *typecase.* The typecase consists of an array of compartments, each of which contains theoretically identical *typesorts*. A typesetter holds the composing stick in the left hand and chooses type with the right, reading the text in the copy and composing that text, letter by letter and line by line in the composing stick. Since the image will be reversed in the printing process, a compositor sets lines upside down, left to right, a process that seems more difficult when it is described than it actually is when performed.[3]

When the compositor has set a number of lines (three? five?) in the composing stick and justified them (if they are to be flush right), the type is transferred to a tray called a *galley,* and the type set in these galleys is then used to compose pages. In the nineteenth century, a proof could be taken from these galleys before the pages were set up. In the early hand press period, galleys were simply a step in composing pages, since it was not possible to print a readable sheet from them.[4]

The process of arranging these pages such that they will be printed in proper sequence is called *imposition.*[5] During the process of imposition, additional, extra-textual matter must be added: folio numbers, signatures, running heads, ornamentation. The set-up pages are then locked together with wooden wedges (what is called *furniture*), and what is called the *forme* is ready to be inked.

The term of most significance to bibliographers in this procedure is the *forme*. In a bibliographical sense, the term *forme* means "what is printed on one side of the sheet"; it also refers materially to the physical unit of that type set up in pages and arranged to be printed—two folio pages, four quarto pages, or eight pages in octavo, twelve in a duodecimo. The forme is the basic unit of printing. At least in theory, each impression of each forme should be identical. In practice, given the stresses on material, fallibilities of human endeavor, and deliberate correction, this is not the case.

A *proofsheet* might be printed from a forme, and any necessary adjustments made: individual typesorts could be adjusted or the surface on which the individual sheets are placed to be printed (the *tympan*) modified to produce an evenly printed sheet. Examples of printed proofsheets are shown in chapter 10, figure 10.2. If the forme to be printed is the reverse side of sheets already printed, part of this proofing involves *making register,* that is, arranging the forme on the bed such that the print block on one side of the sheet is aligned with the print block on the other.

The process by which sheets, already printed on one side, are printed on their reverse sides is called *perfecting*. A sheet is positioned on the tympan by a series of *points* that leave small holes on each sheet. Having been through the press once, each sheet will thus have a number of small holes positioned in exactly the same place in relation to the printed text. When the pile of sheets (called a *heap*) is turned over, these same points can be repositioned in such a way as to guarantee the precise positioning of the sheets (already printed on one side) on the tympan when they are perfected. Proofsheets can be taken until the forme is in the correct position.[6]

After the forme is printed, the type is broken up and *distributed* (or *redistributed*), meaning, it is placed typesort by typesort back into the typecase. Some printed elements that can be reused are not broken up (for example, running heads) but transferred to a new forme. This theoretically could be done for other elements of a text as well (whole words or phrases, perhaps), but I know of no cases where that has been demonstrated.

Because of the pressure of the platen, the forme to be printed must have an even surface. When a forme consists only of a partially printed page, type is placed in the blank sections that will not be inked. This is called *bearing type* and will leave *blind impressions,* that is, impressions that are not inked, but which can be seen and even read with a raking light.[7] Reading and attempting to identify the text of bearing type occasionally will reveal a passage from the text being printed, or a passage from another text being printed at the same time; this information is even more occasionally useful in determining the order or manner in which a book was printed or what other books were printed at the same time in the printer's shop.

Order of Printing

Type is expensive and heavy, and a typecase contains only enough type to keep the printing process going efficiently. Early books were not kept "in type"; and in books where quires consisted of several sheets, there was generally not enough type to keep even a single quire set in type while the next quire was being set.[8] Keeping large books in standing type was made possible in the nineteenth century through the process of *stereotyping*, whereby papier maché impressions were made of each typeset page or forme; these impressions could be easily stored and later used as molds for casting complete formes.[9]

The simplest way of printing a book was a method called *seriatim* printing, that is, setting and printing a book page by page in sequence. This procedure could only have been used for folios, and, with few exceptions, was used only by the earliest presses. In this method of printing, the basic unit of printing would be the page rather than the forme. The printer sets page 1r, prints it, breaks up and redistributes the type, sets 1v (its verso), prints that, breaks up the type, sets 2r, prints that, etc. To print a single folio sheet under this method requires four independent operations of the press and four independent settings of type.[10]

In seriatim printing, each separately printed page is typographically independent of any other page in the book, including its facing conjugate page. In a folio in 6s, the sequence of printing would be 1r, 1v, 2r, 2v . . . 6r, 6v, even though 1 and 6 are conjugates. Also in this hypothetical folio, as many as three active heaps of sheets would be involved during the printing of any quire.

The seventeenth-century printing press as described by Moxon, by contrast, used a "rolling carriage," whereby an entire side of a sheet could be printed as a unit. To print a forme this way requires two pulls of the press; the carriage holding the forme is repositioned under the platen, but there is no movement of the type within the forme (Moxon, sec. 24.7).[11] In a folio in 6s, 1r is set and printed at the same time as 6v; these two pages constitute a forme (see the visual representation of a folio in 6s in fig. 1.7). With this press, there would be a number of ways of printing such a book, but all would require six separate operations corresponding to the six formes: for example, beginning with the inner forme of the innermost sheet 3v.4r, followed by 3r.4v, 2v.5r, 2r.5v, 1v.6r, and finally 1r.6v. No matter how the printer chooses to print this, the first page of the quire (1r) must always be set up and printed with the last (6v).

This method has several implications. In the case of the folio in 6s, the compositor must set 6v with 1r, and 6r with 1v, since leaves 1 and 6 are physical conjugates. A theoretical printer with unlimited type could set up all the pages in sequence, as if printing seriatim (page by page); the pages could then be arranged in formes and the full quire printed. In practice, few if any books were printed this way: a typecase did not contain sufficient type to keep these twelve folio pages in standing type. Before setting up any particular forme (say, 1r.6v), the printer had to know the amount of text in other formes of that quire: leaf 6 cannot be set without knowing what is on leaves 1–5, and leaves 3 and 4 cannot be set without knowing how much text is on leaves 1 and 2.

The solutions involve several processes: the printer or editor first needs to estimate the amount of text to be printed on each page of the quire. To do this, the estimated text of the final printed pages is marked off in the copytext in a process called *casting off* (Moxon, sec. 22.9). If the printer is using a printed text as copytext, casting off is fairly easy, as long as the copytext itself is printed consistently. And there are many cases where such a printed copytext was copied page for page, and even line for line.[12]

A manuscript copytext presents more difficulties, and evidence of inaccurate or careless estimates are easy to find. If you look at the end of almost any printed section of a sixteenth- or early seventeenth-century book, you will see the type adjusted at the end of that section; it will be either spread out or compressed to accommodate the predetermined amount of text planned for that section, whether the section is a page, a forme, or an entire quire. The extra space and peculiar column shapes on the inner forme of the 1532 Chaucer (fig. 4.1) indicate such a casting-off error.

Casting off is not simply a matter of the limited type in a typecase. The time involved in casting off copy is insignificant compared to the labor of typesetting and type distribution in conventional printing, and increasing the amount of type in a typecase would increase the printer's overhead without saving appreciable labor time. In a standard seventeenth-century quarto, each quire consists of one sheet, and there would be enough type in a typecase to enable the printers to set the text seriatim (that is, set type for all eight pages of a quire) if they chose to do so. But they often continued to cast off pages in these cases, just as they did when producing folio quires.[13] The process of casting off thus served several functions. As any modern printer or publisher can testify, it is a good idea to know the exact length of any printing project before embarking on it. And it is also a good idea to adjust the text block of individual pages to avoid wasteful blank leaves: the ideally efficient printed text will end at the bottom of the last page of a standard quire.

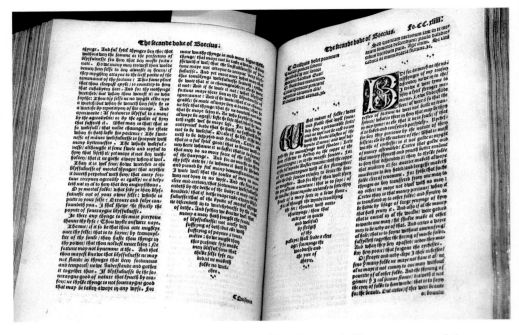

FIGURE 4.1. Geoffrey Chaucer, *Works* (London, 1532). Photo courtesy of the William Andrews Clark Memorial Library, University of California, Los Angeles.

Evidence of Printing Procedures

The method of printing will in most cases leave evidence. As noted above, a printer can print a quire in various ways—beginning from the inside sheets (3.4 of a folio in 6s) and working to the outside (1.6), or beginning with the inner forme of each sheet (iv.6r before 1r.6v). If a book has not had its pages washed in a later restoration, the type impressions of the second impression can be felt or seen when lit with a raking light; these will reveal which side of the sheet was printed last (type impressions are visible on the border of the text block in fig. 5.2). Some bibliographers further believe they can identify pieces of type in a typecase, a broken letter for example. By painstakingly following the appearances of that individual typesort in a printed book, they can determine at what point following the printing of a forme its type was distributed; this, in theory, will show how much type a printer might have had and how the printing proceeded.[14]

Running heads and certain extra-textual aspects of a printed page (e.g., rules and ornaments) can also be useful in this regard. Because the running heads are independent of the text, they were often not reset at all but rather reused as units. It is fairly easy to distinguish the versions of the same running head, and again, this, along with the reappearance of other printing elements such as a reused ornament or rule, often provides some information as to the order in which pages were printed.[15]

Error, States, and the Evidence from the Process of Perfecting

A set of sheets is going through press. At some point in the printing, the printer takes a sheet off for correction (described in Moxon, sec. 22.8). If there are errors, the press can be stopped to correct them in the set type. But some sheets have already been printed, and different copies of the book will thus end up with different readings on the same page; some will contain the original reading, others the corrected reading. If it takes an entire day to print off all the copies for one forme, there are many opportunities to check the printed sheets for error, since one way to ensure the existence of error is to search for it. There are also many opportunities for typographic catastrophe: type can break or work itself free in the forme. If this occurs, the press must be stopped and type either reset or the forme adjusted.

The result of each act of correction is the creation of what bibliographers call a *state;* one state is produced before the act of correction, a variant state after the act of correction.[16] Each printed forme (one side of a sheet) will potentially exist in a number of such states. If the printer makes one correction (or set of corrections) there will be two states in the final printed formes. If the printer makes two, there will be three states. In addition to states created by deliberate acts of correction, there may be accidental states: if a piece of type works loose during the printing process or moves in some discernible way, the result will be different states in the final printed formes. There may or may not be evidence of these states, since for many early books, we may be looking at fewer than a dozen book-copies of the hundreds that came off press, and there is no way of knowing whether these copies and their sheets are representative of the entire edition.

The way a bibliographer finds these states is through the laborious process of collation, that is, the visual comparison of different copies.

Early bibliographers simply placed two copies of the book side by side and read them, looking back and forth between two copies (what Randall McLeod calls the "Wimbledon Method");[17] they were thus able to find and record only textual differences, that is, differences in words or spellings. Modern bibliographers, beginning in the early twentieth century, began to compare pages optically: McKerrow laid a ruler diagonally across the same page of two copies; even if the two pages were textually identical, a change in setting of any line would reveal itself as a difference in where that line intersected the ruler. Later, Charlton Hinman developed a machine that projected and overlaid visual images of corresponding pages from two book-copies. If the pages were identical, the composite image was perfect. Any difference between the two copies would cause a flickering movement or a three-dimensional effect at that point of difference. Other collating machines, much simpler and cheaper than Hinman's, have been developed by Randall Macleod, Carter Hailey, and Gordon Lindstrand. I call my own method the "Human Hinman": I place two copies of a page in front of me, cross my eyes, and visually superimpose the two images. Variations appear as three-dimensional portions of the page.[18] A bibliographer or editor who finds a variant in the two copies then checks the same page of all copies and records which variant those other copies show.

A Practical Problem: The Logic of Variation in the Perfection Process

Variant states can exist on both sides of the sheet, and a standard bibliographical task would be to determine the order of these states; this is not as obvious as it may seem in that acts of correction can result in incorrect readings. What is the relation between the sequence of states on one side of the printed sheets (the inner forme) and the sequence of states on the reverse side (the outer forme)?

In and of itself, the problem of varying states is of small consequence. Methodologically, however, it underscores the difficulties in transforming the evidence (in this case, the patterns of variation in physical books) into the historical processes that produced that evidence. To what extent does the apparent disorder we see in the evidence reflect real historical disorder in the processes that produced it?

Each sheet will show two sets of states, one on each of its two surfaces: the inner forme will show one set of states; the outer forme will
show another. How those two sets of states appear to relate to each
other is a function of the process of perfecting. The sheets go through
the press in a particular order as they are printed on one side. They are
then turned over, and go through the press again. Do they go through
in the same order (as claimed by Gaskell)? or a different order (as
claimed by McKerrow and Fredson Bowers)?[19]

The order in which they go through the press is indicated in part by
the existence of states (state 1, state 2). There are then two questions
that must be kept distinct: (1) how does the sequence of states on the
inner forme relate to the sequence of states on the outer forme? and
(2) how do these sequences relate to the mixture of states in different
sheets of the same book-copy? that is, how do the states shown in one
book-copy relate to those in another book-copy from the same edition?

Individual book-copies show mixtures of states: sheet A might
show an early state for that sheet; sheet B might show a late state; even
a single sheet could show an early state on one side and a late state on
the other. Yet bibliographers such as McKerrow and Bowers were mis-
led by this apparent disorder to assume a comparable disorder in the
printing process. From the mixtures of states in individual sheets of
particular book-copies, they concluded that there was a random mixing
of sheets prior to perfecting to account for it. But the situation is far
more complex.

The following illustrates a hypothetical case of identical sheets
from nine copies of the same book (copies numbered 1–9). Keep in
mind that the problem here is to determine the relationship between
the way these sheets are printed and the resultant variants in each of the
nine copies. Let us assume that there is a stop-press correction on each
side of the sheet, producing two states for each forme and further that
these states are such that we can identify the order in which they were
produced (this is not always so easy in practice!). The vertical line
shown below indicates the difference of states. For example, in the inner
forme, the copies 1–6 show an early state; the copies 7–9 a late state. In
the outer forme (the reverse of that sheet), copies 1–4 show an early
state; copies 5–9 show a late state:

sheet X, inner forme: 1   2   3   4   5   6 | 7   8   9
sheet X, outer forme: 1   2   3   4 | 5   6   7   8   9

For this sheet, book copies 1–4 exhibit early states on both sides; copies 7–9 exhibit late states on both sides. But copies 5 and 6 have early states for the inner forme and late states for the perfected side, the outer forme. Note that contrary to what some bibliographers claim, the existence of books with such "mixed states" (book-copies 5 and 6) does not prove any irregularity in the perfecting process. In our hypothetical case, the sheets are printed in exactly the same order on the outer forme as they are on the inner forme: 1–9.

There is, however, a rule that applies to such mixed copies: in our above example, where the order of sheets is regular, there can be no copies that show a late state for the inner forme and an early state for the outer forme. Thus, for a sheet with two states on each side there will be three possibilities that individual book-copies will show: early states on both sides; late states on both sides; and *either one* of two mixed states, that is, early states on the inner forme mixed with late states on the outer form *or* late states on the inner forme mixed with early states on the outer forme. But all copies with mixed states will have the same mixed states. In the above example, since copies are found that mix the early state of the inner forme with the late state of the outer forme, none will be found that mix the late state of the inner forme with the early state of the outer forme. Violations of this apparent rule do occur. But these anomalies happen with such low frequency that they are as likely to reflect errors made by the scholars who define states in the first place as actual historical anomalies in the printing process.

Certain book-copies provide evidence that obscures rather than clarifies what is going on at press. Consider, for example, a case where a printer corrects a correction, or somehow changes one modification of the text back to the original reading. Suppose a printer corrects a reading *the* to *that,* and later corrects *that* to *the:*

state 1: the
state 2: that
state 3: the

There are three states for the sheet in the print-run. But to the bibliographer, there will be only two states; late state 3 must be classified (erroneously) with state 1. This is only one of many cases where even the most diligent scholar will create classifications at odds with the historical events at press that produced such variants.[20]

II. Analytical Bibliography and the Study of Printing Mechanics

Early English and American bibliographers justified the study of printing mechanics and the minutia of stop-press correction in terms of a higher purpose, which was to discover "what the author wrote." Printing was simply one more process intervening between the reader and the author; the bibliographer labored to understand printing in order to "undo" it, make it transparent, and remove its pernicious influence on the text. McKerrow, commenting in 1927 on his earlier "Notes on Bibliographical Evidence":

> I pointed out that in all work [transmitted by printing] there has intervened between the mind and pen of the original author and the printed text as we now have it a whole series of processes, often carried out by persons of no literary knowledge or interests . . . and that a thorough understanding of these processes was a necessary preliminary to any attempt to reconstruct from the printed book the text as originally conceived by its author.[21]

This approach to bibliography made it part of textual criticism, that is, bibliography was in the service of editorial matters—constructing the definitive text.

The study of the workings of the press in order to determine such matters became known as *analytical bibliography*. This is often defined, at least by Anglo-American bibliographers, as one of three fields of bibliography. The other two are *enumerative bibliography* (the compilation of book lists, whether of a library or a field) and *descriptive bibliography* (the identification and description of the constitutive elements of an edition). In practice, the three fields are interdependent, but even under this categorization, analytical bibliography is subordinate to descriptive bibliography: one describes the working of a press in order to understand how particular editions came into being, editions to be catalogued and described under the other branches of bibliography.[22]

For textual critics in the early twentieth century, analytical bibliography seemed to provide a way of eliminating the variation found in printed texts and getting back to a more stable, authorial original text. Just as textual criticism seeks the earliest text on the theory that it is closer, for better or worse, to the author's original, so did early print historians imagine that the handwritten original in the printing house was probably closer to Shakespeare than were the final products of the press. If there were different versions of a printed page, it was important to determine which came first and which of the variant readings is closest to what the author wrote, or, perhaps the next best thing, to determine what the author *did not* write, that is, to understand how particular errors were introduced at press.

By the late twentieth century, all this had changed; the once disparaged variant gained respectability. Rather than eliminate variation, editors welcomed it. The seminal work by Jerome McGann was central in this shift, redefining what we think of as a text as one that incorporates these variants, whether they are variants produced by the author, or variants produced from edition to edition. The text of Byron that has been read for a century and a half is not a fixed, definitive one but a very messy and thoroughly variant one—a conglomerate of bad texts, careless texts, re-edited texts, even abridgements. McGann's "public text," unlike the once-imagined "authorial text," includes all versions.[23]

Parallel with this shift in editorial theory came a shift in bibliography and in the status of analytical bibliography. Even for descriptive bibliographers, analytical bibliography was secondary: understanding the workings of a press was necessary for understanding the evidence of states, issues, and editions (see chapter 11). But as the variant became welcomed in textual criticism, the mechanics by which it was produced also became welcome to bibliography, as seen in the amusing and often bizarre work of Randall McLeod.[24]

Once an ancillary field, analytical bibliography became an autonomous field of study. Reconstituting historical events, even trivial ones, requires logical and methodological thinking about the use of evidence whatever the field of scholarship. Analytical bibliography was thus no longer to be justified on the basis of its results. Press mechanics would be studied not in order to serve textual criticism or other bibliographical fields but rather simply because "it was there."[25]

III. Examples and Levels of Variation

The processes of printing result in many kinds of variation: stop-press correction within a single edition; variation from edition to edition based on errors of casting off; misreading of copy; correction of copytext; even the absence of copytext. Anyone who examines two editions of the same text will find variation; and for early books, anyone who examines two presumably identical book-copies of the same edition will find variation as well.

Let us consider some examples. All involve variation produced at press; some are stop-press corrections within an edition, others are variations found in a sequence of editions. They can be organized according to various hierarchies, but it is not always possible to map one hierarchy (errors involving letters, phrases, entire passages) onto another (typesetting errors, stop-press corrections, deliberate editorial corrections from edition to edition).[26] Some of the variants noted below involve clear error; for others, determining or proclaiming error involves a series of assumptions about much grander things such as authorial intentions (we just *know* what William Shakespeare must have meant) or aesthetics (phrase X is just *better* than phrase Y) or even political concerns (Shakespeare *must/could not* have shared our ideological concerns).

1.   Errors Involving Single Letters

1.a. In the early *Hamlet* first quarto (Q1), some variants are matters of turned letters: a letter is set upside down. Some of these are obvious to any proofreader: an upside down *b* or *h* is clearly a typesetting error. But others are not: an upside down *u* looks like an *n*; an upside down *w* can be read as an *m*.

Q1 (1603) in *Hamlet* reads: "Then Honesty can transforwe Beauty." Obviously, the word "transforwe" is not a word. Nor is the "w" a *w* in Q1. It is an *m* that has been turned upside down. To transcribe this as I have done above is to transcribe not what was typeset but what might be read by a careless (and illiterate) reader. These would be unremarkable were it not for a modern edition of Q1 that transcribes these turned letters as their mistaken variants, that is, they are transcribed as they could have been mistakenly read by an illiterate or incompetent proofreader.[27]

There are several possible origins of such an error. A compositor could insert the letter incorrectly in the composing stick; a letter could be jarred loose and reset incorrectly on a forme. But the most likely source for this error is the process of type distribution. After the printer broke up a page of type, a worker placed each typesort in the appropriate box of the typecase; that worker looked at an *m*-sort, read it as a *w*-sort, and placed it in the wrong compartment. A later typesetter, wanting a *w*, reached into the *w* compartment and retrieved the wrong letter.[28]

1.b. A similar case is described by McKerrow as "muscular error,"[29] an error that results from the compositor reaching into the wrong compartment of the typecase or misdistributing type to an adjacent compartment. McKerrow is skeptical of this kind of error, which was first discussed by William Blades in 1872 and more recently by Randall Macleod.[30] Theoretically, such errors involve letters that are in adjacent compartments and depend on the "lay" of the typecase (*a* for *o*, *b* for *l*). The presumed errors of most interest to Blades were those where the resultant text made some literal sense: "Were they not *forc'd* with those that should be ours" (*Macbeth*); Blades conjectures "farc'd"; "I come to thee for charitable license, . . . to *booke* our dead" (*Henry V*). Blades conjectures "looke."

Whether typesetting errors show up in a printed text depends on whether they pass proofreading. From what little is known of early proofreading, the customary standard seems to be "making sense"; anyone who corrects proof knows that this is still the overriding factor.[31] If words appear as words and their meaning is coherent, it does not matter whether they conform to copy. Ordinary proofreading, thus, either of the printed page or even of the composing stick itself, would not reveal the kinds of errors discussed below where the erroneous reading makes marginally acceptable sense in its immediate context (that is, the words were real words, even if the syntax was garbled).

1.c. In *Othello,* the 1622 quarto reads as follows:

> Speake . . .
> . . . of one whose hand,
> Like the base *Indian,* threw a pearle away,
> Richer than all his Tribe.

The First Folio (1623) reads:

> . . . Of one, whose hand
> (Like the base Iudean) threw a Pearle away
> Richer then all his Tribe . . .[32]

This seems at first glance to be a conscious correction, especially in its modernized spelling. But the way the Folio reading is transcribed by modern interpreters (*Judean*) obscures the obvious source of this variant. The original variant is not a substantive one involving the words *Judean* and *Indian;* it involves only "literals"—a single letter. At some point in editorial history, *u* was misread as *n,* or *n* misread as *u* (or either *n* or *u* was set upside down in the printing shop). To transcribe the *I* as *J,* as many modern scholars do by convention, makes this variant appear grander than it is.[33]

2. Correction and Miscorrection

2.a. The 1561 edition of Chaucer has two versions of Chaucer's poem to his scribe, "To Adam Scriveyn." In one, Chaucer refers to his poetry as "my makynge"; in the other, his poetry is described as "my mockynge." Both readings make perfect sense, and one of these is likely a conscious correction. We know which of these two readings is "correct," or at least there is a consensus among Chaucerians about that: Chaucer wrote *makynge.* But in terms of the 1561 edition, which of the two readings is the correction? There are two possible answers. The first hypothesizes a corrector who was not an expert in Middle English; he did not know that Chaucer's word "making" meant "poetry writing," The corrector thus changed *makynge* (which made no sense to him) to *mockynge;* Chaucer was viewed as a satirist and a religious reformer in the sixteenth century, and this word was appropriate to such a writer. The second imagines a corrector who did know Middle English and was familiar with Chaucer as well. This corrector recognized *mockynge* as an error and corrected it to the original *makynge* found in early manuscripts. Either of these explanations is possible; and both reveal a sixteenth-century reader of Chaucer changing the original word *makynge* to *mockynge* in accordance with early sixteenth-century notions of Chaucer as a satirist and reformer. The question for printing history is only: Was this reading *produced* at press (as a correction)? or was it *corrected* at press, that is, changed back to the original?[34]

2.b. A famous passage in *King Lear* reads as follows in the 1608 quarto:

> Q: see how yon Iustice railes vpon yon simple theefe, harke in thy eare handy, dandy, which is the theefe, which is the Iustice.

Lear's point is obviously that without robes, a justice is indistinguishable from a defendant, just as in the game "handy-dandy," one does not know which closed fist holds, say, a marble. The 1623 Folio reading, however, obscures this:

> F: See how yond Iustice railes vpon yond simple theefe. Hearke in thine eare: Change places, and handy-dandy, which is the Iustice, which is the theefe.

What's this about "changing places"? The *Oxford English Dictionary*, quoting this passage, believes it has something to do with the game "handy-dandy," but no other reference to this game supports that.

The origin of this phrase seems to be a corrector's instruction. There are two ways of saying what Lear means: "which is the justice, which is the theef?" and "which is the theef, which is the justice?" At some point in the printing and proofreading of the Folio, an editor decided that the order in which these words were given should be changed and wrote "Change places" into the margin, probably with a transposition sign of some kind. The compositor dutifully followed the transposition order: theef/justice changed places (note that the order of these in Q is different from the order in F). That same compositor then, less dutifully, set the editor's instructions into the text as well.[35]

3. An extreme example is Hamlet's soliloquy in Q**ı** (1603):

> To be, or not to be, I there's the point,
> To Die, to sleepe, is that all? I all:
> No, to sleepe, to dreame, I mary there it goes,
> For in that dreame of death, when wee awake,
> And borne before an euerlasting Iudge,
> From whence no passenger euer retur'nd,
> The vndiscouered country, at whose sight
> The happy smile, and the accursed damn'd.
> But for this, the ioyfull hope of this,
> Whol'd beare the scornes and flattery of the world,
> Scorned by the right rich, the rich curssed of the poore?
> The widow being oppressed, the orphan wrong'd,
> The taste of hunger, or a tirants raigne,
> And thousand more calamities besides,
> To grunt and sweate vnder this weary life,
> When that he may his full *Quietus* make,
> With a bare bodkin, who would this indure,
> But for a hope of something after death?
> Which pusles the braine, and doth confound the sence,
> Which makes vs rather beare those euilles we haue,
> Than flie to others that we know not of.
> I that, O this conscience makes cowardes of vs all,
> Lady in thy orizons, be all my sinnes remembred.

If we see this as a radical variant, we may, as Shakespeareans have done, invoke radical solutions: the memorial reconstruction by an actor, for example; a different play altogether. But it might also be possible to see this as simply a more extreme variant of those processes of variation found throughout printing.

Conclusion

The processes that produce such errors are often banal; but the process of sorting them all out is much more complex. What we are confronting here is more basic than the specific cases a bibliographer might tabulate. We might be tempted to characterize these cases as evidence of the complete unknowability of the past, an unknowability that in turn can be a source of great comfort. If scholars cannot "know" in any absolute sense, then they seem to be relieved of the responsibility of attempting to know. But what the study of the processes at press and the implications for authorship and literature suggests is something more unnerving: the past is finally not completely unknowable; it is, instead, extremely and frustratingly obscure.

CHAPTER FIVE

. . .

Page Format and Layout

I. General Definitions

The technical term *format* in bibliography and printing history refers to how sheets of paper are folded to produce the leaves of the book. The format of a book, in a bibliographical sense, would be a folio, a quarto, a duodecimo; these are discussed in earlier chapters. This technical use of the word in bibliography is unfortunate, because format in the bibliographical sense is quite different from what most readers commonly think of as the typographical and visual format of a book: how the words and type are displayed on a page or page opening. I will use the term *page format* to refer to this here, although for some printers, most famously William Morris, the basic visual unit was not the single page but the page opening, consisting of two pages. The visual appearance of the page is something readers evaluate or interpret before they begin to read the printed words: are there two columns? or one? is the type large? or small? are the margins cramped? what is text? what is commentary?

That there is no clear and agreed-upon bibliographical term to describe this most obvious and most often experienced aspect of books is odd. Even in a book as comprehensive and reader friendly as John Carter's *ABC for Book Collectors,* there is, as far as I can tell, no term given for the typographical and visual format of a book. An unambiguous French term is *mise-en-page.* The two English terms used for this aspect of a book, *page format* and *layout,* are best regarded as synonymous, but in certain contexts, they might usefully distinguish two different levels of visual arrangement on the page. For example, "page format" could be defined as the abstract pattern: single column or double column; size of margins; type size etc., what in the printing trade might be referred to as the "template." "Layout" might then apply to more local matters: the particularities of how the words are arranged to fit into a general page format or template. But there is no fast distinction between such levels, and book historians and bibliographers have no consensus on how they are to be described; even the preliminary definitions of the above pair of terms could be reversed. Moreover, anything discussed within the compass of such terms will clearly blur into matters of typography (the subject of chapter 6).

As a preliminary example, when we distinguish the Shakespeare 1623 First Folio from the contemporary quartos, we see the most immediate difference in page format and layout: the folio is in double columns, with framed borders. It includes running heads, foliation. It also contains distinct typographical aspects. The quarto, by contrast, is in a single-column squarish block. This seems a logical and natural way of printing books of this size, although it is not at all universal. Single- and triple-column folios are common, and many quartos are printed in two columns. There may be a material or psychological reason to limit the width of a line; modern readers claim to have difficulty reading the large text blocks in early folios printed without columns. But this may also be a matter of pure convention.

Page format also includes what is commonly called justification. The earliest books printed by Caxton show left justification, but "ragged right." Later Caxton volumes are justified right and left. For these books, "ragged right" may have been a matter of typesetting convenience, at least, as long as we assume that the mechanics of typesetting were roughly the same for fifteenth-century books as for seventeenth-century books: the compositor only had to set the line, letter by letter, until there was no space left; blank quads could be used to fill the line. To produce right justification requires a more complex final step: after setting the line of type, the compositor must add blank spaces to the interior of the line to adjust the line to the correct length.[1] But we do not know enough about fifteenth-century typesetting to carry this beyond mere speculation. Perhaps right justification was regarded as pointless innovation: there is nothing comparable in manuscripts; written lines cannot be adjusted once completed, and even carefully planned manuscripts can have only crude right justification in comparison to printed books.

Different conventions have also applied to the treatment of run-on lines and headings. A modern printer places these on the next line by convention. Fifteenth-century printers followed the conventions of manuscript production and placed the run-on portion on the right, wherever space was available. The run-on portion of a line could appear above or below that line, to the right of the preceding or following lines.[2]

Printing turned some elements of manuscript format into pure decoration, such as the once functional *guide rules*. In manuscript production, page format is determined prior to the actual writing of that manuscript: the text block is marked out and each line ruled, in pencil, pen, or dry-point; the text is then written within those guide rules. In printed books, such guide rules have a different function: rules separating running heads from text or notes from text are printed in some books; red borderlines were occasionally added as decoration to individual book-copies after printing.[3]

Functions of Page Format

Page format can serve a number of functions, distinguishing text from footnotes, quoted text from gloss, quoted from original material. A fifteenth-century legal text is shown in figure 5.1: Gratian, *Decretum* (Basel: Richel, 1476). Here, elements of format guide the reader: various levels of text (main text, gloss, and notes) are distinguished by position, color, and size and style of typeface. Note that there are no page or foliation numbers, features added to such books only in the sixteenth century, and the running heads give only the briefest of orientation distinguishing one of five "books."

Figure 5.2 is a contemporary scholarly text: Guillermus [William of Paris], *Postilla super epistolas et evangelia* (Nuremberg: Koberger, 1488); this provides material for sermons on the text of Paul "for all wishing to understand the Epistles." The material is arranged not according to the order in the New Testament but according to the order in which readings are chosen for the liturgy. The open page concerns text for the first

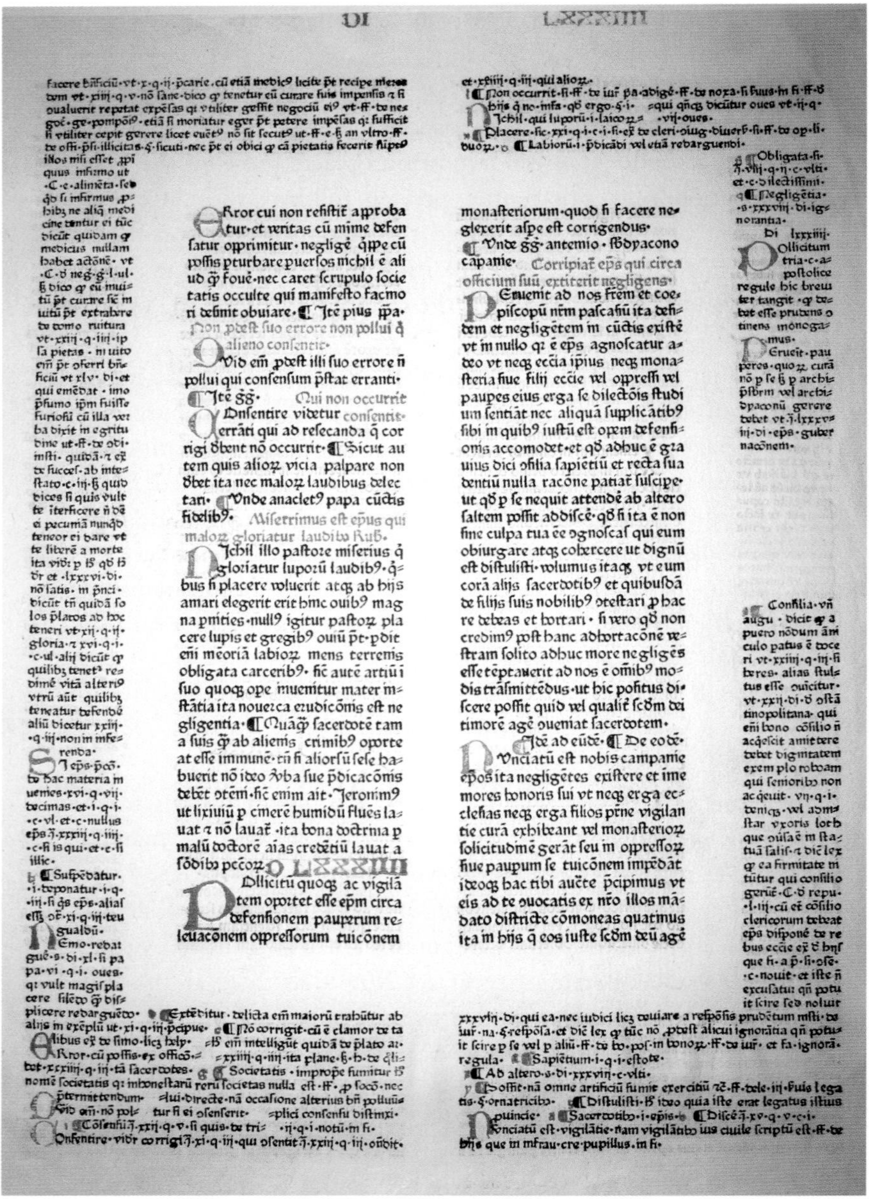

FIGURE 5.1. Gratian, *Decretum* (Basel: Richel, 1476). From Konrad Haebler, *German Incunabula: 110 Original Leaves,* 2 vols. (Munich, 1927), pl. 27. Photo courtesy of the George J. Mitchell Department of Special Collections & Archives, Bowdoin College Library, Brunswick, Maine.

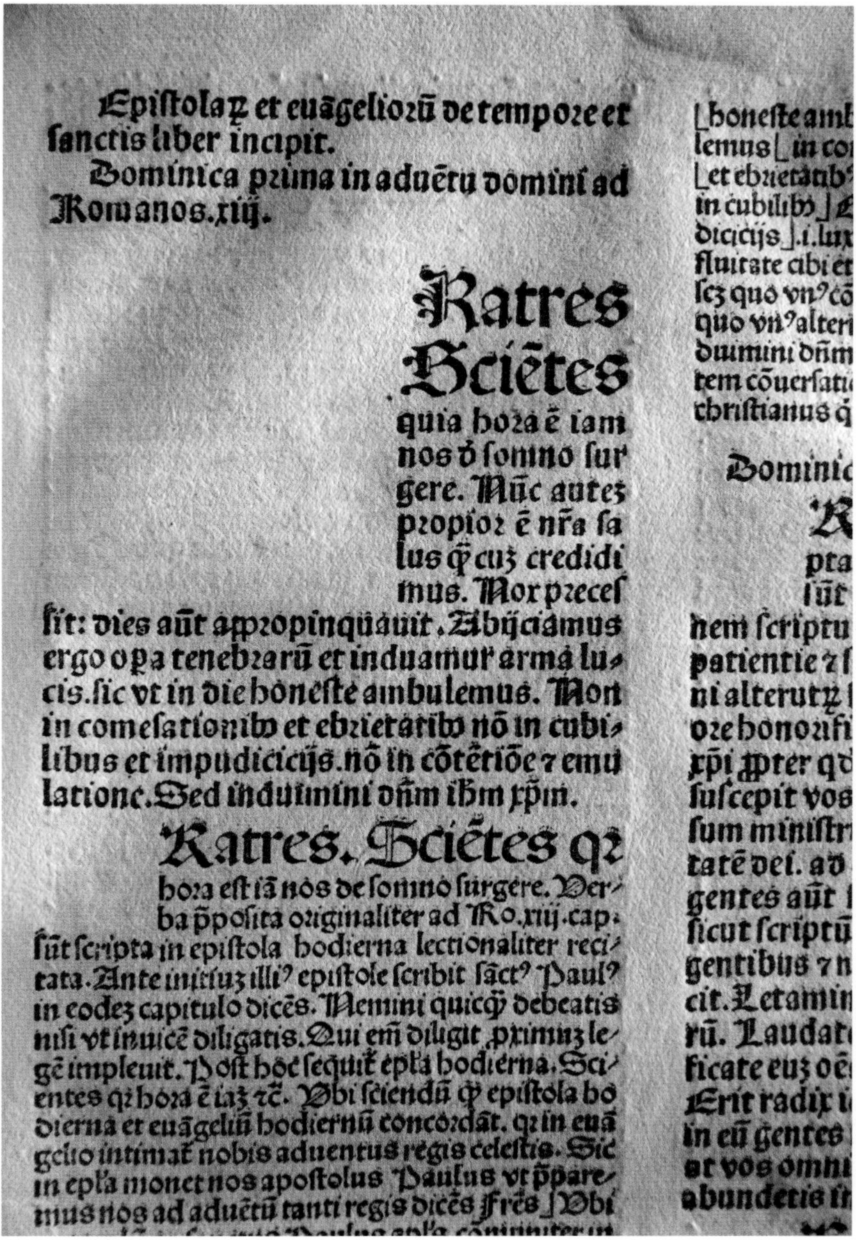

Epistolaꝝ et euāgeliozū de tempoze et
sanctis liber incipit.
Dominica pzima in aduētu domini ad
Romanos.xiij.

Ratres
Scietes

quia hoza ē iam
nos ð somno sur
gere. Nūc autez
propioz ē nr̄a sa
lus q̃ cuz credidi
mus. Mor przecef
sit: dies aūt appzopinquauit. Abijciamus
ergo opa tenebzarū et induamur armā lu,
cis.sic vt in die honeste ambulemus. Non
in comesationib et ebzietātib nõ in cubi,
libus et impudiciciis.nõ in cõtētiõe ⁊ emu
latione.Sed induimini dr̄m ihm xp̄m.

Ratres. Scietes qz

hoza est iã nos de somno surgere. Ver,
ba pposita originaliter ad Ro.xiij.cap,
sūt scripta in epistola hodierna lectionaliter reci,
tata.Ante initiuz illi? epistole scribit sāct? Paul?
in eodez capitulo dicēs. Memini quicq̃ debeatis
nisi vt inuicē diligatis.Qui em diligit .pzimuz le
gē impleuit. Post hoc sequit epl̄a hodierna. Sci,
entes qz hoza ē iaz ⁊c. Vbi sciendū ꝙ epistola bo
dierna et euāgeliū bodiernū concozdat. qz in euã
gelio intimat nobis aduentus regis celestis. Sic
in epl̄a monet nos apostolus Paulus vt ppare,
mus nos ad aduētū tanti regis dicēs frēs Vbi

[honeste amb
lemus [in co
[et ebzetātib]
in cubilib] ⁊
diciciis].i.lux
fluitate cibi er
sez quo vn? cõ
quo vn? alteri
duimini dr̄m
tem cõuersati
christianus q̃

Dominic

R
pta
lūt
nem scriptu
patientie ⁊ s
ni alterutz l
oze bonoūfi
xp̄i apter q̃
suscepit vos
sum ministr
tatē dei. ad
gentes aūt
sicut scriptū
gentibus ⁊ n
cit. Letamin
rū. Laudat
ficate euz oē
Erit radix i
in eū gentes
et vos omni
abunderis in

FIGURE 5.2. Guillermus [William of Paris], *Postilla super epistolas et evangelia*
(Nuremberg: Koberger, 1488).

Sunday of Advent (reading from Romans 13). The format here clearly involves the size of type, the text and its heading in the first section in larger size ("Fratres Scientes quia hora est . . ."), the gloss and its heading, in the second section, in smaller type.

In a modern book, we have so internalized these conventions of format that we think little about them. But an open page of Thomas Warton's *History of English Poetry* (1774–81) (fig. 5.3) shows how complex these conventions are. Indentation and justification distinguish verse from prose, quoted material from text. In the footnotes, quotation marks (on the left) serve the same function. Type size distinguishes text from notes, and also the catchword.

The choice of page format involves economic factors as well, but these cannot be isolated from textual function and aesthetic matters. In terms of material economy, excess white space is to be avoided, since the cost of the paper required for that unused space is the same as the cost of the paper on which words appear. For the printer, labor costs might be a competing factor: it costs the same to have a worker typeset or a scribe write a paragraph on a half page as it costs to have that worker produce the same paragraph on a full page. Readers, however, might find wide margins useful in some cases (e.g., for making annotations in schooltexts or scholarly texts). Aesthetic considerations are also a factor, but these cannot be quantified. Apparently, contemporary readers were not as bothered by the large, type-filled folios produced by English printers in the late seventeenth century as are some twentieth-century print historians, who consider this period the nadir of English typography.[4]

II. Representation of Verse in Manuscript and in Early Print

In literary texts, one of the functions of page format is to distinguish prose from verse and to indicate as well the basic structure of verse—lines, stanzas, even the boundaries of autonomous works. The styles of right justification, less significant in manuscript production, become a conventional mark of this difference in print (ragged right = verse; justified right = prose). In addition to the ordinary use of uppercase letters to indicate proper nouns, or, at certain points of history, significant

Ibunder bloe and blodi,
An hys moder ftant him bi,
Wepand, and Johan:
Hys bac wid fcwrge ifwungen,
Hys fide depe iftungen,
Ffor finne and louve of man,
Weil anti finne lete
An nek wit teres wete
Thif i of love can [1].

In the library of Jefus college at Oxford, I have feen a Norman-Saxon poem of another caft, yet without much invention or poetry [m]. It is a conteft between an owl and a nightingale, about fuperiority in voice and finging; the decifion of which is left to the judgment of one John de Guldevord [n]. It is not later than Richard the firft. The rhymes are multiplied, and remarkably interchanged.

Ich was in one fumere dale
In one fnwe digele hale,
I herde ich hold grete tale,
An hule [o] and one nightingale.

[1] MSS. Bibl. Bodl. B. 3. 18. Th. f. 101. b. (Langb. vi. 209.)
[m] It is alfo in Bibl. Cotton. MSS. CALIG. ix. A. 5. fol. 230.
[n] So it is faid in Catal. MSS. Angl. p. 69. But by miftake. Our John de Guldevorde is indeed the author of the poem which immediately precedes in the manufcript, as appears by the following entry at the end of it, in the hand-writing of the very learned Edward Lwyhd. " On part of a broken " leaf of this MS. I find thefe verfes writ- " ten, whearby the author may be gueft " at.
" Mayfter Johan eu greteth of Guldworde tho,
" And fendeth eu to feggen that fynge he nul he wo,

" On thiffe wife he will endy his fonge, " God louerde of hevene, beo us alle amonge."
The piece is entitled and begins thus ; *Ici commence la Paffyun Ibu Crift en engleys.* I hereth eu one lutele tale that ich eu wille telle
As we vyndeth hit iwrite in the godfpelle, Nis hit nouht of Karlemeyne ne of the Duzpere
As of Criftes thruwynge, &c. It feems to be of equal antiquity with that mentioned in the text. The whole manufcript, confifting of many detached pieces both in verfe and profe, was perhaps written in the reign of Henry the fixth.
[o] Owl.

E

That

nouns, many manuscript and printed works employ an uppercase letter to indicate the beginning of a line of verse; prose employs them only at the beginnings of sentences. Historically, these vaguely defined conventions sometimes find themselves at odds with the text they are supposed to support, and that is the subject of the section below.

Medieval Verse

Medieval manuscripts have various conventions for representing verse. In Old English manuscripts, verse lines were simply run on, with the limits of each single verse indicated by a raised dot. Old English scribes wrote vernacular verse this way even though they must have been accustomed to seeing classical verse written out in what we now regard as more standard line forms. The earliest printed editions of Old English represented the verse by half lines, although there was no precedent for this in medieval manuscripts;[5] twentieth-century editions define a typographical line as a pair of half lines separated by a space, although again there is no precedent for that in Old English manuscripts.

The first English poem to be written in manuscript in what could be called modern lines is the twelfth-century "Owl and the Nightingale."[6] The thirteenth-century Harley MS 2253 contains poems in French, Latin, and English, along with prose pieces; the English verse is lineated in modern fashion, as French and Latin verse had always been lineated, even though it is not always easy to see where one poem ends and a new one begins. Stanzaic structure in late medieval English manuscripts is often indicated by marginal brackets on the right (examples include the often-reproduced Towneley MS and sections in the Ellesmere MS of Chaucer's *Canterbury Tales*). In printed editions, the only remnant of this convention is the bracket used to indicate a rhyme triplet in English heroic verse (as for example in Dryden's *Fables* of 1700).

Function of Initial Capitals

A notable feature of early printed verse is the separation of initial capitals from the remainder of the line, as in the Aldine edition shown in figure 5.4. The appearance of this might well relate to the process of manuscript production. The scribe has as a copytext a text in verse. To

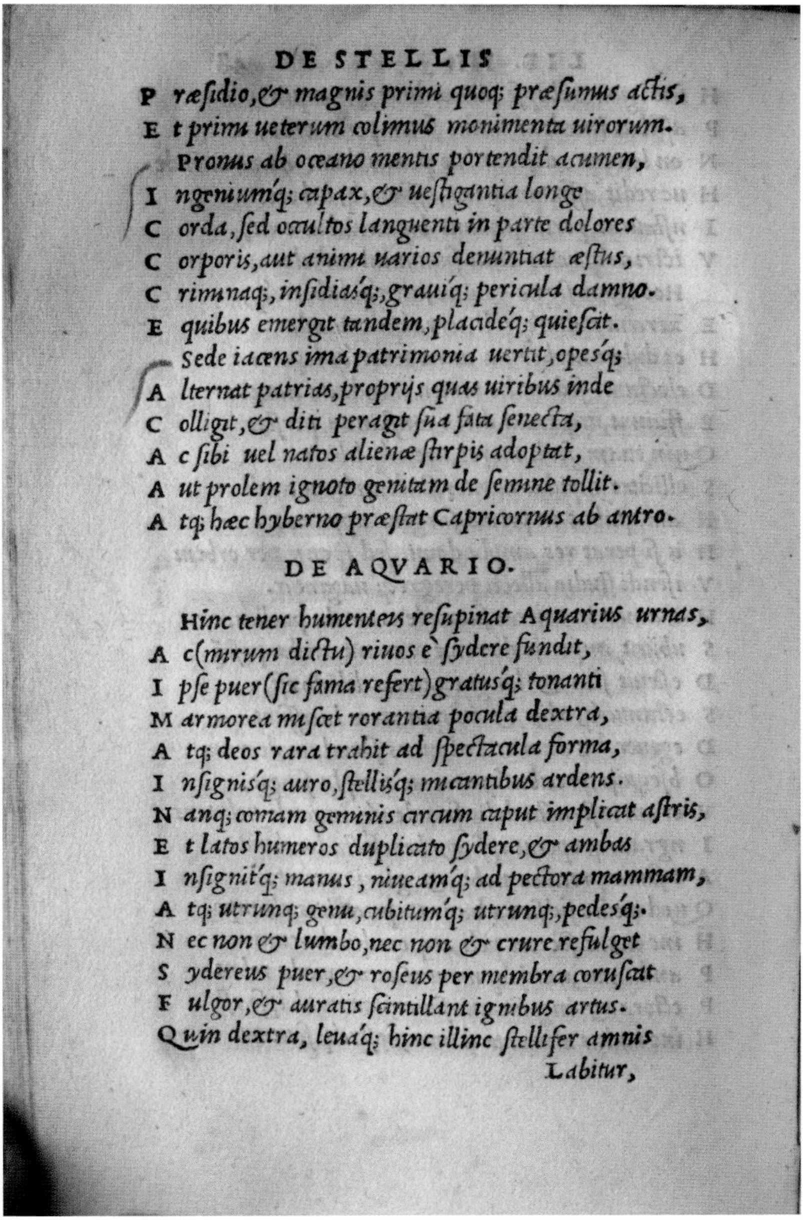

P ræſidio, & magnis primi quoq; præſumus actis,
E t primi ueterum colimus monimenta uirorum.
Pronus ab oceano mentis portendit acumen,
I ngeniumq; capax, & ueſtigantia longe
C orda, ſed occultos languenti in parte dolores
C orporis, aut animi uarios denuntiat æſtus,
C riminaq;, inſidiaſq;, grauiq; pericula damno.
E quibus emergit tandem, placideq; quieſcit.
Sede iacens ima patrimonia uertit, opeſq;
A lternat patrias, proprijs quas uiribus inde
C olligit, & diti peragit ſua fata ſenecta,
A c ſibi uel natos alienæ ſtirpis adoptat,
A ut prolem ignoto genitam de ſemine tollit.
A tq; hæc hyberno præſtat Capricornus ab antro.

DE AQVARIO.

Hinc tener humenteis reſupinat Aquarius urnas,
A c (mirum dictu) riuos e ſydere fundit,
I pſe puer (ſic fama refert) gratuſq; tonanti
M armorea miſcet rorantia pocula dextra,
A tq; deos rara trahit ad ſpectacula forma,
I nſigniſq; auro, ſtelliſq; micantibus ardens.
N anq; comam geminis arcum caput implicat aſtris,
E t latos humeros duplicato ſydere, & ambas
I nſigniſq; manus, niueamq; ad pectora mammam,
A tq; utrunq; genu, cubitumq; utrunq;, pedeſq;.
N ec non & lumbo, nec non & crure refulget
S ydereus puer, & roſeus per membra coruſcat
F ulgor, & auratis ſcintillant ignibus artus.
Quin dextra, leuaq; hinc illinc ſtellifer amnis
Labitur,

FIGURE 5.4. Jovianus Pontanus, *Opera* (Venice: in aedibus . . . Aldi Manutii, 1533). Photo courtesy of the George J. Mitchell Department of Special Collections & Archives, Bowdoin College Library, Brunswick, Maine.

guard against one of the most obvious of errors (skipping a line, or re-
peating it), the scribe first copies the vertical series of initial letters.
With those initial letters in place, the scribe can write out the lines. Any
major error (a skipped or repeated line) will quickly become apparent
and can be corrected.

Like many conventions of manuscripts, this once-functional practice has become purely ornamental. Only if the compositor sets type
directly on the forme, rather than in a composing stick, could the separation of initial capitals be useful. If a compositor is working with the
unit of a page, the initial uppercase letters for each line could then be set
first. If the compositor sets type in a composing stick and consequently
sets the initial capital with the rest of the line, the extra space serves no
function other than to allude to or continue the visual presentation of
a medieval manuscript. This convention is found only in early printed
editions, and I assume the invention and general use of the composing
stick, whereby lines are typeset in units of three or four lines rather than
on the page, made it impracticable.

Representation of Verse in Early Printed Editions

Terence and Shakespeare are two of the most popular poets in western
literary history, and the representation of verse in their early editions
shows the problems both faced and created by early printers. In the
fifteenth century alone, there are some seven hundred manuscripts of
Terence and over one hundred printed editions. No other literary author, even Virgil, has comparable numbers. Shakespeare's status as a
major English author was secured in his lifetime, and printers took
advantage of this, producing four folio editions in the seventeenth century and dozens of quarto editions of individual plays. But secure as the
reputations of these authors were, the most basic form of the words they
wrote was often in question.

Terence

The early printed texts of Terence are wildly diverse, although Terence
scholars, unlike Shakespeareans, have not reacted to these variant texts
by claiming that Terence wrote multiple versions of any of his plays or
that any editor ever thought he did so. Schoolboys from the Middle

Ages through the eighteenth century used Terence as a model of speaking in Latin. Yet even while schoolmasters beat the minutia of his phrases into their students, neither master nor student was clear on what constituted verse nor on the principles of its construction.[7]

Many fifteenth-century editions of Terence print his text as prose, including the earliest printed edition, the Strassburg edition of Johannes Mentelin.[8] When these books were reprinted, some of the reprints correctly ignored the irrelevant prose line breaks. Others, however, interpreted the line breaks as verse breaks and presented passages transcribed line for line from earlier prose editions as verse, even though this pseudo-verse was of course unscannable by any metrical principles. Later editions in turn often slavishly reproduced this imaginary verse structure, since there were no reliable authorities either for Terence's text or for the verse he used. Not until the 1505 Giunta edition, based on the collation of the Bembo manuscript by Politian, was a text established that could scan according to a defensible set of metrical principles.[9]

The verse form thus provided no brake on the corruption that was inevitable in these much-copied texts. Scribes or printers trying to produce clean texts of Terence could not be certain their copytexts were correct, nor did they have a clear and regular verse pattern for Terence they could use to smooth out any errors they might find. The result was metrical cacophony. Even the most diligent students of metrics working through Terence could not know for certain whether any of the lines they were studying were metrically correct. It is one thing to scan verse when you know the verse form and know also that the line you are trying to scan is correct and scannable; it is quite another when the verse form is unknown and you do not know whether that form is correctly represented in the lines you are looking at.

Shakespeare

It is with the problems faced by early printers of Terence in mind that we should look at variant representations of verse in Shakespeare. Variants in Shakespeare texts exist on many levels: there are stop-press variants in the different copies of the same edition, as well as variants between each printed version. As we saw in chapter 4, these variants can involve single letters, words, or even entire passages. In ordinary textual criticism, variants are distinguished as "accidental" or "substantive" (see coda below). Here, I will look at variants that involve the visual lines in which the words are printed: for verse, this would be called its colometry.

For *King Lear,* as with many Shakespeare plays, the text of the 1623 Folio can differ significantly from the text found in the quarto editions. The text in the two *Lear* quarto editions of 1608 and 1619 is more or less the same; editors speak of a "Q text," as if that text were a single thing represented materially, although imperfectly, in the two quarto versions. I provide here what is called a "diplomatic" transcript of a passage in the two quartos; my line breaks reproduce those in the printed text:

> *Bast.* Thou Nature art my Goddesse, to thy law my seruices
> are bound, wherefore should I stand in the plague of custome,
> and permit the curiositie of nations to depriue me, for that I am
> some twelue or 14. mooneshines lag of a brother, why bastard?
>
> (Q1)

> *Bast.* Thou Nature art my Goddesse, to thy law my seruices
> are bound, wherefore should I stand in the plague of custome,
> and permit the curiosity of Nations to depriue me, for that I am
> some 12. or 14. moone-shines lag of a brother: why bastard?
>
> (Q2)

The textual or literal differences here are minute and from a literary point of view inconsequential. More significant are the line breaks. That these breaks are the same can only mean that one version was copied from the other, or both were copied from the same printed source.

These line breaks are clearly of primary importance to the printer. The differences in the text (the form "12." as opposed to "twelue") are the result of efforts to keep line breaks the same. One of these printers or compositors (we do not know which one simply from comparing these texts) was willing to sacrifice matters of text in order to produce the correct or most convenient format.

The differences between the quarto and folio texts of *King Lear* are more significant than those between Q1 and Q2. Here is a diplomatic transcript of the same speech shown above in the 1623 Folio:

> *Bast.* Thou Nature art my Goddesse, to thy Law
> My seruices are bound, wherefore should I
> Stand in the plague of custome, and permit
> The curiosity of Nations, to depriue me?
> For that I am some twelue, or fourteene Moonshines
> Lag of a Brother? Why Bastard? Wherefore base?
>
> (F)

Which of these versions, Q or F, is Shakespeare's? Or which is a more accurate version of what Shakespeare wrote or meant? Did Shakespeare write this speech as verse? or as prose? Do we say that the editor or compositors of the quarto compressed this speech into prose to save space? or do we say the editor of the 1623 Folio set this as verse to elevate it? We are so familiar with this speech that we have difficulty imagining the prose version to be anything other than an error.

But is it?

Some scholars have argued that the variation between the folio and quarto versions of *King Lear* are not ordinary; they indicate, rather, that Shakespeare wrote two plays: one like the folio version (called the "Tragedy of King Lear") and the other like the quarto versions (called the "History of King Lear").[10] But even those who hold this view do not argue that Shakespeare wrote two versions of Edmund's Nature speech, one in verse and one in prose. The Oxford Shakespeare, somewhat incongruously, prints the quarto version of this speech in verse, despite the fact that both quartos print it as prose; the bizarre consequence of this is that the form of F (a play called the "Tragedy") is used as an overriding authority for the form in Q (according to its editors, a different play altogether entitled "History").[11]

The situation in Terence suggests that we should regard the F text with some skepticism: even when fifteenth-century editors of Terence rightly determined that a passage set as prose in their copytext was verse, they did not set it correctly. The strange unscannable lines in some early Terence editions mean only "This text is verse." The same argument could be made of the Shakespeare First Folio (F). F obviously has a source, in some passages, apart from what we see in Q. But there are other sections that are obviously intelligible only as direct settings of Q (see the example in chapter 4, III.2.b). The metrical form of Edmund's Nature speech found in F is not regular. Nor does the placement of the speech in F (as the final section of a printed page, precisely where most adjustments to problems in casting off were made) give any confidence that the metrical representation found here is correct, even if we concede that Edmund is speaking in verse in the first place.

Coda: Accidental and Substantive Variants and the Importance of Page Format

Among the major assumptions in traditional textual criticism are the following: (1) Only error is important in tracing filiation and the relationship between manuscript and printed versions. That is, error has a traceable lineage; the "correct" reading, by contrast, could come from anywhere. (2) Substantive variants (readings involving words) are more important than accidental ones (variant readings involving spelling). Both of these basic editorial assumptions are challenged by considerations of page format.

The distinction above, between substantives and accidentals, was articulated in a classic article by W. W. Greg, considered one of the pioneers in modern analytical and descriptive bibliography.[12] The difference is deceptively simple: a substantive variant is one that involves a lexical item (*horse/donkey*). An accidental variant is one that involves a nonlexical item such as mere spelling (*horse/hors*). According to Greg, accidental variation in multiple versions of the same text can be the result of compositorial or scribal habits, even "house style." Neither a printer nor a scribe was concerned with duplicating the particularities of spelling in a copytext. Thus similarities of spelling tell us little about whether one manuscript was copied from another or is in any way related to it. If one group of manuscripts reads "horse" and a second group reads "hors," we can say nothing about their textual relations. Substantive error, however, is another matter. If the correct reading in a text is "horse," we can assume that there is a direct relation among all those that read (erroneously) "donkey." Scribes and printers would not change a substantive reading capriciously, and classical textual criticism must assume that in most cases such error or change does not arise independently among multiple versions.

This is an important distinction and has proven of great use in textual criticism. But where Greg privileged the higher, substantive levels of variation (lexical variation as opposed to spelling variation), the above section shows that the lower subtextual level might be even more useful in determining the origin and history of versions of texts. Greg did not consider this level in detail because in most of his studies the errors he noted were only textual: either he was collating two different printed editions (the Chester Plays) or, when collating copies from the same edition, he used the "Wimbledon" method noted above; that is, he looked back and forth between two copies. Thus, reset lines, broken type, and all elements of page format would not be included in his notes.

To illustrate this, consider the various versions of Edmund's speech from *Lear* quoted above. We know Q1 and Q2 of *King Lear* are closely related, not because they are textually the same, both in terms of substantives (lexical readings) and accidentals (spelling relations and conventions), but because the line breaks are identical. According to Greg, typesetters and scribes presumably followed the words of their copytext because they respected those words; since they were not so concerned with the spelling of their copytexts, they often used what was convenient. So far so good. But in terms of page format, there is a paradox: scribes and typesetters may well have *followed* the subtextual format for the same reason, that is, because it was a matter of editorial indifference to them. Q2 copied the line format of Q1, not because it was important but because it was not. Reproducing the copytext line for line made it easier to cast off copy, and perhaps easier to typeset a new edition. Accidentals followed the principles set out by Greg: the difference between *fourteen* and *14* being of no importance, the typesetter chose what was more convenient to set in a line.

Many prose texts from early printed editions provide examples. Where line endings of two separate editions of the same prose text correspond, there is almost certainly a direct relation—one served as copytext for the other. Thus the reason scholars know the Shakespeare Second Folio is printed from a copy of the First Folio is not because they agree in terms of substantives (which they generally do) but because so many arbitrary and inconsequential details of material structure are identical, whether page breaks or the line endings of many prose passages.

What this also suggests is that what textual critics refer to as "shared error" is not always decisive in determining filiation, that is, the relation between versions. Even where a textual critic can determine error, it is not always the case in these early books that shared error is the primary evidence for filiation: agreement in substantive errors may well be the result of contamination, where a reading from one text is imported into another text by writing that in the margin. In the case of early Terence editions, the decisive evidence for textual affiliation might well be the correct reading, rather than shared errors. Until the eighteenth century, correct colometry and the substantive readings that support it seem to be absolute proof of affiliation; the verse format is more reliable in determining the relation of one version to another than is substantive error, for which there are as many sources as correct readings. In Terence, any correct reading found in a printed edition up until, say, 1700 (whether that involves substantive readings or verse format), is almost certain evidence that the edition goes back to the Giunta edition, where the now-standard readings and colometry of the Bembo manuscript were first printed.

CHAPTER SIX

. . .

Typography

Matters of page format and layout, discussed in the previous chapter, blur into and in many ways include matters of typography; both involve the intended appearance of the text to a reader. Page format, like the text it contains, is an unlocalized abstraction embodied in book pages and the words on those pages; type, in early print production, by contrast, is something that existed materially in a physical typecase. Type could be bought and owned, and it could materially change over time, deteriorating from a once pristine or idealized form.

In the preceding chapter, we saw how visual format can be associated with genre: scholarly books are often in more complex formats than are popular books. Such associations at first glance seem stronger for typography, and even the names given to classes of type support this: the terms *gothic* vs. *roman*, for example, uphold centuries-old clichés about the difference between medieval and modern, romantic and classical. One can see these various typefaces functioning on a page from 1602 Chaucer (fig. 6.1). Blackletter, or gothic type, is used for quoted material in Middle English; italic for Latin; roman for text.

Distinctions such as these, found in individual books, give rise to statements such as those by Lucien Febvre, writing of fifteenth- and sixteenth-century typestyles: "The distinctive story of roman was a triumph of the humanist spirit, the story of a victory [over gothic script] which deserves telling."[1] This is an enthusiastic version of a commonplace in book and cultural history. According to this assertion, the "rise

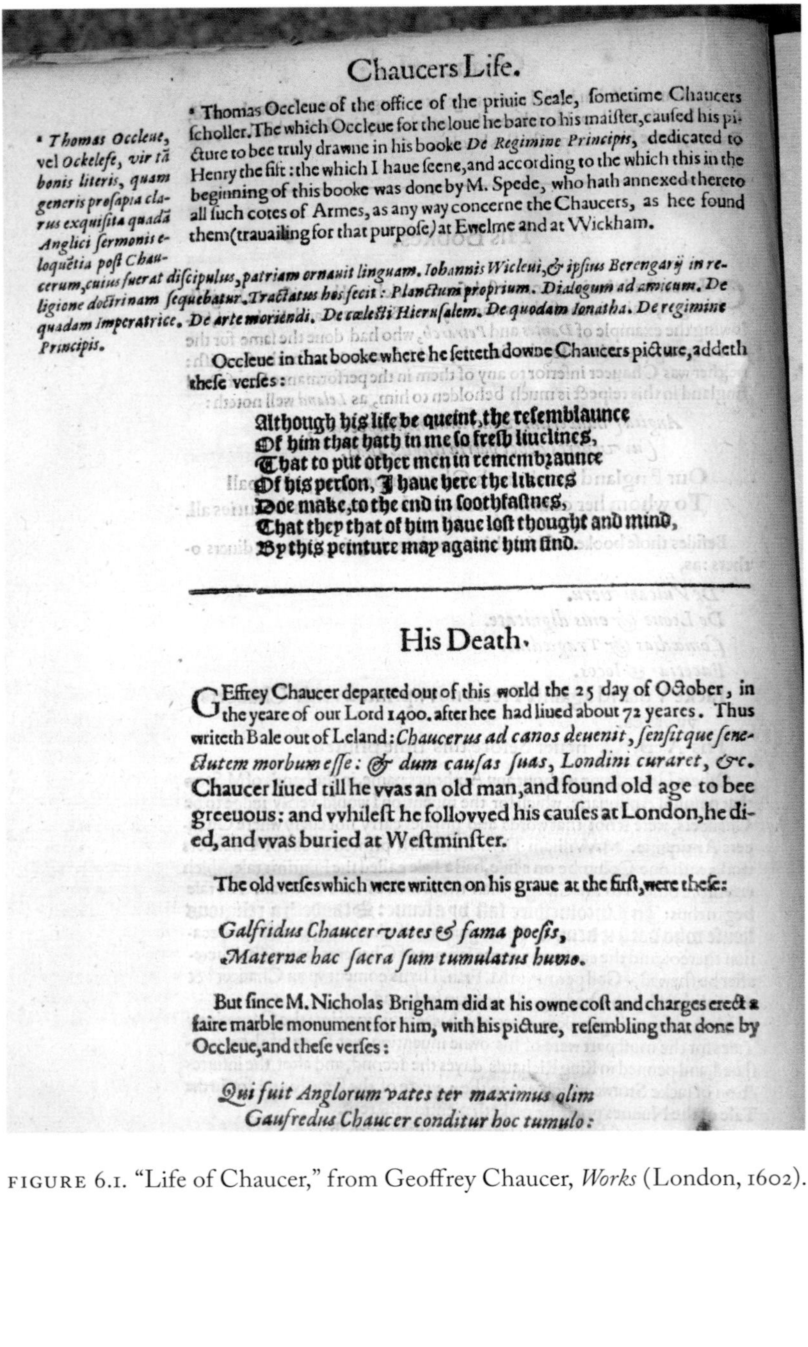

Chaucers Life.

* Thomas Occleue,
vel Ockelefe, vir tā
bonis literis, quam
generis profapia cla-
rus exquifita quadā
Anglici fermonis e-
loquĕtia poſt Chau-
cerum,cuius fuerat diſcipulus,patriam ornauit linguam. Iohannis Wicleui,& ipſius Berengarij in re-
ligione doĉtrinam fequebatur.Traĉtatus hos fecit : Planĉtum proprium. Dialogum ad amicum. De
quadam imperatrice. De arte moriendi. De cæleſti Hierufalem. De quodam Ionatha. De regimine
Principis.

* Thomas Occleue of the office of the priuie Seale, fometime Chaucers
fcholler.The which Occleue for the loue he bare to his maiſter,cauſed his piĉture to bee truly drawne in his booke De Regimine Principis, dedicated to
Henry the fiſt : the which I haue feene,and according to the which this in the
beginning of this booke was done by M. Spede, who hath annexed thereto
all fuch cotes of Armes, as any way concerne the Chaucers, as hee found
them(trauailing for that purpoſe) at Ewelme and at Wickham.

Occleue in that booke where he fetteth downe Chaucers piĉture, addeth
theſe verſes :

> Although his life be queint,the reſemblaunce
> Of him that hath in me ſo freſh liuelines,
> That to put other men in remembzaunce
> Of his perſon, I haue here the likenes
> Doe make,to the end in ſoothfaſtnes,
> That they that of him haue loſt thought and mind,
> By this peinture may againe him find.

His Death.

GEffrey Chaucer departed out of this world the 25 day of Oĉtober, in
the yeare of our Lord 1400. after hee had liued about 72 yeares. Thus
writeth Bale out of Leland: Chaucerus ad canos deuenit, fenſitque fene-
ĉtutem morbum eſſe : & dum cauſas ſuas, Londini curaret, &c.
Chaucer liued till he vvas an old man,and found old age to bee
greeuous: and vvhileſt he follovved his cauſes at London,he di-
ed,and vvas buried at Weſtminſter.

The old verſes which were written on his graue at the firſt,were theſe:

Galfridus Chaucer vates eſ fama poeſis,
Maternæ hac ſacra ſum tumulatus huuio.

But ſince M.Nicholas Brigham did at his owne coſt and charges ereĉt a
faire marble monument for him, with his piĉture, reſembling that done by
Occleue,and theſe verſes :

Qui fuit Anglorum vates ter maximus olim
Gaufredus Chaucer conditur hoc tumulo:

FIGURE 6.1. "Life of Chaucer," from Geoffrey Chaucer, *Works* (London, 1602).

of humanism" is supported or documented by the change from gothic to roman and italic type; gothic type is intellectually backward in some way, whereas roman type is modern.

There are other much more disturbing versions of this myth. In 1933, the National Socialists had declared "Fraktur" the official German type; in 1941, the policy was suddenly reversed in an edict by Martin Bormann on behalf of the Führer:

> To define or regard the so-called gothic script as a German script is false. In truth, the so-called gothic script consists of Schwabacher-Jewish letters. . . . Today, the Führer . . . has decided that Antiqua-Script [roman] is to be designated as the normal letter. . . . The use of the Schwabacher-Jewish letters by authorities will from now on cease.[2]

Is the about-face on the cultural value of gothic script a mark of the moral bankruptcy of Nazism? an index of the arbitrary nature of totalitarian power? or finally a matter too trivial to discuss in the context of Nazism? To what extent can typestyles be said to "mean" or be declared to "mean"? To answer such questions, we cannot simply choose which narratives are appealing (like that of Febvre) and which are not (Bormann). We must consider what type is as well as the nature and function of type classification. Febvre's statement tells us something about the twentieth-century mythology of "humanism"; Bormann's statement tells us something about totalitarianism. Neither tells us very much about type.

I. Typeface, Typefont, Typecase

In the illustrations below, we can identify the various types used by Aldus Manutius or the English printers Thomas Berthelet and John Baskerville and speak of them without ambiguity. But the generic term *type* refers both to material (the physical typesorts in a printing house) and to an abstraction (for example, "italics"). What bibliographers generally consider a basic term in typographical study is the *typefont;* this is a unit that can be measured, described, and its examples pointed out. But what they mean by the term of course are the repeatable impressions made by the material typesorts that constitute that typefont in printed books. To define or to imagine what a typefont is and how it differs from what could be called a typeface involves consideration of the processes of typefounding.

The first detailed description of type manufacture and typefounding is from Moxon's seventeenth-century manual *Mechanick Exercises on the Whole Art of Printing*.[3] In Moxon's description, the process of type manufacture begins with a calligraphic or typographical model, from which an artisan cuts a set of *punches,* one for each letter. Punches, formed of hard material, are then struck into softer *matrices* (the punches, thus, are technically called *patrices,* although this term is very rarely encountered). These punched matrices are trimmed and "justified"; each is fitted into a mold, and from this mold individual typesorts are cast. As many typesorts are cast as will be used in the final set of type and stored in a *typecase.* Thus more sorts for the letter *e* will be produced than for the letter *g.* Although a filled typecase contains many typesorts for each letter, it constitutes only one example of the *typefont* cast by the matrices. The same set of matrices might be used to cast new sorts or even a new set of typesorts: if the type body of these new sorts is the same size as the original set, these will necessarily be considered the same typefont; if the individual letters are cast on a larger body, the two will be different and may be legitimately considered either as variants of the same font or as two separate fonts. If the two are not distinguishable in terms of size, they may in some cases be distinguishable due to eccentricities and variation in individual typesorts.

A typecase can be understood as the contents of the physical case used by a typesetter for one typefont; it consists of the number of typesorts thought to be required for basic printing efficiency. A typecase in this sense would be the unit owned, stored, and either manufactured or purchased by a printer.[4] Even though bibliographical discussions do not follow a rigorous set of distinctions, a hierarchy of terms can be imagined that reflects the methods of type manufacture: each one of these terms corresponds to a physical and material element in the process of typefounding:

A *typeface* is the abstraction embodied in the physical punches; it is thus the style of type, as well as the pattern the punch-cutter follows or the pattern implied as the punch-cutter works.

A *typefont* is embodied in a set of matrices.

A *typecase* is a physical set of *typesorts* produced by these matrices.

Thus one might speak of a typeface such as "Aldine italics," meaning italic type of various size like that found in books printed by Aldus Manutius. In this instance, there is clearly a useful distinction between typeface (an abstraction) and typefont (a particular size of Aldine italics).[5]

Theoretically, typographical terminology could be defined to correspond with stages in the typefounding process. In practice, the ambiguity of our technical terms is the inevitable product of our imperfect and incomplete knowledge about how such things as typesorts were produced and distributed historically and how that history is embodied in the ink on the pages of books. Typefonts can be mixed, modified, and set in such eccentric ways as to be unrecognizable; and an idealized language cannot match the contradictions and obscurities of the evidence.

A type impression and a physical typesort can be described in the same language (fig. 6.2). Kerned letters are those whose letter form extends over the "shoulder" of the typesort and fits over the body of the adjacent type. Early type reveals different ways of setting accents. In some typefonts, accents are cast with the letter; they may be made from separate matrices and punches or, more likely, with matrices formed from multiple punches. In some fifteenth-century type, vowels that took accents were cut at half height. These could then be used with accents with a small letter indicating a footnote or sidenote; an example can be seen in the legal text shown in figure 5.1.

II. Basic Classifications of Type (Paleographic Categories)

Early typefonts are divided into identifiable categories, in what might be called a taxonomy of typography. These categories and the names describing them are derived from terms used in paleography—*textura, roman, italic, bastard, rotunda*.[6] The meaning of that language is modified when applied to typography, sometimes to fit changes in historical style, sometimes due to the mechanics of type manufacture. At certain points in history, the classifications make logical sense; for example, an

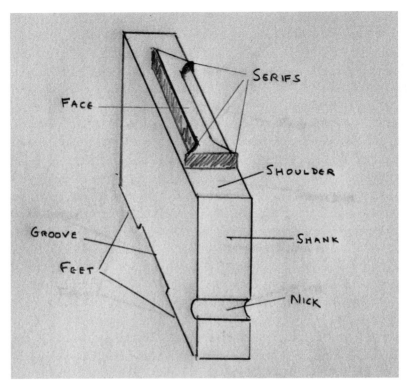

FIGURE 6.2. Typesort.

English printer of the seventeenth century might have a blackletter typefont to oppose a roman typefont (see fig. 6.1 above). But these distinctions are not universal, and typographical oppositions that function coherently in one printer's inventory of type might not even exist in the inventory of another.

Most typographical manuals distinguish fifteenth- and early sixteenth-century type according to three broad categories: roman, italic, gothic. Gothic is then divided into subcategories, generally three: textura (= English blackletter), rotunda, and bastard.[7] What might be regarded as typical examples are shown in figure 6.3, a sixteenth-century English text. Terms such as *fere-humanistica* or *gotico-roman* describe those varieties that mischievously do not conform to these categories. The typeface used in the legal text in figure 5.1 could be classified this way.

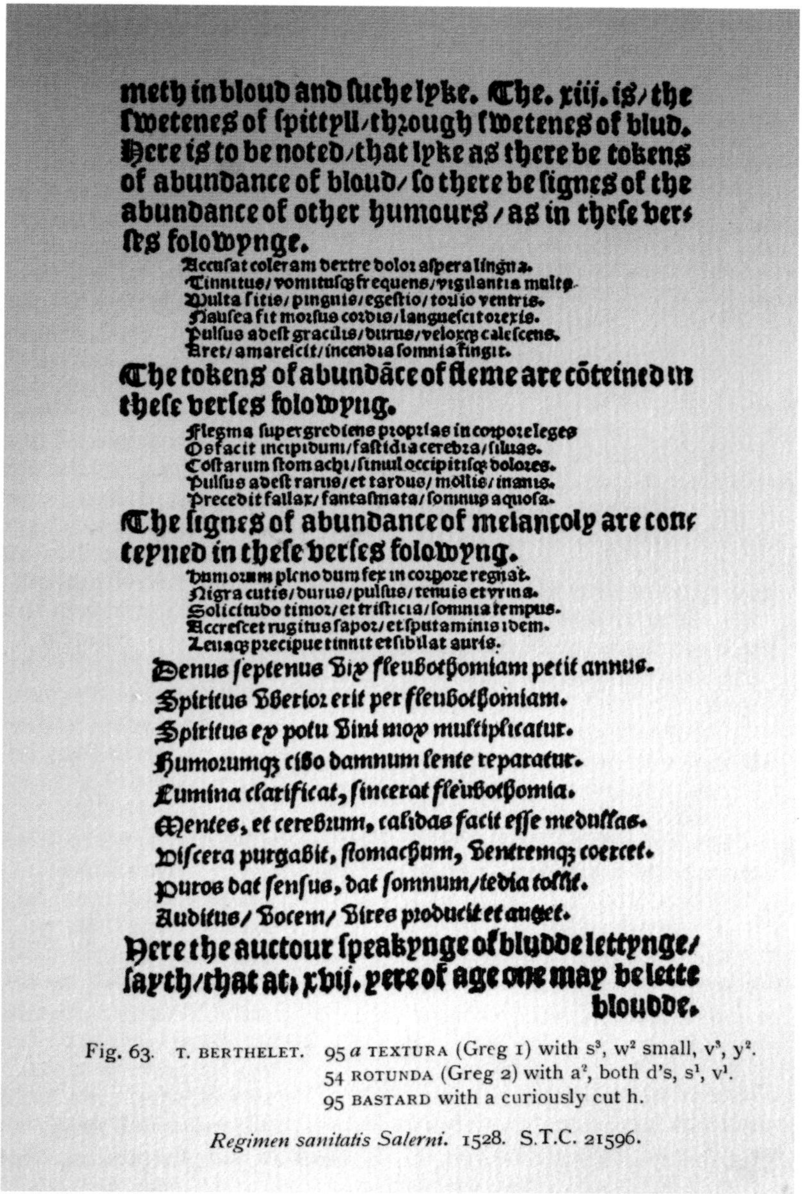

meth in bloud and suche lyke. The. riij. is / the
swetenes of spittpll / thzough swetenes of blud.
Here is to be noted / that lyke as there be tokens
of abundance of bloud / so there be signes of the
abundance of other humours / as in these verses folowpnge.

  Accusat coleram dertre dolor aspera lingua.
  Tinnitus / vomitusqz frequens / vigilantia multa.
  Multa sitis / pinguis / egestio / torrio ventris.
  Nausea fit morsus cordis / languescit orexis.
  Pulsus adest gracilis / durus / veloxqz calescens.
  Aret / amarescit / incendia somnia fingit.

The tokens of abundāce of fleme are cōteined in
these verses folowpng.

  Flegma supergrediens proprias incorporeleges
  Os facit incipidum / fastidia cerebra / saluas.
  Costarum stomachi / simul occipitisqz dolores.
  Pulsus adest rarus / et tardus / mollis / inanis.
  Precedit fallax / fantasmata / somnus aquosa.

The signes of abundance of melancoly are con-
tepned in these verses folowpng.

  Humorum pleno dum fex in corpore regnat.
  Nigra cutis / durus / pulsus / tenuis et vrina.
  Solicitudo timor / et tristicia / somnia tempus.
  Accrescet rugitus sapor / et sputaminis idem.
  Leuisqz precipue tinnit et sibilat auris.

Denus septenus Bir fleubotßomiam petit annus.

Spiritus Bßerior erit per fleubotßoiniam.

Spiritus ex potu Bini mox multiplicatur.

Humorumqz cißo damnum sente reparatur.

Lumina clarificat, sincerat fleubotßomia.

Mentes, et cerebrum, calidas facit esse medullas.

Viscera purgabit, stomachum, Bentremqz coercet.

Puros dat sensus, dat somnum / tedia tollit.

Auditus / Bocem / Bires producit et auget.

Here the auctour speakpnge of bludde lettynge /
sayth / that at, rbij, pere of age one may be lette
                               bloudde.

Fig. 63. T. BERTHELET. 95 *a* TEXTURA (Greg 1) with s³, w² small, v³, y².
                        54 ROTUNDA (Greg 2) with a², both d's, s¹, v¹.
                        95 BASTARD with a curiously cut h.

Regimen sanitatis Salerni. 1528. S.T.C. 21596.

FIGURE 6.3. Varieties of gothic. F. S. Isaac, *English and Scottish Printing Types*,
2 vols. (London, 1930–32), vol. 1, fig. 63.

Any discussion of such types can provide convenient examples to make these categories appear more fixed and coherent than they are: textura is squarish (it is often called "Missal type" after the style of textura found in early liturgical books); rotunda is rounded; bastard is characteristic of vernacular texts. But while early printers shared our sense of some of these classifications (roman vs. textura), they may not have shared others, or they may have represented typographical oppositions differently. Caxton had no roman font, for example, and what a contemporary printer might represent as the opposition textura/roman, Caxton represents as the opposition textura/bastard: in his translation of Boethius (ca. 1478, Goff B813), Latin is printed in textura, English in bastard. The typographical distinctions seen in the 1528 edition of the *Regimen sanitatis* in figure 6.3 (textura vs. rotunda vs. bastard) are represented in the later editions of Berthelet (1530–41) by completely different typefaces (textura vs. italic).

Implications and Ambiguities of Type Classification

Medieval writing styles did not stay firmly fixed and distinguished according to the technical language of paleography. Scribes are never bound to one style and can vary a style, modify it, or combine features from different styles, even in the course of a single page. To the paleographer, this means that many styles are not pure; they are bastardized, in the sense that they mix elements of textura (or "formata") and cursive.[8] When used of printing types, however, the category "bastard" does not refer to such mixtures; it becomes rather a hardened subclass of gothic, associated with vernacular printing in French or Dutch.[9] Based on examples such as seen above in figure 6.3 or below in figure 6.4, bastard can be defined by a number of easily discernible features: slanting letters, looped ascenders, single-story *a,* etc.

Equally problematic is the classification known as rotunda. Paleographically, this refers to a style of handwriting associated with medieval Italian legal texts from the Bologne region. In printing, that classification is a useful one for the typestyle of the fifteenth-century Venice printer Ratdolt or, distantly, the sixteenth-century typefont used occasionally by the English printer Berthelet (fig. 6.4). But students of French typography prefer the term *lettre de somme* to describe this type,

(vt dicitur) rerum euentus necessario contingit/
sed potius dicendum est/quod ea que nos prospe
ra et aduersa in hoc mundo vocamus/ secundum
merita et demerita hominum/ digno dei iudicio
proueniunt.

℧ And netheles yet somme men wryte
And sayn fortune is to wyte/
And some men holde opinion
That it is constellacion/
whiche causeth all that a man dothe
God wote of bothe whiche is sothe/
The worlde/as of his propre kynde
was euer vntrew/and as the blynde
Improperly be demeth fame
He blameth/that is nought to blame
And preyseth / that is nought to preyse
Thus whan he shall the thynges peyse
Ther is deceyt in his balaunce
And all is that the varyaunce
O fys/that shulde vs beter auyse
For after that we fall and ryse
The worlde ariste / and falleth with all
So that the man is ouer all
His owne cause of wele and wo
That we fortune clepe so
Out of the man hym selfe it groweth
And who that other wyse troweth/
Beholde the people of Israel
For euer/whyle they dydden welle
Fortune was them debonayre
And when they dydden the contrayre
Fortune was contraryende
So that it proueth wele at ende
why that the worlde is wonderful
And may no whyle stande full/
Though that it seme wele beseyn/
For euery worldes thynge is vayne
And euer goth the whele about/
And euer stant a man in doute/
Fortune stant no whyle stylle
So hath ther no man his wylle
Als far as any man may knowe
There lasteth no thynge but a throwe
Boetius.
O quam dulcedo humane vite multa amaritu
dine aspersa est.

℧ The worlde stante euer vpon debate
So may be syker none astate/
Now

Now here/now there/now to/nowe fro
Now vp/now doun/the world goth so
And euer hath done/and euer shall
wherof J fynde in specyal
A tale wryten in the byble
whiche must nedes be credible
And that as in conclusyon/
Seyth/that vpon diuisyon
Stant/why no worldes thing may laste
Tyl it be dryue to the laste
And fro the fyrst reygne of all
Vnto this daye howe so befall
Of that the reygnes be meuable
The man hym selfe hath be culpable
whiche of his gouernaunce
Fortuneth all the worldes chaunce

Prosper et aduersus obliquo tramite uersus
Immundus mundus decipit omne genus
Mundus in cuentu uersatur, ut alea casu,
Quam celer in ludis iactat auara manus.
Sicut imago uiri uariantur tempora mundi,
Statque nihil firmum preter amare deum.

℧ Hic in prologo tractat de statua illa/qua rex
Nabugodonosor viderat in somnis/ cuius caput
aureum/pectus argenteum/venter eneus/ tibiee
ferree/pedum vero quedam pars ferrea/quedã
fictilis videbatur: sub qua membrorum diuersitate
secundum Danielis eppositionem huius mundi
Variatio figurabatur.

℧ The high almyghty purueyaunce
Jn whose eterne remembraunce
From fyrst was euery thynge present
He hath his prophecye sent
Jn suche a wyse/as thou shalt here
To Daniel of this matere
Now that this world shal torne & wede
Tyll it be falle vnto his ende
wherof the tale tell J shall
Jn whiche is betokoned all
℧ As Nabugodonosor slepte
A sweuen him toke/the whiche he kept
Til on the morowe he was aryse
For therof he was sore agryse
Tyl Daniell his dreme be tolde
And prayed hym fayre/that he wolde
A rede what it token may
And sayde/a bedde where J lay
We thought J seyghe vpon a stage
wher

referring to the handwriting seen in a manuscript of St. Thomas's *Summa;* the same term is found in Daniel Updike's influential *Printing Types.* This *lettre de somme* is a small script, and as long as examples are conveniently chosen, a typographical category can be usefully derived from it (see fig. 6.3 above). The large rotundas of Ratdolt or the beautiful sixteenth-century rotundas of Berthelet in figure 6.4 are in no way related to this smaller *lettre de somme,* nor do they serve the same function.

John Gower's *Confessio Amantis,* shown in figure 6.4, was printed twice in the sixteenth century, once in 1532, again in 1555; editions of Chaucer were printed in 1532 and again in 1542 and 1550. All of these editions are in the same format (large, double-column folios); they are "the same" in any cultural sense: Chaucer and Gower were the "great medieval English authors" and marketed that way in these large folio editions. But the typefonts used are from different families. The 1532 Gower is printed in what is technically a rotunda. The 1555 edition (set line for line from the 1532 edition) is printed in a textura. There is obviously no difference in the function of these typefaces. The folio Chaucer of 1532, printed in the same format, is printed in what is technically a bastard (see fig. 4.1), the editions of 1542 and 1550 in textura. There is clearly no significant literary or cultural difference in these various editions, even though they are printed in all three major families of gothic type.

Not only do the functions of various categories of type vary from region to region, some typefaces are regional, for example, the German Schwabacher or the now standard Fraktur, which developed from it. Both are technically forms of gothic. Yet these types do not partake of the typographical systems of other European regions, nor is it accurate to say that the broad distinctions of one region (for example, the distinctions implied by English books alternating blackletter and roman) are analogous to those in another (the German choice of, say, Schwabacher). Those who attempt to translate such categories from one culture to another, or from one language to another, are often left in a muddle. English translators of Febvre's often dithyrambic analyses of type use the term *blackletter* to translate all three subclasses of gothic in French—*lettre de forme, lettre de somme, bâtard.*[10]

III. Fifteenth- and Sixteenth-Century Type Classification

In the fifteenth century, identifiable typefonts (that is, fonts distinctive in terms of style and size) can in the majority of cases be associated with individual printers, implying that printers either made their own type or had it made specifically for them. The influential bibliographer Henry Bradshaw saw the history of early printing as a history of type-fonts,[11] and the library shelves of the British Museum under the direction of Robert Proctor in the late nineteenth century were rearranged to reflect this. Books printed in the same types were grouped together: editions were organized by printers, printers by town, and towns by country, both on the shelves themselves and in *Catalogue of Books Printed in the XVth Century Now in the British Museum* (British Museum Catalogue, or BMC). These categories and entries within them are arranged by priority of printing date (thus, in Proctor order and in BMC, Germany precedes England, since Gutenberg precedes Caxton; in England, Caxton precedes Wynkyn de Worde). The cataloguing and shelving systems are reflections of the history of physical type: books printed in the typefont known as Caxton type 1 are earlier than those printed in the typefont Caxton type 5.[12]

Fifteenth-century and some sixteenth-century typefonts are now conventionally described by "20-line" measurement, to which may be added a broad classification of the type: 110G (a gothic type measuring 110 mm for twenty lines); 111R (a roman type measuring 111 mm for twenty lines). The central task for incunabulists (those who study fifteenth-century books) in the nineteenth and early twentieth centuries was to identify the presses of various books, since perhaps half the fifteenth-century books had no explicit indication of printer. If fifteenth-century printers tended to cast their own type or have it made especially for them, a "one type/one printer" rule is a useful working assumption; quantifying these types is a good place to start, even if the units themselves are superficial (there is no essential characteristic linking "all gothic types with 20-line measurements of 110 mm").

Proctor measured typefonts "from the top of the short letters in line 1 to the bottom of the short letters in line 20."[13] Some reflection will reveal that this method will not tell you what a 10-line measurement for the same type is. A better method was adopted later and is now used in all type-measurements: twenty lines are measured from the bottom of line 1 to the bottom of line 21. Thus, the appropriate 20-line measurement of any fragment of text containing four, five, or ten lines can be found by extrapolation. Unfortunately, it is not possible to translate a 20-line measurement from one system to the other. Proctor's measurements cannot be converted into the measurements in BMC, even though the British Library method of cataloguing books is Proctor's own, and it is often more frustrating than amusing to be confronted by cases where the measuring system is not clearly identified.

A second system of identification was developed by Konrad Haebler in *Typenrepertorium der Wiegendrucke.* Haebler classified uppercase *M* into some forty varieties for gothic type (for roman type, the defining typesort was a *Qu*). If the assumption that an uppercase *M* is associated with a particular lowercase font is accepted (cases where it is not will quickly reveal themselves), then again, type identification is mechanical: you identify the *M* from Haebler's chart, and look to the index for the 20-line measurements associated with it. You can then cross-check the reference in various facsimile collections, such as *Veröffentlichungen der Gesellschaft für Typenkunde des XV. Jahrhunderts* (= VGT) or Konrad Burger's *Monumenta Germaniae et Italiae Typographica,* or, more accurately, you do that if these collections happen to be available and if, more rarely, they are accessible on an open library shelf.[14] In theory, most fifteenth-century gothic types can be identified this way; in practice, the collections of facsimiles are not readily accessible, even in rare book libraries, the indexes, both in Haebler and in VGT, maddeningly difficult to use, and not all the measurements in Haebler's *Typenrepertorium* correct.

Fortunately, for the earliest period (fifteenth-century books in general and sixteenth-century books printed in England), more useful resources are available. The British Museum Catalogue (BMC) organizes books in Proctor order (country > town > printer > date). In an index preceding each volume, the typefonts used by each printer are listed, and each is illustrated in a separate section of facsimiles. Each font is classified (gothic / roman / semi-gothic / bastard) and given a 20-line measurement. Because of the limited number of fifteenth-century editions, for a gothic type with, say, a 20-line measurement of 94 mm, searches usually result in a manageable number of candidates. The BMC does not have a general index, but if you can "ballpark" the type as, say, German, all you have to do is scan the table of contents of volumes I–III looking for a 94G (= a gothic type with a 20-line measurement of 94 mm) or, to be safe, 93–95 mm. If the origin of the type is not apparent (German? French? Italian?), that will only mean scanning the table of contents in an additional volume or two. The relevant facsimile images can then be compared against the original example. In this purely mechanical method, almost any fifteenth-century type can be identified, that is, dated and associated with its printer.

For sixteenth-century English books to 1558, the same technique can be used with the plates in Isaac's *English and Scottish Printing Types*. Isaac's indexes are systematic, and organized according to three categories: 20-line measurement; *s*-type; and *w*-type. You measure the type, match the *s* or *w* to Isaac's key, and refer to the plates. Even though types were becoming increasingly standardized in the sixteenth century, Isaac's plates seem to be comprehensive: even the smallest fragment of English printing of this period can be identified.

For works after the early sixteenth century, the identification of a printer is rarely a central problem for bibliographers: most books, except seditious ones, are signed, that is, their printer is explicitly named. Type, however, is becoming standardized, and more a product of typecasters than of printers; there is, consequently, no easy way to identify with precision seventeenth-century English types, and often no hard way either.

Practical Exercise in Type Identification

As an example, how would an incunabulist identify the fifteenth-century types shown in figures 5.1 and 5.2 or in the fragments in chapter 10 (figs. 10.1–10.2)?

(1) I measure the type; there are several typefaces in figure 5.2, Guillermus [William of Paris], *Postilla super epistolas et evangelia*, printed by Koberger in 1488; two are easily measureable: 72G and 83G (the 83G must be measured in 10-line units).

(2) If the binding gives me no place to start, I simply start with Germany.

(3) I look in the introductory pages to the "Facsimiles" volume of BMC ("Facsimiles, Parts I–III") and find all those types with roughly the same measurement; Koberger seems to have fonts with these measurements (p. 15).

(4) I look now to the facsimile page that illustrates each of these types and compare them with the types I am trying to identify (here, facs. XXXIX).

(5) I now look back at the main entries in BMC for books printed in the same types (here, the description of Koberger's types in BMC II, 410). The date ranges for these types are given (1487–88 for 72G; 83G is a cut-down version of 92, 1485–88). If the British Library has the book, it will be described among their holdings (here, BMC II, 432). At that point, it is a matter of checking a copy of the book or a facsimile image, if available, in an online catalogue such as that from the Bayerische Staatsbibliothek.[15] If the British Library does not own this book, things are more complicated. But well over half the examples of unidentified early printing I find (these are generally fragments in early bindings) are easily identified this way.

Ornaments, Initials, Uppercase Letters

Uppercase letters are included in a different physical case from lowercase letters. Thus, the same uppercase letters can be used in different fonts, provided that the typesort body itself is roughly the same height. The association between uppercase and lowercase fonts is strong enough to permit systems like Haebler's classification of uppercase M in *Typenrepertorium* to work. Other identifying elements include initials and ornaments. In the earliest period, these are usually woodcuts, although some ornaments and initials may be cast. The difference is a significant one: if an initial or ornament is cut, every identifiable instance of this block will involve the same physical piece of type; if it is cast, multiple examples of this initial could exist, although likely not in the same printing house.

Initials are usually easily identifiable: they are produced in sets, and each initial in a set will have the same dimensions and style. Even catalogues that give only the dimensions of cut initials are often sufficient to identify them. Standard collections of facsimiles such as VGT contain plates of these initials. Identification of an initial might be enough to identify a printer, although initials, like type itself, could be borrowed from other printers.

The most curious example of an initial is the *factotum*—a woodcut ornament in which any uppercase letter could be set (fig. 6.5). The advantage is the reduction in the number of ornamental initials a printer needs: why would a printer purchase a complete set of initials when, say, the *x* or *y* initial is almost never used?

Typographical Variants in Early Type: Letter and Typesort

In modern type, the fundamental unit of any typefont is the letter: each letter is represented in each size by one set of interchangeable typesorts. In early type, however, this is not the case. As in medieval handwriting, letterforms differed according to context. Certain letter combinations were ligatures (two letters set as one piece of type as they were written as a unit by a scribe)—*æ*, for example. Two forms of *r* were generally used, a standard form and a special form, shaped like an arabic 2, used after letters with a right-facing bowl such as *b, o,* or *p* (see fig. 6.6, page from the Gutenberg Bible, first column, line 13, "quattuor"; the use of this form is clearly inconsistent). The system used by Gutenberg, following scribal practice seen in midcentury texturas of Missals, was especially complex: a different letterform with no left serif was required to follow any letter with "right extension" such as *c, t, e,* or *f,* effectively doubling the number of typeforms required (see fig. 6.6, variant *e* and *i* in first column, line 2). Yet not all printers and typesetters understood the nuances of the distinctions embodied in their typecases. And in late uses of early types, these forms are often misused, that is, typesetting and the typecase are at odds.[16]

The difference between handwriting and printing is fundamental here: a scribe does not need to use any significant mental energy to produce two different *r*'s or *i*'s in different contexts. Ligatures themselves are developed to make writing more efficient. Yet these features became cumbersome when incorporated into print. To produce the two *r*'s, the two or three different *i*'s, and various ligatures under classical procedures of typesetting requires additional work at every step: more

...could arise:
...he was, and so wily of seruise,
There was no man no where so vertuous,
He was the best begger in all his hous:
And gaue a certaine ferme for the graunt:
And none of his brethren came in his haunt.
None of his widdow had but a shoo,
(So pleasaunce was his In principio)
Yet would he haue a ferthing or he went,
His purchase was better than his rent:
And rage he couth as it were a whelpe,
In louedayes there coud he mikell helpe,
For there he was nat like a cloisterere,
With a thredbare cope, as a poore frere,
But he was like a maister or a pope:
Of double worstede was his semy cope,
So rounded as a bell out of presse.
Somewhat he lisped for his wantonnesse,
To make his English sweet vpon his tong,
And in harping, when that he song,
His eyen twinckled in his head aright,
As done the sterres in a frosty night.
This worthy frere was called Huberde.

The Marchaunt. vii.

Marchant was there with
a forked berde,
In motley, and high on
his horse he sat,
Vpon his head a Flaun-
ders beuer hat,
His bootes clasped faire
and fetously,
His reasons spake he full solemnely,
Shewing alway ý encrease of his winning:
He would the see were kept for any thing
Betwixe Middleborough and Orewell:
Well coud he in eschaunge sheldes sell,
This worthy man full well his wit besette,
There wist no wight that he was in dette,
So stately was he of his gouernaunce,
With his bargeins, and with his cheuisaunce,
Forsooth he was a worthy man withall,
But sooth to saine, I not what men him call.

The Clerke of Orenford. viii.

Clerke there was of Orenford
also,
That vnto Logicke had long
ygo:
As leane was his horse as is a
rake,
And he was nothing fat I vndertake,
But looked hollow, and thereto soberly:
Full thredbare was his ouer courtpy,

For he had yet gotten him no benefice,
Ne was nought worldly to haue none office:
For him was liuer han at his beds hed
Twentie bookes, clad with blacke or red,
Of Aristotle, and of his Philosophie,
Than robes rich, or fiddle, or gay sautrie,
But all be that he was a Philosopher,
Yet had he but little gold in cofer,
But all that he might of his friends hent,
On bookes and on learning he it spent,
And busily gan for the soules pray
Of hem, that helpen him to scholay,
Of studie tooke he most cure and hede,
Not a word spake he more than was nede,
And that was said in forme and reuerence,
And short and quicke, and of high sentence,
Sowning in morall vertue was his speach,
Gladly would he learne, and gladly teach.

The Sergeant at law. ix.

Sergeant of law ware and wise,
That often had ben at the peruise,
There was also, full rich of excel-
lence,
Discreete he was, and of great reuerence:
He seemed such, his words were so wise,
Iustice he was full often in assise,
By patent, and by plaine commissioun,
For his science, and his high renoun,
Of fee and robes had he many one:
So great a purchasour was no where none:
All was fee simple to him in effect,
His purchasing might not been in suspect,
No where so besie a man as he there was,
And yet he seemed busier than he was:
In tearmes had he case and domes all,
That fro the time of king William was fall,
Thereto he coud endite, and maken a thing,
There coud no wight pinch at his writing:
And euery statute coud he plaine by rote,
He rode but homely in a medley cote,
Girt with a seint of silke, with barres smale,
Of his array tell I no lenger tale.

The Frankelein. x.

Frankelein there was in his com-
panie:
White was his berd, as is ý daisie,
And of his complexion he was san-
guine,
Well loued he by the morow a sop in wine:
To liuen in delite was euer his wonne,
For he was Epicures owne sonne,
That held opinion, that plaine delite
Was very felicitie perfite.

In

FIGURE 6.5. Factotum. Geoffrey Chaucer, *Works* (London, 1602).

Duos cherubin ĩ singulis summita-
ribus .piciatorij:extendentes alas·et
tegentes propiciatoriũ:seq; mutuo et
illud respicientes. Fecit et mensam de
lignis sethim·in longitudine duorũ
cubitorum·et ĩ latitudine unius cubiti:
que habebat in altitudine cubitum ac
semissem. Circundeditq; eã auro mun-
dissimo ꝫ fecit illi labium aureum per
gyrũ: ipsiq; labio coronam auream·
interrasilem quatuor digitoꝛ:et supr
eandem·alteram coronã auream. Fu-
dit et quatuoꝛ circulos aureos·quos
posuit ĩ quatuor angulos p singlos
pedes mense cõtra coronam: misitq;
in eos uectes ut possit mensa portari:
ipsosq;quoq; uectes· fecit de lignis se-
thim·et circundedit eos auro. Et uasa
ad diuersos usus mense· acetabula-
fialas·et sciatos et thuribula ex auro
puro: ĩ quibz offerenda sũt libamina.
Fecit et candelabrum ductile·de auro
mundissimo.De cuius uecte:calami-
scyphi·speruleꝫ: ac lilia procedebant·

cum omnibz uasis suis. Fecit et altare
thymiamatis ꝺe lignis sethim·p quadrum singlos habens cubitos et in
altitudine duos:e cuius anglis pro-
cedebant cornua:uestiuitq; illud auro
purissimo·cũ craticla ac parietibz·et
cornibz. Fecitq; ei coronã aureolam
per gyrũ:ꝫ duos anulos aureos sub
corona p singula latera:ut mittãtur
in eos uectes· et possit altare portari.
Ipsos autem uectes fecit de lignis se-
thim:et opuit laminis aureis. Cõp-
suit ꝫ oleũ ad sanctificationis ungtũ:
ꝫ thymiamata ꝺe aromatibz mũdissi-
mis·ope pigmẽtarij. XXXVIII
Fecit et altare olocausti de lignis
sethim· quinq; cubitorum per
quadrum. Et cuium ĩ altitudine:cui9
cornua de angulis procedebant:opr-
ruitq; illud laminis eneis. Et in usus
eius parauit ex ere uasa diuisa:lebetes·
forcipes·fuscinulas·uncinos·ꝫ igni-
um receptacula. Craticlamq; eius in
modum retis fecit eneam:et subter eã

FIGURE 6.6. *A Noble Fragment: Being a Leaf from the Gutenberg Bible* (New York, 1921). Photo courtesy of the William Andrews Clark Memorial Library, University of California, Los Angeles.

punches, more matrices, more typecasting, and an increase in the size and complexity of the typecase. A conventional typecase must contain all letter variants and contain enough of them so that a forme can be typeset no matter how many of these variant sorts happen to be required. In addition, each typesetter must understand fully the conventions of handwriting variants on which that particular complex typecase was based. A comparison of the implied typecases for Caxton's early fonts and more streamlined later fonts shows that many of these alternate forms and ligatures were dropped as unnecessary.[17]

Variant and Mixed Fonts

The term *variant font* could refer to several different situations. In the classic description of typecasting by Moxon in the seventeenth century, different fonts could be produced with the same set of matrices: unless these matrices were adjusted in the mold in exactly the same way, these two fonts could well have different measurements. They would be variants, although it might be difficult to quantify these relations.

A second example involves an apparent mixed font, that is, a single typecase made up of two or more independent fonts. There are many early typefonts that were completed with others. Early English books required the letter *w*. French and Dutch fonts did not need or include this letter, and when these fonts were used for English, *w*'s from other fonts were used to make up this lack. The page opening from the 1532 Chaucer in figure 4.1 shows several of these *w*'s in use.

Fonts could also evolve, and a classic case involves Caxton type 2 and its closely associated variant Caxton type 2*. These two fonts can be distinguished; type 2* is a modification of type 2. Yet scholars disagree on how this difference is to be described, and the lack of consensus here may indicate uncertainty in the methods of casting early type. It is generally agreed that Caxton 2* is a "recasting" of Caxton 2. Yet what does this mean? Were the punches modified? Were matrices modified? Can we even speak of classic punches and matrices here? William Blades, in 1861, identified these modified fonts and suggested that Caxton recast his type 2 using the typesorts as punches. George Painter in 1976 dismissed this theory as preposterous but provided no details as to why it is unreasonable. I assume Painter is thinking of conventional type manufacturing, whereby sorts are softer than the matrix material, itself much softer than the punches used to form these matrices. Thus, Painter explains type 2* as a new casting by the typecutter Veldener, made (perhaps?) not by trimming old typesorts but by trimming the original punches of type 2.[18] But it is quite possible that no reasonable explanation can or should be sought purely in terms of seventeenth-century typefounding. We do not really know how Veldener made type. And as the most recent studies of type used in the Gutenberg Bible show, the same can be said of the earliest example of movable type as well.[19]

III. Modern Classifications of Typefonts and Typefaces

As typefounding becomes an important craft in the sixteenth century, the influence of typecutters exerts itself. Styles of roman type become identified by their designers: Garamond, Caslon, Baskerville, etc. Differences in these styles are purely aesthetic, and there are few who would argue that the difference between Caslon and Baskerville type in the eighteenth century is meaningful or functional in a text the way that the difference between blackletter and roman might be. A printer chose as a roman type one of these styles but did not use these styles in opposition. Modern typefounders developed a universal language of "point size." In nineteenth-century typographical manuals, sizes are indicated by a hierarchy of terms—in English, pica and "English"; in Italian, *nompariglia, garamone, Silvio, testo,* etc. When these terms were combined with the terms for the style, the type could be referred to systematically; for example, "English English" (!), a blackletter font of a particular size.[20] The reason for this standardization has to do with the development of the typefounding industry: as typefounding was taken out of the hands of the printers, there needed to be a language with which printers and type manufacturers could communicate, whether in the standardized language one finds in a "Specimen Sheet" or in the "point sizes" of modern typographers.

Old Style and Modern Face

Early eighteenth-century English type differs from nineteenth-century type in several striking details: the width or weight of the strokes that make up the letter, the contrast between thin and thick lines (modern face shows sharp contrasts), the angle of the serifs (slanted in old face; squared in modern face). Compare the Caslon Specimen Sheet in figure 6.7 with the later modern face type from the Bodoni Press in figure 6.8. The difference is described variously; Updike characterizes it as old style vs. modern face. These broad distinctions lead to the description of late eighteenth-century type by Baskerville's press as "transitional," although obviously, it could not have been classified that way or seen that way when designed (fig. 6.9).[21]

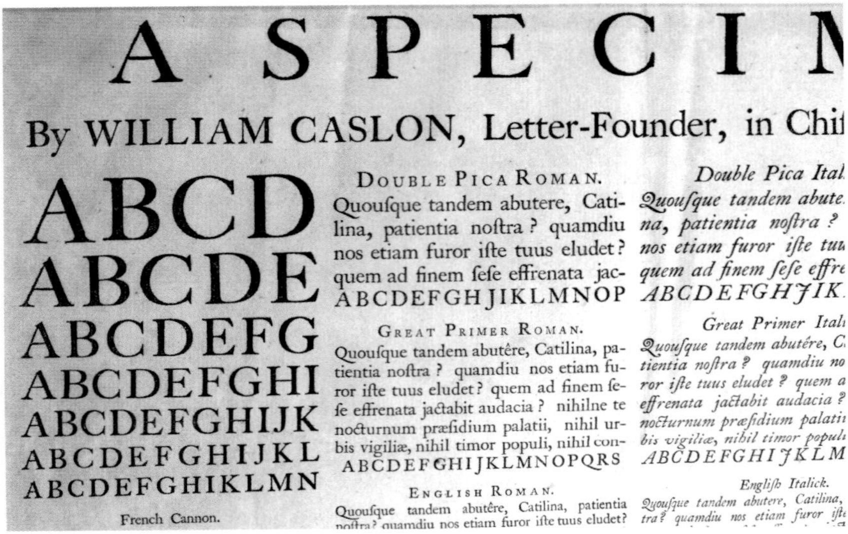

FIGURE 6.7. Specimen Sheet, William Caslon. Photo courtesy of the William Andrews Clark Memorial Library, University of California, Los Angeles.

How important such details were to printers is not certain, but they are occasionally of use to the bibliographer. In the early twentieth century, Thomas Wise produced a number of forgeries, the most famous a putative first edition of E. B. Browning's *Sonnets*. In one of the great bibliographical mystery tales of the twentieth century, John Carter and Graham Pollard revealed these as forgeries in part by minute examination of the type. To Carter and Pollard, the typeface used by Wise was too late to appear in a book printed in 1847. It is significant that the forger himself missed this detail completely: to the expert contemporary bibliographer Wise, the distinction was invisible.[22]

The types designed by William Morris in the late nineteenth century are another example of the evolution of typographical history. Morris's types are self-conscious imitations of fifteenth-century types, such as those in the fifteenth-century books owned by Morris from the Augsburg region. They imply both a history of type and an ideological interpretation of its history, one that rejected contemporary design of type. Morris's influence on modern type design and on fine press printing had little to do with the accuracy of the history he was promoting.[23]

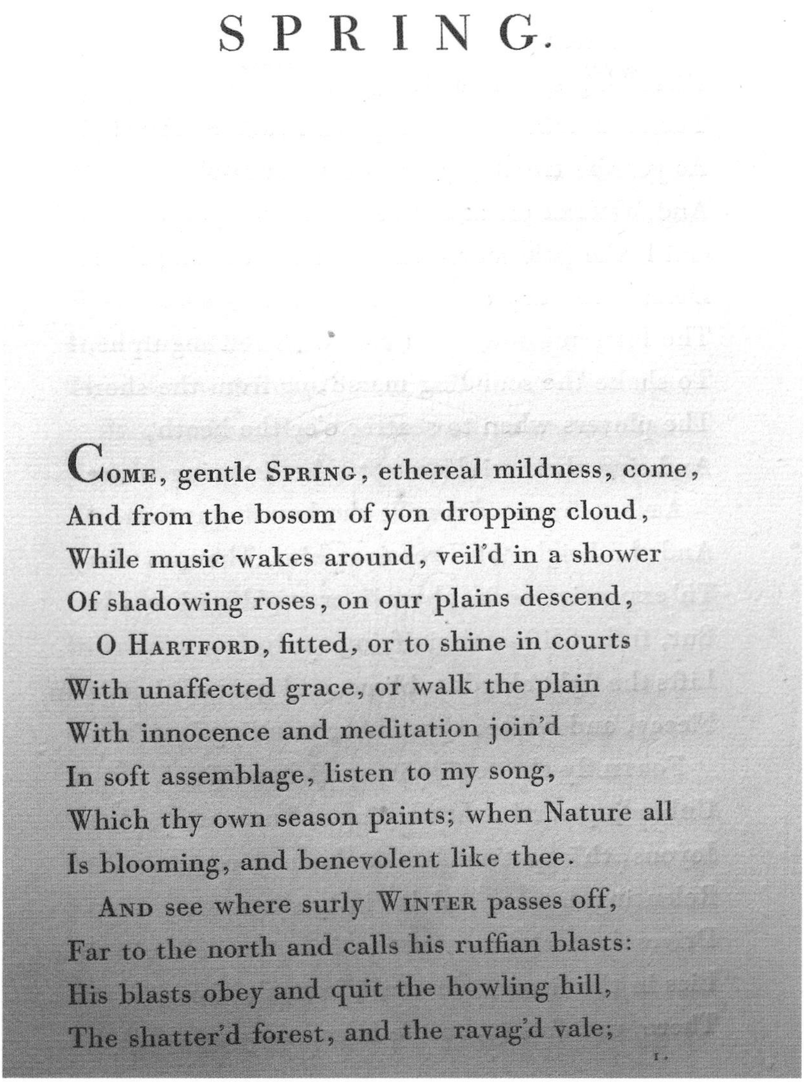

SPRING.

COME, gentle SPRING, ethereal mildness, come,
And from the bosom of yon dropping cloud,
While music wakes around, veil'd in a shower
Of shadowing roses, on our plains descend,
  O HARTFORD, fitted, or to shine in courts
With unaffected grace, or walk the plain
With innocence and meditation join'd
In soft assemblage, listen to my song,
Which thy own season paints; when Nature all
Is blooming, and benevolent like thee.
  AND see where surly WINTER passes off,
Far to the north and calls his ruffian blasts:
His blasts obey and quit the howling hill,
The shatter'd forest, and the ravag'd vale;

FIGURE 6.8. James Thompson, *The Seasons* (Parma: Bodoni Press, 1794). Photo courtesy of the William Andrews Clark Memorial Library, University of California, Los Angeles.

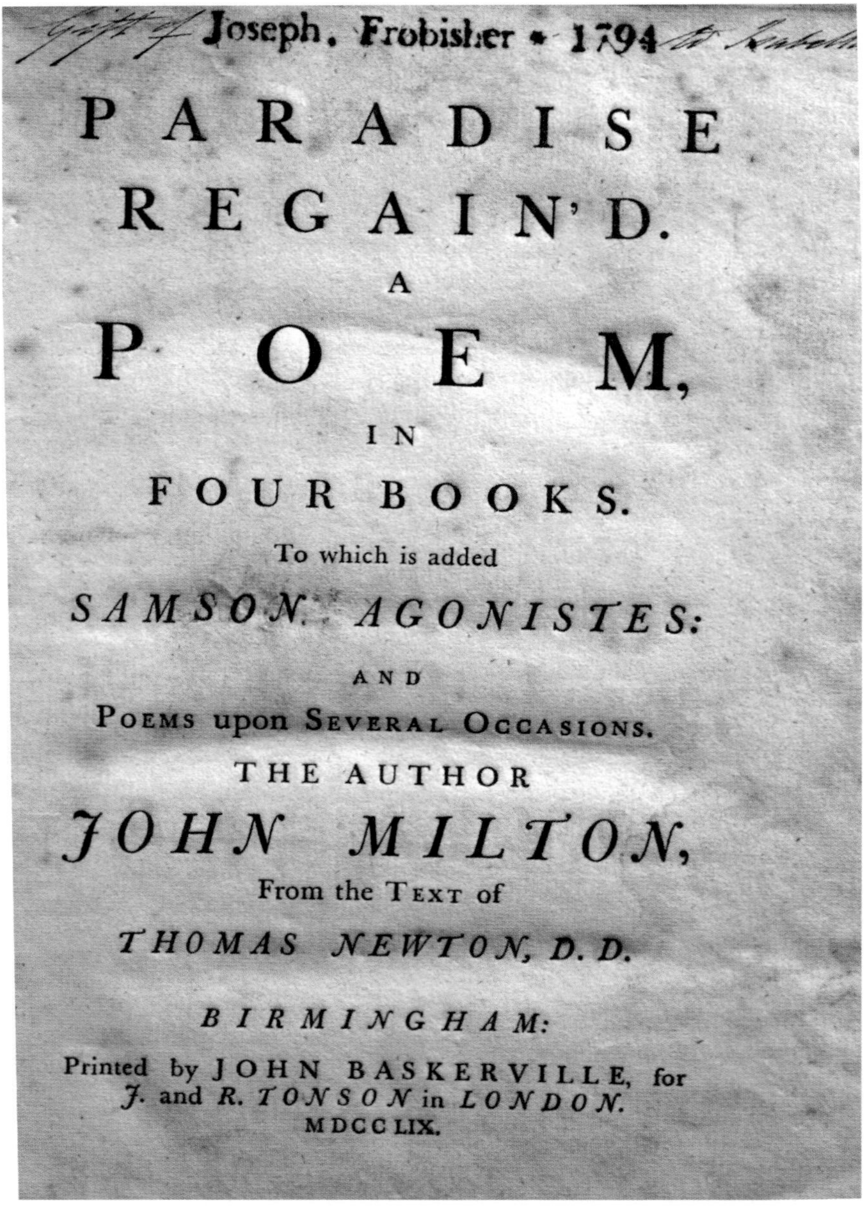

Joseph. Frobisher • 1794

PARADISE

REGAIN'D.

A

POEM,

IN

FOUR BOOKS.

To which is added

SAMSON AGONISTES:

AND

Poems upon Several Occasions.

THE AUTHOR

JOHN MILTON,

From the Text of

THOMAS NEWTON, D.D.

BIRMINGHAM:

Printed by JOHN BASKERVILLE, for
J. and *R. TONSON* in *LONDON.*
MDCCLIX.

FIGURE 6.9. John Milton, *Paradise Regained* (Birmingham: Baskerville, 1759).

Conclusion

Students of early books have been eager to see in typestyles differences of content, as if distinctions of type could mean something in the same way one could speak of meaningful differences between a gothic and a classical arch in architecture. Perhaps variations in type, whether obvious or abstruse, could provide in some way a "key to all culture."

Self-conscious attempts to support large cultural movements by writing styles do exist. The handwriting associated with fifteenth-century humanists was copied from eighth-century Carolingian manuscripts, which the humanists mistakenly imagined were related to original Roman writing. Reviving that style thus defined an entire class of handwriting as gothic, one that could be dismissed along with all the nefarious but undefined gothic ideas it was used to represent.[24] The fact that the early humanists were wrong in associating this Carolingian script with the handwriting of classical Rome did not undermine the pervasiveness of the myth they fostered. Early Italian printers followed the currents of contemporary manuscript production, cutting roman and italic types in imitation of this handwriting, enabling such grand typographical narratives as Febvre's, quoted at the beginning of this chapter.[25]

Yet cases like this cannot be generalized, and the typographical history involved is an obstinate one. Febvre was committed to the notion of a sixteenth-century victory of humanism long before he considered that narrative in terms of typestyles (gothic vs. roman); he seems never to have considered how that typographical narrative might be documented or quantified.[26] The best one can say is that in certain books, perceivable differences in typefonts can support semantic or ideological differences assumed to be in those books. They can rarely, if ever, create those differences.[27]

There simply is no hard and fast rule governing the meaning of typefonts. They were deployed in particular printing shops and deployed in certain cultures, and typesetters themselves were limited to the "vocabulary" of type that happened to be in the printer's typecases. At times, distinctions seem to operate intelligibly: in late seventeenth-century England, blackletter was reserved for legal documents, Bibles,

Middle English; roman and italic was used for classics in the late fifteenth century. Certain combinations seem unimaginable: one would not expect to see a classical text printed in textura (although the early Donatus grammars were so printed). Certain German typefonts (Schwabacher and Fraktur) can effectively be used only for German; bastard is used only for vernacular French and English. Yet when readers confronted something that from a typographical history is bizarre (Rabelais in roman type?), there is little evidence that they thought much if anything of it, even though modern scholars, in retrospect, find important cultural transformations manifested in such changes.

Excursus: The Presumed Efficiency of Aldine Italics

Aldine italics (shown in fig. 5.4) are occasionally cited as a model of efficiency: italics were used not for ideological reasons but rather because more readable text could be set in italics than in other typefaces.[28] Is there any truth to this? The test below is one anyone can do. I had hoped to compare a book set in Aldine italics with the same text set in roman type of comparable size. This proved far more difficult than I imagined. I thus settled on a simpler test: how does an arbitrary prose passage in Aldus's type compare with an arbitrary prose passage in any other contemporary roman type of similar measurement? The short answer is that there is no significant difference.

An Aldine 79I (an italic with a 20-line measurement of 79 mm) has in many books a column width of 64 mm, and the number of characters per line for this font is in the neighborhood of 39–42 mm (see the Horace, 1519). A 1536 glossed Horace (Venice: Tacuinus) has two roman fonts: the text is 90R, the gloss 77R. Comparing the line widths of the verse suggests little to no difference in efficiency (line widths 38–50 mm in a 79 mm type vs. line widths of 45–60 mm in a 90 mm type). Comparing the prose produces similar results. The Aldine uses 79I type; the 1536 uses 77R. The Aldine line width is 64 mm, and this holds roughly thirty-nine to forty-one characters. For, say, 63 mm of text width in the 1536 Horace, the number of characters used is thirty-eight to forty-one. There is no gain in efficiency. I obtained the same result using the Aldine 74I in the 1502 edition of Valerius Maximus and comparing it with the roman fonts in the 1494 edition by Pincius.

I tested a number of typefonts this way, always with the same results. For some, the italics were slightly more "efficient" (maybe two or
three characters per line); for others, the roman seemed more efficient.
The differences were negligible. There is no question that the Aldine
italics *look* more efficient: they are lighter, and there are many kerned
letters. But that apparent efficiency is illusory.[29]

The question of efficiency, however, has a second part. A type can
be more efficient than another in the sense that it takes up less space
or requires fewer characters. But that is only meaningful if translated
into legibility. A type from which our own type is derived may well
seem more readable than one that is less familiar to us.[30] I personally
found the roman type in all my comparisons far more legible than any
of the Aldines (I expected the opposite result). Whether this was a
matter of the washed pages of the Aldines I used, the darkness of the
roman, or my own dislike of italics generally, I do not know. Legibility
of type is not a quality inhering in type but a function of a reader's reading experience. And there is no legitimate way a reader in the twenty-
first century can judge the readability or legibility of a fifteenth- or
sixteenth-century type to contemporary readers.

CHAPTER SEVEN

• • •

Illustrations

Techniques and Applications

What I mean by illustration in this chapter consists of all the extra-literary matter included in what we call the book's text: woodcuts, engravings, lithographs, even hand-drawn illustrations and certain kinds of early color printing. The processes of printing with type and the processes of illustration have parallel but distinct histories, and book illustration is only a small part of the history of woodblock printing, engraving, and lithography; sophisticated techniques in basic methods of printing from woodcuts and copper engravings existed well before the development of movable type in the mid-fifteenth century. In part because of these disparate histories, illustrations in books, whether included as pure ornaments or textual elaborations (e.g., ornamental capitals), full-scale illustrations, or even title pages, have a less secure relation to the book than do textual portions printed with letter-press type.[1]

Some illustrations are printed with the text; others may be printed separately and collated and bound with all copies of the completed edition (see the instructions for placement in the upper right of figure 7.4 below); some are hand drawn in individual copies; there are cases of illustrative paper constructions folded into a book. Illustrations found in book-copies may be separable from the original book; they might be added to individual copies ("tipped in") at a later date. This chapter will look at standard methods of illustration and some of the implications they have for bibliographical study.

I. Relief, Intaglio, and Planographic Techniques

There are three standard techniques in printing illustrations for books: *relief* (ink is applied to the raised portion of a block, as in a woodcut; standard letterpress type is an example); *intaglio* (ink is applied to and transferred from the incised portions of the block, as in engravings or etchings); *planographic* (the illustration is drawn on a flat block and ink applied through various chemical processes; lithographs are the most important examples in book history).

Relief (Woodcuts)

For early books, illustrations are most commonly created with wood-cuts. Woodcuts are relief cuts; a woodblock line is what is left when all else is cut away. Woodcuts and other relief cuts produce a surface that is not unlike the surface formed by set type. No matter what size wood-blocks might be, as long as they are roughly the same depth as a piece of type, they can be set with type in a forme, inked with type, and printed off in the ordinary processes of printing on a standard printing press. Under a magnifying glass, the appearance of a relief line is obvious: it is exactly the same as what is produced by type. Like type, the raised inked surface of a relief cut is pressed into the paper. Ink, thus, tends to appear built up on the edges of any inked line or surface, something bibliographers call *squash* (fig. 7.1).

The earliest woodblocks were cut cross-grain. In the eighteenth century, better cutting tools were used to cut end-grain woodcuts, producing a finer line, a different aesthetic, and often a different relation between inked and uninked portions (lines are cut into the block and left uninked on an inked background). The most famous artist of the newer style is Thomas Bewick, whose cuts are often called wood engravings because of this relation of incised to raised portions. Ordinary woodcuts from the fifteenth and sixteenth centuries are often characterized as crude compared to these later cuts. But the technical means

FIGURE 7.1. Squash. Guillermus [William of Paris], *Postilla super epistolas et evangelia* (Nuremberg: Koberger, 1488).

to produce fine-lined cuts was certainly available in the early period, as is shown by the woodcuts of Dürer and by woodcuts typical of early Venetian books.

Like type, woodcuts are designed for reuse: they are not necessarily peculiar to particular books and book projects, and their meaning is often determined by textual context. The semantic value of a woodcut can be quite general: de Worde's woodcuts of a scholar (Hodnett nos. 926 and 927) appear in a number of books; the woodblocks for the pilgrims of Chaucer's *Canterbury Tales* first used by Caxton continue to be used in the sixteenth century, although the pilgrims to whom individual blocks are assigned can vary; in the 1561 edition, the new cut used to represent the Prioress is also used to represent the Wife of Bath.[2] What modern readers see as crudeness in these early cuts is perhaps a matter of the stereotypical nature of their content.

Many types of woodcuts had no semantic value at all, for example, large ornamental capitals, tail pieces and head pieces, and ornamental pieces comparable to what modern typographers call "dingbats." Printers owned such ornamental blocks and used them in various projects. Some ornamental or illustrative cuts were building blocks, intended as parts of larger illustrations. One of the more amusing examples is in an

FIGURE 7.2. Terentius, *Comoediae* (Strassburg: Grüninger, 1496). Photo courtesy of the University of Southern California on behalf of USC Libraries.

early Terence edition by Grüninger (fig. 7.2). Terence characters are types; that is, the character of the old man (*senes*) is recognizable from one play to the next. To represent all the characters in Terence plays thus requires only a limited number of woodblocks. These cuts could be variously labeled and combined with other scenic or architectural blocks to construct scenes in different plays.[3]

Books can often be identified by printer based on the stock of cuts or ornaments;[4] and in certain cases dated by the state of the ornament: woodblocks could crack in the pressures of printing and later uses or states of that woodcut will then be apparent through such damage. Although most early relief ornaments, dingbats, and architectural borders are woodcuts, they could also be cast, and this seems certainly true of the small ornament pieces used to construct large ornaments. If the same cut seems to occur in contemporary books by different printers, that apparent "cut" is likely cast.

Intaglio

Intaglio processes are the reverse of relief; that is, the inked line is the result of what is cut out of the original plate. In the process of engraving, a metal plate is incised; ink is then spread on the plate and the plate wiped clean, leaving ink in the incised portion. Until the nineteenth century, these plates were copper; harder, steel plates were used in the nineteenth century. The press required to produce an engraved impression must be strong enough to press the paper into the incisions in order to take the ink (in a relief cut, the paper only needs to be in firm contact with the inked surface), and the pressure is such that most engravings will leave a characteristic *plate line* in the paper. Such a plate line is visible in figure 7.4 below.

Other forms of intaglio printing include etchings and mezzotints—also produced from plates in an intaglio process. Portions of the plate are eaten away by acids (etchings) or roughened with a roller or rocker (mezzotints); these portions take the ink. Mezzotints are able to reproduce degrees of shading represented in etchings and true engravings by cross-hatching. A variant of etching is the aquatint, whereby a rough ground is stuck to portions of the plate prior to an acid bath. Impressions made with engravings and other intaglio processes differ in appearance from those of woodblocks in a number of ways: in an engraving, lines are often tapered to a fine point due to the way an engraving tool cuts through copper. Etched lines, by contrast, are blunt. The two types of lines are readily apparent in figure 7.3. Under a magnifying glass, lines produced by intaglio processes do not show the "squash" associated with relief cuts.[5]

Because the ink is in the cut portions rather than in the raised portions, engravings and other intaglio plates cannot be set with type on a forme used in a printing press but must be printed separately. This means that the printing of engravings is not necessarily within the province of the printer. In the seventeenth and eighteenth centuries, the most common way to incorporate engravings into a book was to print them separately. The engraving would then be pasted onto a blank leaf or bound into a book as a single leaf. Many eighteenth-century books were set by their printers with printed instructions as to the placement of commercial engravings. There are exceptional books that

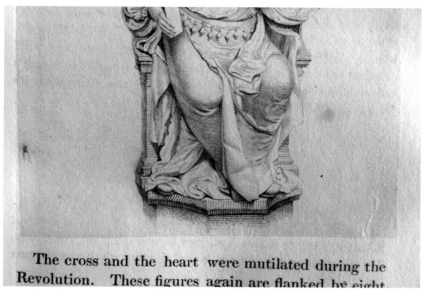

The cross and the heart were mutilated during the
Revolution.   These figures again are flanked by eight

FIGURE 7.3. Etched and engraved lines (shading in figure is engraved; pedestal is etched). Thomas Frognall Dibdin, *Bibliographical, Antiquarian and Picturesque Tour in France and Germany,* 3 vols. (London, 1821), 1:57.

combine letterpress type and engraving on the same leaf, and this, of course, required that the same page go through two different presses; an example is the large Prior folio of 1719 (fig. 1.1).[6]

Engravings and etchings usually identify their artists, perhaps because it is relatively easy to represent writing through these techniques; woodblocks conventionally are not so signed even though the same division of labor applies. A typical seventeenth- or eighteenth-century engraving will identify one or more of three figures: the artist ("inv." for *invenit;* sometimes "pinx." for *pinxit*); the designer (that is, the craftsman who designed an engraving from an original drawing or painting; "del." probably for *delineavit*); and the engraver (that is, the craftsman who actually cut the engraving design into the metal; "sculp." for *sculpsit*). The name of the artist or designer is conventionally placed on the bottom left, the name of the engraver on the right. In figure 7.4, "J. Wale delin." means Wale is the designer of the engraving; "C. Mosley Sculp." refers to the craftsman who cut the engraving.

Plate VII.

Vol. II. facing p. 125

J. Wale delin.

C. Mosley Sculp.

Ye sovereign Wives! give ear and understand,
Thus shall ye speed and exercise Command.

Wife of Bath.

FIGURE 7.4. Engraving attributions. *The Works of Alexander Pope*, vol. 2, *Containing His Translations and Imitations* (London, 1751), pl. VII.

Combined Methods in Early Printed Books

In the earliest printed books, the conventions for illustrations were not set and consequently different techniques are used, occasionally in the same edition. Woodcuts might be set with type; engravings could be printed on the same sheet as letterpress or pasted in later; hand illustrations could be added after printing. The 1477 Dante, printed in Florence, contains two types of engravings: some are printed on the page with text; others are pasted in.[7] A more elaborate example in early printing is the edition of Boccaccio's *De claris mulieribus* by Colard Mansion (1476). Mansion's *Boccaccio* is a luxurious volume in nine books. In some copies, the opening page of each book contains a large, hand-painted miniature. In others, space is left on these pages for hand-colored engravings, which are pasted in. The engravings are larger than the space provided in unillustrated copies, and the type for these pages had to be reset to accommodate them. The left column of this reset page is then printed in red, whereas copies designed for hand-painted illustrations are printed in black only. Only one copy contains all extant engravings, the copy in the Boston Museum of Fine Arts.[8]

In some cases, one method of printing reveals the influence of another, as in the portraits of painters in the seventeenth-century edition of Vasari; see the cameo shown in figure 7.5. The style of the cameos indicates that they were originally engravings, or at least drawn in the style of engravings; but the ink shows that they are woodcuts constructed of two pieces: individual medallions were placed within woodblock furniture and printed with the text.

Planographic Methods: Lithography

In a planographic process, the image is produced on a flat surface. The most common form of this process is lithography, where an illustration is transferred from a flat stone. There are numerous ways of doing this, all based on the principle that the qualities of the stone and the crayon used to draw the image on that stone are different and will attract or repel in opposite ways various chemical solutions and finally the ink used to print the image. The simplest way to make a lithograph is to

RAFAELLE DA VRBINO
PITT. ET ARCHIT.

VITA DI RAFAELLE DA VRBINO
PITTORE, ET ARCHIT.

Vanto largo, e benigno ſi dimoſtri tal'hora il Cielo nell'ac-
cumulare in vna perſona ſola l'infinite ricchezze de'ſuoi re-
ſori, e tutte quelle gratie, e più rari doni, che in lungo ſpa-
tio di tempo ſuol compartire frà molti indiuidui, chiara-
mente potè vederſi nel non meno eccellente, che gratioſo
Rafael Santio da Vrbino, il quale fù dalla natura dotato di
tutta quella modeſtia, e bótà, che ſuole alcuna volta vederſi
in coloro che giù ...

FIGURE 7.5. Giorgio Vasari, *Vite de più eccellenti architetti, pittori et scultori italiani* (Bolonga, 1648).

work directly on the surface of a stone: the artist draws on the stone with crayon; a first solution is applied to the stone and is repelled by crayon; a second solution is applied, whereby the crayon is washed away; the stone is inked, and ink adheres only where the artist's crayon marked the stone. These processes can also be combined with etching, whereby portions of the stone or plate are eaten away by acid.[9] As is the case with engravings, lithographic illustrations must be printed separately from relief type in conventional printing; usually, the lithographic images, like engravings, are tipped in to the completed book.

A lithographic image can be original or it can be made from pre-existent images such as drawings, engravings, or woodcuts, and unlike reproductions produced by, say, engravings, it will maintain the general aesthetic characteristics of these sources.

Photographic Methods

The development of photography in the nineteenth century complicated the matter of illustration and reproduction: photography could be combined with all three classes of illustration, relief, intaglio, and planographic. Photographic processes are of interest for early book history only insofar as they serve to facsimilize early books and provide illustrations of them in other books. Among the more common photographic processes are the following:

(1) Half-tone relief. This is the most common relief print.[10] A screened image reduces the photograph to areas of pure black and white (black dots on a white surface); the image is then etched and printed through a relief process. This method was the normal way of reproducing images with text until the 1960s and still used in newspapers in the 1980s.

(2) Photogravures. The process was developed in the mid-nineteenth century but only began to be used commercially in the 1880s. Machine printing of these images involved a screen, similar to the screen used in half-tone relief prints.[11]

(3) Collotypes and offset lithography. Offset lithography uses the same screen process as intaglio and relief printing. Its advantage for commercial printing was only realized when the text itself

was reproduced lithographically along with the illustration. Off-set lithography involves the same processes as ordinary lithography until the actual printing: ink is not transferred from plate to paper but from plate, to roller, to paper.[12] When lithography is combined with photography, a process developed in the late nineteenth century, accurate copies can be reproduced from any pre-existent image.

II. Early Color Printing

All the processes described above could be used to print in color. For most early books, however, color was added by hand to ordinary black-and-white woodcuts or engravings. Color was thus similar to rubrication as used in manuscript production: after the book was written or printed, it was rubricated; red initials were added, along with rubrics, running heads, and any illustrations.

Examining early books shows that such rubrication is usually the owner's responsibility. For example, many books have rubrication on their initial pages but not on their later pages. For such books, an owner apparently began rubricating a book, beginning with the first page and moving systematically forward before finally losing interest; such rubrication may have been done after the book was bound. By contrast, if a book has the inner leaves of some quire or quires rubricated but not the outer leaves, or if only certain conjugates of a quire are rubricated (say 1.6, but not 2.5 or 3.4), this rubrication was done before the book was bound, and perhaps before it was sold.

Color printing was developed by the earliest printers, although some of their methods may have been no more efficient than hand coloring. By the end of the fifteenth century, two-color printing of text in red and black was routine. For a text requiring red initials or red highlighted words, this was done by setting the type for the entire forme and masking all but the portions to be printed in red. The sheets were then run through the press, and all red portions printed. The masks were then removed; the type used to print the red portions was replaced by blank quads, and the entire heap run through the press again and printed in black using ordinary procedures of printing.[13]

The method used for such printing can generally be determined by examining the pages under a magnifying glass: in any inadvertent overlapping of black and red, black ink will be found printed over red ink. In addition, where masking is imperfect (and nearly all books using this method will show such cases) there will be traces of red ink on type intended to be printed in black, but since black was printed after the type intended for red portions was removed, there will be no cases of black ink on text intended to be printed in red.

In a few cases, the forme was inked in two colors and printed in a single pull. The early books of Caxton and Mansion seem to have had the red portions and black portions inked together and printed simultaneously. In the Mainz *Psalter* (1457) elaborate two-color initials seem to have been put together from separately inked blocks and printed as a unit.[14]

In the eighteenth century, the standard method of colored illustration was hand coloring of engravings that were then tipped in to individual book-copies. William Blake employed a more elaborate system in such books as *Songs of Innocence and of Experience.* Plates etched in relief were inked in multiple colors and the sheets printed from those plates further colored by hand. For mass-produced books, one can assume that individual variations in the colors of engravings are accidental; for Blake's books, one must assume that each copy is unique.[15] By the nineteenth century, processes for printing multiple copies in color were improved, but even the best of these processes still involved completion of the image by hand. Among the most important examples are books by Rudolf Ackermann, printed by aquatint in two colors and finished by hand.

III. The Case of Blockbooks: The Myth of the Transitional

An interesting genre of illustrated early books is the blockbook—books whose pages are printed not from movable type but from large woodblock plates. Blockbooks, particularly those from the fifteenth century, are bibliographically exceptional, and many bibliographers and library catalogues do not classify them as books at all.[16] Blockbook leaves are printed on one side only and usually in folio format; these leaves are folded and put together in codex form, although the forms individual copies take can vary: in some, an image faces a blank; in others, blanks face each other and can even be pasted together. Blockbooks are often found bound together with ordinary letterpress books.

Most early blockbooks are picture books on biblical or religious subjects: Song of Songs, Apocalypse, the Ars Moriendi. In the Biblia Pauperum, the typological relations between Old and New Testament scenes are demonstrated by picturing them together (fig. 7.6). What printed text is required is carved into the block in relief as are the pictorial lines of the illustrations themselves. There is one case of a Donatus grammar printed exclusively from woodblocks, with no movable type (Ulm: Konrad Dinckmut, 1476–80).

The illustrations of the completed books are generally colored by hand, and a comparison of book-copies printed from the same blocks shows that at least some were colored as a group, before retail sale. A small class of blockbooks incorporates sections of movable type, printing their large illustrations on the upper half of a leaf, the accompanying text on the lower half, set in movable type. Only one side of the leaf is used, and the two halves are printed in different types of ink, one for the woodblock and ordinary printing ink for the text; an example is the *Speculum humanae salvationis* (Goff S659).

Blockbooks have been seen as a transitional type of work in an imagined history of printing: they are transitional in the purported rise of literacy (their presentation made abstruse subject matter available to illiterate readers), and transitional as well in the technological development of printing with movable type (carved plates are a transition between handwriting and movable type). They were thus seen as early or primitive in various senses, and because of this, they became involved in various vaguely documented nationalistic histories of the origin of printing.

One of the earliest and most effusive versions of early printing history is by Hadrianus Junius, who in 1568 attributes the invention of the "typographic art" to an otherwise unknown Laurens Janszoon Coster of Haarlem, who created movable types after working on earlier blockbooks, such as the *Speculum*. Coster's materials, according to this narrative, were then stolen by Johannes Faustus (Fust, the partner of Gutenberg) and taken finally to Mainz.[17] Several erroneous histories converge in these and other myths: the nationalist histories that privileged certain works (for example, the Dutch *Speculum*) and the formal-

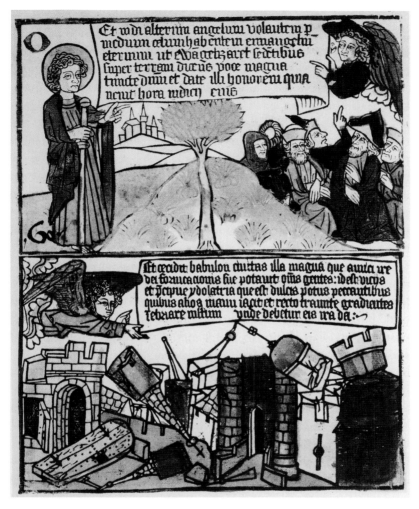

FIGURE 7.6. Blockbook. *Apocalypsis Johannis,* fol. 25v. Reproduced by permission of the Huntington Library, San Marino, California.

ist histories that saw woodblocks as somehow transitional in a grand narrative of the rise of literacy.

Actual history proved much less coherent, and evidence of various kinds, including paper evidence, suggests that most blockbooks were printed in the 1460s and 1470s, well after the invention of printing with movable types.[18] As for their presumed illiterate audience, because blockbooks were bound even in their earliest bindings with normal letterpress books (books that are useless for even marginally literate users), their audience is likely comparable to that for most other fifteenth-century books.

The construction of blockbooks highlights several additional problems dealt with in this study. A blockbook plate is equivalent to standing type, something that was not part of ordinary printing until the nineteenth century and the invention of stereotyping. Compared to type set in a locked forme, woodblock plates are permanent, and there is no need to plan anything comparable to an extended print-run when images are taken from these plates. A handful of exemplars could be printed off at a time or even a single exemplar. Stevenson, considering paper evidence, suggests the figure of five or six as the number taken at one time (that is, the number of copies of each blockbook "issue").[19] Each of these issues could have been planned and its exemplars constructed in different ways: if we define "edition" as an actual set of, say, forty-eight plates, individual book-copies printed from these plates could be printed in quires of 6, or in quires of 4 or 8. This is easily demonstrated by folding three or four sheets of paper into bifolia and arranging a sequence of images on the pages. Determining the possibilities would have been no more difficult for a professional printer in the fifteenth century than for an amateur bibliographer today.

It is difficult to say precisely how we should understand the term *edition* in such cases, and difficult as well to define bibliographically the various formal subgroups based on quire structure and even similarities in colors.[20] One solution is simply to define an edition as constituted by a set of plates.[21] But since the same plates could be put together and used at great distances in time, this means that there is no temporal coherence to the notion of edition, and, given the absence of external evidence for printing procedures, no clear way of speaking of a "re-edition" or "reprint."

PART TWO

History of Books and Histories of Book-Copies

CHAPTER EIGHT

. . .

Bindings

When we confront a painting, most of us look right past the frame to the picture it contains. When reproduced in surveys or textbooks, a painting is stripped of its frame. This is the same way pages of books are pictured in most scholarly articles and even in comprehensive databases such as Early English Books Online (see chapter 12 below). But it is not the way we experience those pages in books we find in a library. Material books do not let us so easily ignore the frames they are in, nor do they allow us to experience the pages the way they are reproduced even in many of the illustrations here (see, for example, figs. 6.3 and 7.6). When we hold a book, especially a rare book, our attention is often consumed by that frame, that is, the binding. Most readers looking at any of the bindings pictured below would quickly describe them as books; no viewer looking at an empty picture frame would describe it as a painting.

I. Basic Binding Structures

Binding histories and handbooks distinguish two processes in binding: the process of *forwarding* and the process of *finishing*. Forwarding consists of all actions that produce a structurally functional binding (e.g., sewing of quires, constructing boards and spine); finishing consists of the final decoration of the completed binding (e.g., decoration of the leather with stamps or rolls). Paradoxically, the most readily apparent characteristics of a binding, and those most useful for identifying it as well, are those involved in finishing, seemingly the more superficial of the two categories. And with few exceptions (the work of Nicholas Pickwood is one), finishing is the primary focus of most binding histories.[1]

Quires may be sewn together or into a binding in a number of ways: in "stabbed" bindings, quires are simply folded, placed together, and sewn straight through the leaves; in Coptic binding (an early binding style not used of printed books), a single thread is passed through each quire and looped through itself to hold the quires together. In classic binding, quires are sewn through their folds and onto perpendicular *cords* (usually between three and five) with the same thread. These cords are attached to boards, and may be reinforced with binding strips (fig. 8.1). A *spine* covers the cords; a *cover* surrounds the boards. A *pastedown* inside the cover hides the attached cords (see fig. 1.2). Covers are generally constructed of one piece, but many books have had spines replaced, and in a large percentage of early books, the cover, spine, and even boards may not be contemporary. Some early books are quarter- or half-bound (leather covers cover only part of their boards).

In early books, the binding is constructed on the book itself; cords are attached to boards, and the cover, including spine, is built up on the book. When such a book is opened, the spine usually remains in contact with the bound edges of the leaves. It is possible to construct the spine such that when the book is open, the spine is no longer in contact with the leaves. Such bindings are found as early as the medieval period; English bindings are typically of this type after 1820. This style of spine is characteristic of a binding type developed in the late eighteenth century, a *case binding*. A case binding consists of a prefabricated case of boards and spine; that is, the cover is not manufactured on the book-copy. This prefabricated case is then glued onto the book, or rather the book is glued into the case. By the mid-nineteenth century, this mass-produced binding becomes, for many editions, part of the book rather than simply an accident of provenance. If the book you are holding is what we call "hard-bound," it is an excellent example of this type of binding.

Bindings from the fifteenth through eighteenth centuries generally consist of wooden boards (oak or beech) covered with some kind of leather. Some early bindings use pasteboards (sheets of paper pasted

FIGURE 8.1. Binding structures.

together); others are bound in limp vellum bindings and are thus analogous in many ways to a modern paperback. There are various materials for covers:

> calf: typical of English bindings, thick, suitable for stamps
> morocco (goat): Italian, does not take stamp well
> pigskin: not often used in England; characteristic of German
>   bindings of the sixteenth and seventeenth centuries
> vellum
> other materials—doe, etc.

The grains and surfaces of these materials are often but not always distinguishable. The websites of the British Library and the Bayerische Staatsbibliothek have excellent color images demonstrating different binding materials. Examples also can be seen in many of the illustrations here (vellum in fig. 1.6; calf in fig. 8.2; morocco in fig. 8.3).

The structures and decorations of bindings are modified by fashion, and those fashions have little to do with the contents of the book: a religious book and a secular book do not usually have distinguishable binding decoration; bindings of any two books from seventeenth-century England, however diverse in content, will be far more alike than the bindings found on different copies of the same text that come from different regions or time periods.

II. Trade vs. Bespoke Bindings

For books printed prior to the mid-nineteenth century, bindings are generally not part of the catalogued book. They are, rather, individual objects attached to individual book-copies. During the hand press period, each binding is handmade, although these handmade bindings may be mass produced. And any individual book-copy is subject to rebinding throughout its life. An important distinction in binding, although not one easy to define, is whether a binding is put on a book before retail sale by what we might call a publisher or a bookseller or ordered or put on a book by a retail buyer.

The most authoritative and influential study of early bindings is still E. P. Goldschmidt, *Gothic and Renaissance Bookbindings* (1928);

Goldschmidt states categorically: "In the fifteenth and sixteenth centuries books were always sold in rough, unfolded sheets, and never otherwise." Goldschmidt means here "sold by the printer/publisher *to* a retail bookseller."[2] Goldschmidt recognizes "trade bindings" (any series of like bindings on the same book) but defines them as products of particular booksellers, who may or may not have been binders.

Goldschmidt's general principle (the sale of early books in rough sheets) extended further than he may have intended and resulted in what Stuart Bennett calls a consensus in mid-twentieth-century scholarship on the English book trade of the eighteenth century: that English books of this period were also distributed and sold in loose sheets, even to retail customers.[3] Such a notion contradicts what most of us experience when looking at these eighteenth-century books; the uniformity of bindings from the period seems inconsistent with a theory that each was commissioned by an individual owner. What would be the point of commissioning a binding if the result was one of the ordinary bindings so commonly found on such books in our libraries? Bennett claims, by contrast, that for a period he defines as 1520–1800 the percentage of books bound before retail sale may be as high as 80 percent and that such "prepublication" bindings can be found as early as the fifteenth century.[4]

The standard term for a binding put on by a publisher or bookseller and sold with the book is *trade binding*. A binding ordered by a customer is a *bespoke binding*. These terms, however, are not precise nor are they universal, since they seem appropriate to bookselling and binding practices more characteristic of the modern period than the early period; Bennett thus proposes for "trade" binding the term *prepublication* binding, which has its own set of attendant problems. What is being distinguished in both cases is a mass-produced, run-of-the-mill contemporary binding such as those in figure 8.2, as opposed to an individual, often aristocratic binding, such as those shown in figure 8.3 below.

Printer, Publisher, Bookseller

To distinguish bindings as we have in the above section implies distinguishing the functions of printer, publisher, and bookseller. Yet this is another case in bibliography where the language of bibliography poses

FIGURE 8.2. Eighteenth-century trade bindings.

or implies distinctions that may not have existed historically with any uniformity. In the sixteenth century, a book in England may have been printed by a certain printer for an entrepreneur, who may in turn have distributed these books to a bookseller. These functions may have been represented by the names in a colophon or, in later periods, on a title page. In some cases, the same person might serve more than one of these functions. Thus, the material evidence of the typefont (the evidence that enables us to assign books to printers in the fifteenth century) does not enable us to assign a book to the entrepreneur who commissions the printing of the book, someone we would be likely to describe as a publisher in the modern sense.

Bennett's proposed term *prepublication* thus depends on an agreement about what publication is; and this, as a means of distinguishing binding types, may simply beg the question. We still need to define at what point a book is published: is this when its sheets leave the press? when it is packed for delivery for booksellers? or when its first retail sale begins? Since it is difficult to define exactly what a publisher is or what the moment of publication is during the hand press period generally, it is equally difficult to categorize material evidence (binding types) based on such abstractions.

The solution implied in many histories of binding, including Bennett's, may be to imagine a continuum, with the buyer at one end and the printer at the other; a fluid and changing institution of publication lies between and to some extent controls these two extremes. The institution of binding then could be said to move historically from the buyer in the earliest period toward the printer in the latest period.

III. Original Binding vs. Rebinding

The discussion in the preceding section refers to what is variously and loosely described as the original or contemporary binding, that is, a binding understood as the first binding put on a book. In the strictest sense, the terms *original* and *contemporary* are different, but the nature of the material evidence makes them often indistinguishable: a printed book-copy may lie unbound for decades; it could also be bound and re-bound soon enough after printing for the rebinding to be contemporary. Because of the vagaries of these terms, often a more general term such as *early binding* is used. The more monumental the book and the earlier the book, the more likely its copies will have been rebound at some point in their histories. Books regarded as valuable in the book trade are no more likely to remain in their original bindings than valuable paintings are likely to remain in their original, deteriorating frames.

The fact that so many of the early books we encounter in libraries are not in their original bindings has produced among most bibliographical scholars a habit of mind that considers bindings and books two separate things. Bibliographical books are thought to transcend their bindings. I can still, in accord with standard bibliographical thinking, take any book on my shelves, rip its binding off, and have it rebound without changing its bibliographical identity. If we look at early English plays in a library such as the Huntington Library or the Clark Library, with a focused interest only in their earliest distribution and form, we soon learn to disregard bindings altogether: the copies are nearly all in elegant, expensive bindings from the nineteenth century, creating a common genre and form these books may not have possessed in the seventeenth century. The morocco-bound quarto volumes shown in figure 8.3 from the Clark Library reflect nineteenth-century English aesthetics and the importance early English drama had for nineteenth-century English collectors and their American counterparts of the twentieth century. But these bindings tell us little about institutions surrounding English drama in the seventeenth century.

IV. Resources for Studying Bindings

The study of book structure, the nature of editions, and the institution of printing had begun in earnest by the seventeenth century. Bookbinding, however, remained a craft only marginally related to the study of books, that is, the content of books and the basic processes of printing. Early collectors spent a great deal of attention on the bindings that they commissioned, but binding history in and of itself did not become an object of bibliographical study until the nineteenth and twentieth centuries. For the collector, the original binding was simply the package or frame in which a book appeared, and this frame could be modified to accord with the decor of the building where the book would be displayed.

One consequence of this history is that of the numerous studies on binding, there is as yet no comprehensive survey that will make a general reader comfortable with binding history. Students of bookbinding must leap into this field at a sophisticated level: Goldschmidt's *Gothic*

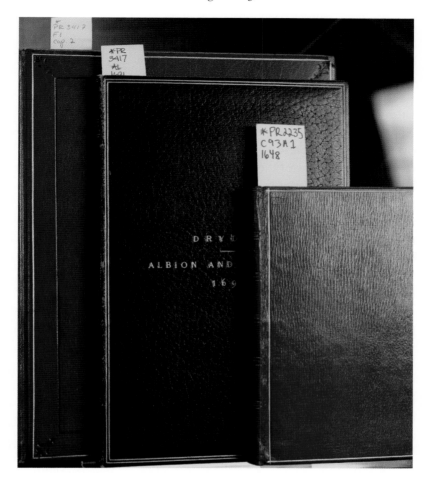

FIGURE 8.3. Morocco bindings. Photo courtesy of the William Andrews Clark Memorial Library, University of California, Los Angeles.

and Renaissance Bookbindings may be the best place to start, no matter what level of scholarship, although it is not in any ordinary sense introductory. Most histories and collections of bindings, including Goldschmidt's, have concentrated understandably on monumental, decorated bindings. The earliest histories of bindings were often belletristic and just as often unreliable, even when they dealt with such important figures in binding history as Grolier.[5] Until recently, there was no book that gave a good survey of ordinary run-of-the-mill bindings. Pearson's excellent *English Bookbinding* (1995) has corrected that for English bindings, but there is nothing comparable to Pearson's study for other regions.[6]

There are, then, limited ways of studying the field, either in a theoretical or practical sense. You could perhaps read every book on bookbinding available; after a hundred of these, you might be in a position to critique or at least reread the first. Alternatively, you could call heaps of rare books out of one of the few libraries that will permit you to do so, hoping for the best. But this is not something that can be done easily, and without guidance, you might be as bewildered as before, satisfied only to have handled the books themselves. A congenial librarian who will describe these bindings for you is the best possible resource, and some of us have been lucky in this regard; but those librarians with time on their hands, expertise, and a collection of old books ready to hand are in short supply.

Among the best readily available printed resources on bindings are present-day illustrated sales and auction catalogues, even though these will not put the actual books in your hands. Many contain full-color, high-quality photographs of books whose bindings are described in detail, since bindings about which nothing is known are unlikely to be pictured. Book dealers are able to invest the time and money required to obtain reliable descriptions and photographs of expensive book-copies, as can be easily seen by glancing through a recent Maggs Bros. catalogue or the stunning catalogues produced by Phillip J. Pirages.[7] If you view a thousand pictures of bindings in auction catalogues, and read the descriptions of them, you will be in excellent shape for describing, dating, and evaluating the next ones you encounter. Some of these auction catalogues are of such high quality they qualify as reference books.[8]

Online, browsable, catalogues and collections are also available. Scott Husby has developed a website, Bookbindings on Incunables in American Library Collections, that surveys early bindings; it contains selections of bindings from each library with minimal notes (http://www.bibsocamer.org/BibSite/Husby/). The British Library also has a database of bindings, with very brief notes for each entry (http://www.bl.uk/catalogues/bookbindings/). Both collections show pictures of binding covers rather than pictures of bindings; and neither the notes nor the images provide much information about structure, endpapers, or marks of ownership and use. Nonetheless, the hundreds of color illustrations can at least be browsed and can be searched in various systematic ways, by country, by century, etc. The British Library database presents its bindings differently from the way similar bindings are shown in sales catalogues. Examples are chosen for convenience and coherence; those of the auction catalogue, by contrast, are more serendipitous and are chosen according to what happens to be available for sale. Neither of these methods is inherently superior to the other and each has its advantages.

V. Identification and Classification of Early Bindings

Bindings from certain regions and certain periods have been more heavily researched than those of other regions and periods. They are studied not because of their relative importance but rather because of accidents of political and aesthetic history. For fifteenth- and sixteenth-century bindings, the most attention has been paid to German bindings, and the reasons for this are various. Early German bindings use recognizable binding stamps that enable the bindings from particular binders to be identified and catalogued. Early Italian binders, by contrast, did not develop these distinctive marks. Later history also is a factor. When German monasteries were secularized in the late eighteenth and early nineteenth centuries, vast numbers of German books, many of them in their earliest bindings, came on the market. In contrast to books in university or aristocratic libraries, they had not been subject to wholesale rebinding, and many ended up in reasonably accessible public and private libraries.[9] Binding histories must concentrate on what can be studied; and "what can be studied" is not necessarily a representative sample of "what was once there."

Most of the bindings in the early period of printing are localized; they are products of particular monasteries or products of particular booksellers. They are thus associated with the retail end of the book trade and unrelated in a direct way to the locale of printing. The difference between the place of printing and the place of binding is an indication of movement of books through the book trade: German and Italian books are often found in English bindings but rarely the reverse. Liturgical books, geared to particular regions, will show a closer relation between printer and owner than will a classical text. Widely distributed Italian classical books will appear in bindings from any region.

Identification of Fifteenth- and Early-Sixteenth-Century Bindings

Some features of early binding indicate date or region; others can identify the bindery. Among the gross features that may distinguish early from late are the existence of clasps (most early books have these) and the relation of boards to the leaves (on early bindings, these are the same size as the book block itself with no overlap). Titles of early books may be written on the fore-edge (i.e., the edge opposite the spine). Most early bindings are decorated in some fashion: such patterns of decoration are regional, and often patterns are identifiable. For English bindings, such differences have been laid out in a table by Pearson.[10]

Other features are also regional: in a rule attributed to J. Basil Oldham, English and French bindings have clasps on upper cover, catches on lower cover; German and Dutch bindings, by contrast, have clasps on the lower cover, catches on the upper cover.[11] Unfortunately, the restorers of such bindings are not always attuned to this detail, and mistakes can be made, that is, original boards may be reattached backward. Materials also tend to be regional: most early English bindings are in calf; morocco is used in Italy; pigskin is found only in German bindings.

The stamps of many of these bindings are distinctive, and there are several catalogues that can be used to identify them. If the binding is German, its stamps can often be found in one of two resources: the standard catalogue of bindings by Ernst Kyriss and the two-volume catalogue of binding stamps known as the Schunke-Schwenke catalogue. If the binding is English, there are catalogues of binding rolls and binding stamps by Oldham, Strickland Gibson, and others.[12] Catalogues of binding stamps are generally more reliable and less maddening to use than are catalogues of watermarks, in that what they provide is an exact match or no match at all. A binding stamp is made of solid metal, and, unlike the wires that form watermarks, these do not change. Nor is the leather of a binding subject to shrinkage as is paper.

To use the Schunke-Schwenke catalogue, you start with an actual stamp or a rubbing of a stamp. The object pictured in the binding stamp must then be identified (it helps to skim the catalogue and get a sense of the possibilities—lily, griffon, dragon—along with the German names for such things). Within these categories, stamps are arranged by shape and then by size. If the stamp is recorded, identification is relatively simple, the whole process hampered only by a rather serious irony: stamps in the catalogue are reproduced by rubbings, which produce a slightly blurred image; this blurring has been made worse in the printing by a mysteriously bad process of reproduction, such that each image in this catalogue appears slightly out of focus.

Typical Sixteenth- and Seventeenth-Century Bindings

In the sixteenth century, there begins to be a sharp difference between run-of-the-mill bindings and aristocratic bindings. The often illustrated, heavily decorated bindings by Grolier are much different from the more modest bindings pictured, for example, in figure 1.6. Vellum bindings become routine, and entire library shelves were filled with such bindings.[13] Additional ornamentation developed, for example, the textured and decorated edges found in sixteenth- and seventeenth-century French and Italian bindings known as *gauffered* edges. Other peculiarities of ornamentation include fore-edge paintings; in some cases, these illustrations on the fore-edge of a book are only visible when the binding is relaxed and the pages fanned; some reveal different paintings when the pages are fanned in opposite ways.[14]

By the eighteenth century, at least in England, most bindings are the trade bindings or prepublication bindings documented and described by Bennett and Pearson. These can be dated according to style, but there is little need to do so: a trade binding is by definition contemporary with the printed work it houses. Thus, in these cases, and only in these cases, a rough date for the binding can be given simply by looking at the book's date of publication.

Conclusion: Bindings and Restoration

The eighteenth and nineteenth centuries made books objects of interest; they became collectible. Earlier aristocratic bindings (for example, by Grolier) seem quite naturally to be found on books contemporary with that binding; by the eighteenth century, aristocratic bindings are more likely to be associated with older, collectible books. Books owned by major collectors were routinely rebound, often in high quality morocco; see the examples in chapter 9 below from the libraries of the Earl of Pembroke (Thomas Herbert, 8th Earl, 1656–1733) and John Ker, Third Duke of Roxburghe (1740–1804). Such rebinding campaigns were not confined to aristocrats: major library collections (Cambridge University Library is a famous example) were also subjected to wholesale rebinding.

What one might call the bibliographical aesthetics of the latter half of the twentieth century to the present are different: proprietors of major collections no longer wish to leave their institutional mark on a book. Bindings tend to be preserved when possible or restored. This can mean the preservation and restoration of boards only, and occasionally boards are transferred to books they never belonged to. This new respect for the relation of bindings to the overall history of the book has its own attendant ironies. In a working library such as the Huntington, books that cannot be reasonably restored or preserved are likely to be rebound in simple, serviceable bindings. Such libraries have no incentive to rebind lavishly any books other than particular display copies, since the vast majority of their books are never seen by anyone other than scholars. In recent years, many rare book libraries have adopted the policy of storing rare books inside individual cardboard boxes. For the preservationist, this means books and the materials of book-copies are better preserved. For the scholar, this means that more of them are invisible, since bindings that could be once found by scanning shelves can now only be discovered through catalogue searches. It also complicates the two histories of the physical book-copy and the book. The modern nondescript binding or the cardboard box that renders many book-copies visible only in the catalogue reduces those book-copies to books, since without detailed copy-specific description, they are interchangeable with any other copy of a different provenance.

* * *

CHAPTER NINE

Marks in Books

Provenance

I. Book History vs. Book-Copy History

Certain features of ordinary books belong almost entirely to the history of book-copies, not to the history of books in the sense of editions and printing variants found in those editions. These features include ownership marks, accidents of history affecting book-copies, damage and repair, sophistication by restorers, and, for early books, binding. All of these features are included within the field of *provenance.* Provenance study deals with the history of any material book following publication and distribution, that is, all records of its appearance in a modern scholar's hands, in a dealer's catalogue, or in a modern or contemporary library. For most books, provenance includes facts of binding as well; even for books of the nineteenth century and later when books are marketed bound in prepublication bindings, binding facts are rarely considered part of the edition in a purely bibliographical sense.

In provenance study, what might be called bibliographical facts are incidental and secondary: format, typography, authorship, even such abstruse matters as ideal copy (chapter 11) are important only insofar as they pertain to the history of an individual book-copy. A book within the study of provenance is not an exemplar of forces within printing or editorial history but rather a cultural or economic object with a history of ownership, analogous to any other art object.

Books do not generally survive at random, and although there may be no Grand Narrative of Provenance, that is, no elegant coherence to the way books escape destruction, there are factors that bear on such survival. Books written by Shakespeare, Gutenberg Bibles, books printed by Caxton, illustrated books, books about automobiles—these might be valued by collectors or reflect a culture's sense of history, for example, the importance of the category "early English books." Early grammar books and popular novels, however plentiful, might have been read to death or later abandoned as valueless. Other books have found their way into a modern archive due to political and economic events of the nineteenth century.

What is on a collector's bookshelves in the nineteenth century is neither a random nor a representative selection from printing history; rather, it can give us a sense of "what was considered valuable" during that period, and perhaps "what was considered history." And these books in turn constitute what later bibliographers see, perhaps wrongly, as the basic facts of printing history. As we noted in chapter 2, a book's survival, which may mean only its presence in an archive, is in some cases a product of the ratio of a book's mass to nineteenth-century transportation costs.

The basic distinction between book and book-copy can be considered as a problem in how we view provenance. Provenance might be seen as something that needs to be transcended: it is that history of individual copies that stands between us and the book those copies represent. It can also be considered the essence of book history itself, something the original conception and publication of the book only initiates.

The majority of scholarly works classified as works on provenance focus on major or aristocratic collectors. In English, there are two excellent general studies of provenance so understood, the now classic study of the great English collectors by Seymour De Ricci (1930) and the more recent *Provenance Research in Book History* by David Pearson (1998).[1] These studies define what amounts to the canon in English provenance research: lists of great collectors and their unique marks of ownership—the Earl of Pembroke and the Dukes of Roxburghe and Devonshire, to name a few. Many of these collectors left or sold their books to public and university libraries: Samuel Pepys's books are now in Magdalene College, Cambridge. The books of Bishop Moore, which included several Caxton volumes, went to Cambridge University Library through George I. The books of Robert Harley went to the British Museum, along with his manuscripts, and unlike these manuscripts were subsequently auctioned off on the retail book market. Others sold their books on the open market; large portions of the collections of the Earl of Pembroke and Robert Hoe are now at the Huntington Library.

But there are other collectors, less well studied, who have influenced the way books have survived as well, and their books will be found in rare book libraries everywhere, for example, the run-of-the-mill books of obscure owners such as those books pictured in my conclusion (figs. C.1 and C.2). It may be an interesting intellectual exercise to identify the individual owners whose marks are recorded in such books, but often, the way it is interesting is not immediately obvious.

The emphasis in this chapter will be less on the owners in and of themselves than on the way these owners exist in what might be called a dialectical relation with the original books: the nature of early printing affects what the owner wishes to collect; but what the owner wishes to collect also affects our understanding of early printing and in many cases materially changes the evidence that constitutes the field of early printing history.[2]

II. Owners of Books and Marks in Books

Most of the ownership marks a modern scholar will encounter identify libraries far more modest than those of the Duke of Roxburghe or the Earl of Pembroke. An example of the unsystematic way books have been collected and the unsystematic way their owners have been recorded can be found in one of the most bizarre books in bibliography, W. Carew Hazlitt's *Roll of Honour*.[3] It is impossible to give a sense of the nature of this work by simple description. I quote the initial entries of the first column of a random page, here, p. 149:

> Richmal Mangnal, Schoolmistress. 1759–1821. Daughter of James
>   Mangnall of Hollinhurst, Co. Lancaster.
> Peter Manigault of the Inner Temple and of South Carolina, Barrister at Law.
> Isaac George Manley, R.N. Admiral of the Red. Accompanied
>   Capt. Cook in his first voyage.
> John Manley, Barrister at Law, Esq.

John Manley, R.N., Plymouth.
Joseph Henry Manley of Cork.
Timothy Manlove. 17th Century.

There are thousands of entries like this, with no index, notes, or sup-
portive material of any kind; the printed entry constitutes the sum total
of what Hazlitt has to say about each owner. Hazlitt's approach reflects
the nature of the subject: those luminaries most represented in provenance studies cannot be typical book owners, nor, given a list such as
his, does there seem any point in trying to determine or define what a
typical book owner would be.

The great collectors have had a significant impact on the material
nature of individual book-copies. The binding of a Pembroke book,
even the atypical example in figure 9.2 below, is immediately obvious to
anyone who has seen one. And the great American collector of the late
nineteenth century, Robert Hoe, rebound most of his books in elegant
bindings, imitating those of earlier aristocratic collectors.

Each of these owners has a use for a book, and some have obvious
attitudes toward a book's provenance. For early Italian books, it seems
to have been customary for a new owner to remove the coats of arms of
previous owners. Both Pembroke and Hoe likewise removed signs of
prior ownership. Yet when the Duke of Devonshire purchased books
from the library of the Duke of Roxburghe in the late nineteenth century, all marks of the duke's ownership were retained, as were his handwritten annotations. The Devonshire arms were simply added to the
distinctive Roxburghe binding.

This process is not confined to important owners. Even run-of-
the-mill books will show evidence of a series of owners, and in some,
each new owner has crossed out the mark of an earlier one. In addition
to collectors, scholars have also left their mark in books: Gabriel Harvey's annotations to Spenser are now a canonical part of scholarship in
early English literature.[4] Politian also left an identifiable signature on
most of the books he owned.[5] And much lesser scholars (schoolboys?)
have left their marks in books, as shown in the Terence in figure 9.1.

The books of some of these owners have been identified and are
well known. But indexing books by ownership and recording their
provenance has never been done and perhaps cannot be done in any

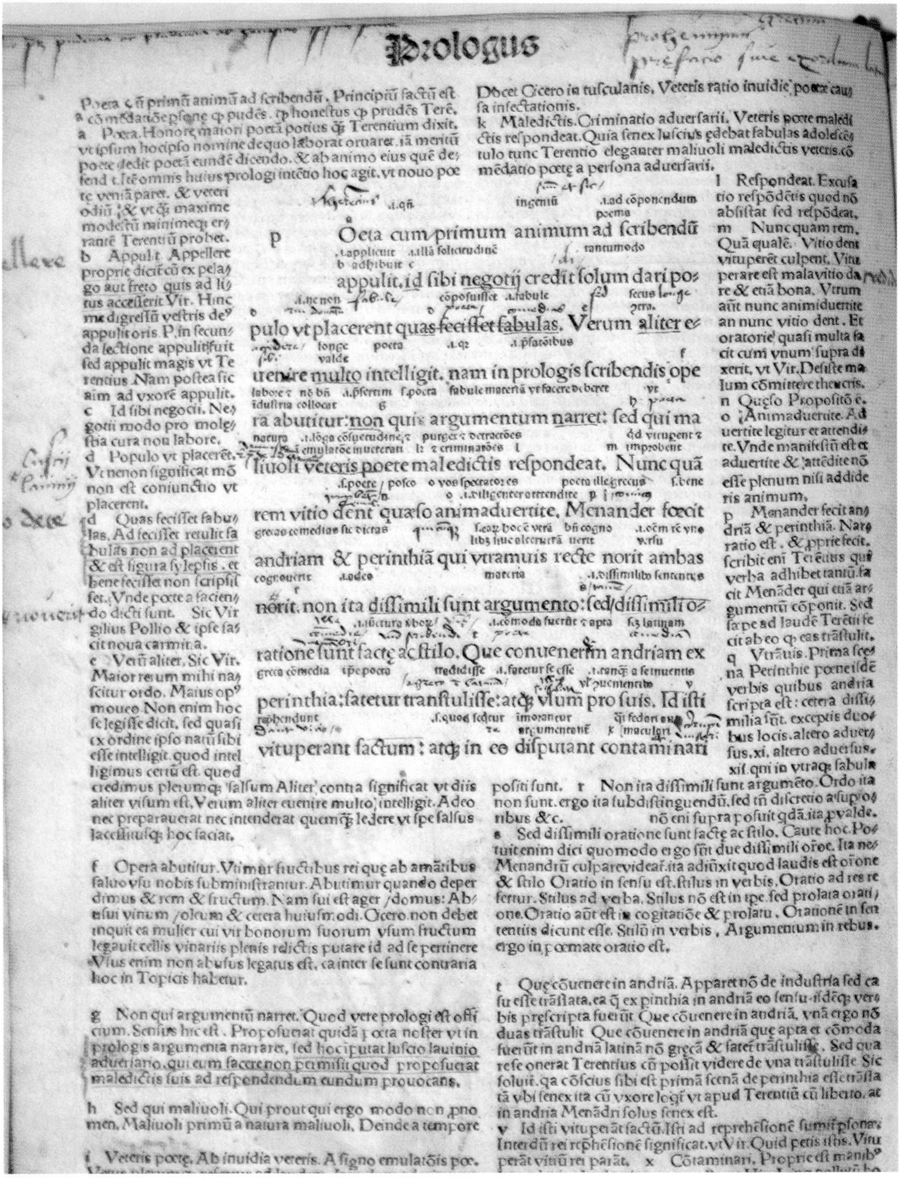
Prologus

Poeta cum primum animum ad scribendū appulit, id sibi negotij credidit solum dari populo vt placerent quas fecisset fabulas. Verum aliter euenire multo intelligit. nam in prologis scribendis operam abutitur: non qui argumentum narret: sed qui maliuoli veteris poete maledictis respondeat. Nunc quā rem vitio dent quaeso animaduertite. Menander fecit andriam & perinthiā qui vtramuis recte norit ambas norit. non ita dissimili sunt argumento: sed dissimili oratione sunt factę ac stilo. Que conuenere in andriam ex perinthia: fatetur transtulisse: atq; vsum pro suis. Id isti vituperant factum: atq; in eo disputant contaminari

FIGURE 9.1. Terentius, *Comoediae* (Strassburg: Grüninger, 1499). Photo courtesy of the University of Southern California on behalf of USC Libraries.

systematic way. There are no public union catalogues showing "books owned by person X" comparable to the many catalogues listing "books written by (or printed by) person Y." The provenance of books in certain areas (fifteenth-century books) is better recorded than in other areas, but the best indexes, even of these books, are private indexes.[6] For some owners, individual scholarly studies have provided lists of known books although few of these lists are really complete.[7] Particular libraries also have provenance lists, which vary wildly in quality and scope. The information on provenance from the Huntington Library and the Folger Library for early English books is available in their online catalogues. Excellent published provenance lists are also available for the incunables in Staatsbibliothek in Munich, the Bodleian, and the University Library at Freiberg.[8] But even in these cases, ownership is sometimes defined in a limited way and often does not include the owner or agent who actually put together portions of the collection as a unit. Twentieth-century booksellers, important as they may be for the books in any collection, rarely are included in provenance indexes.

III. Three Book Owners: Earl of Pembroke, Leander Van Ess, Otto Vollbehr

The following section concerns three important but quite different sources for books now housed in the Huntington Library. Thomas Herbert, Eighth Earl of Pembroke (1656–1732), is an aristocratic collector familiar in provenance studies, and of the three, the only one likely to be included in a basic work on provenance or book collecting. Less well known is Leander Van Ess, a Benedictine scholar of the early nineteenth century, whose extensive collections are now housed in the Huntington Library and in the Burke Library of Union Theological Seminary. The third is a book dealer of the twentieth century, Otto [von] Vollbehr. I choose these owners first because of their wildly divergent attitudes toward what books are and what books are for, and second, because it is their diverse attitudes that resulted in a large portion of early books in the Huntington collections. Although these owners are interesting in their own rights, they are considered here from a bibliographical standpoint: what do their books tell us about book history and how has the ownership of these books created and transformed what we consider bibliographical evidence?

Earl of Pembroke

Thomas Herbert, Eighth Earl of Pembroke, amassed his library in the early eighteenth century. Books from this library are very distinctive. They have characteristic bindings in two styles: in red morocco and in calf. The gold tooling marks are various but repeated in series. In the Huntington Library, these eighteenth-century books are further encased in nineteenth-century boxes, built so tight around the books that air holes need to be drilled to enable the books to be removed from them. There is a second major collection of Pembroke books at the Scheide Library in Princeton, and Pembroke books can also be found in private hands, occasionally coming up for auction.

A typical Pembroke book, thus, announces its Pembroke provenance but rarely reveals signs of earlier ownership. Pembroke sought out clean copies, and if the copies he found were not clean enough, he had them washed. Each of his books contains on its flyleaf an exact penciled inscription of what was to be stamped on the label on the spine. And each has two sets of shelfmarks, corresponding to two different arrangements in Pembroke's library. Theoretically, these marks could be used to reconstruct the library of the earl at Wilton House in Wiltshire, an intellectual exercise that would be interesting, but onerous. They indicate where books were shelved, and from them one can get some general idea of the categories Pembroke employed ("classics"; "early printing"). The titles and the way they were shelved show what Pembroke felt to be of value: book history meant "monuments in printing history" and "dissemination of the classics." Even a partial list of the incunables from his collection at the Huntington reveals these tendencies. His library contains several Caxtons, an early blockbook, and many first editions of classical texts.

Pembroke's view of cultural history relating the technology of printing and dissemination of the classics is still found in most twentieth-century printing histories, where the theme of "the rise of humanism" resonates perhaps more loudly than it should. But the value of these books for historians and collectors has changed. Many of the books collected by Pembroke are less significant from the standpoint of modern bibliography than they would have seemed to him. Fifteenth-century folio editions of classical authors are still valuable, but they are not rare, nor are they now considered the most significant books in western cultural history.

To Pembroke, book-copies were clearly of greater value if pristine, that is, unused and uncut, with wide, untrimmed margins. This seems reasonable enough, but there are many ideological assumptions built in to such a presumably innocent view of books and what constitutes their value. Pembroke's books completely remove the intervening history or had little record of that history to begin with; they are, in essence, museum pieces documenting a moment in fifteenth-century cultural history preserved in the eighteenth-century collection. The time between these two moments in history has been deliberately and systematically effaced. Printing, thus, is not a part of living history but a part of preserved history.

In many cases, washing a book will leave its pages with characteristically flat and dull surfaces: the impressions of the type can no longer be felt, and the page surface often has a grey sheen. In most Pembroke books, pages seem bleached and have that much desired but ill-defined characteristic of "crispness" so often alluded to in nineteenth-century sales catalogues. But things do not always work out as planned. An extreme example is the Huntington Pembroke book pictured in figure 9.2, where the process of cleaning and restoration that once produced a pristine book has now proven catastrophic. The leaves are so brittle and fragile that the book cannot be handled—a consequence of the chemicals used to clean it in the eighteenth century. Nor does there seem to be any way to halt its inevitable deterioration. No other Pembroke book I have seen has suffered damage comparable to this.

The book poses a very interesting set of questions: Pembroke himself wished to erase and essentially fix history; what should the modern restorer or librarian do in this case? Because this book is not unique, the copy does not need to be saved in order to preserve an exemplar of the edition. If it were to be preserved (it is or was, after all, a valuable book), a legitimate question would be "what state should one preserve it in?" Should a restorer try to undo the obvious damage done by the eighteenth-century restorer? that is, return the book to the notion of The Pristine current in the eighteenth century? Or should the preserva-

FIGURE 9.2. Pembroke binding. RB 104595. Reproduced by permission of the Huntington Library, San Marino, California.

tionist attempt further restoration? perhaps place the remnants of the leaves in plastic covers? or clap a faux fifteenth- or sixteenth-century stamped binding on it? Or would either approach just reinforce the very ideological assumptions that led to the damage in the first place? Both imply that intervening history (whatever has occurred in the eighteenth through twentieth centuries) is merely decay and destruction and that the purpose of restoration is the erasure or undoing of that history. The lover of history thus acts to destroy history. Is not that book, in all its unrestored stupor, a far more valuable item in history than any of the exquisitely bound companion volumes from the Pembroke library where it was once housed?

Leander Van Ess

Leander Van Ess was a Benedictine scholar in the early nineteenth century whose books appear in two forms. Some have their original bindings; of those in the Huntington Library, these are the best source for early run-of-the-mill sixteenth-century bindings, and none I have seen has been restored. Others are in nineteenth-century pasteboard pamphlets. Some of these later bindings were the work of the libraries that de-accessioned the books before coming into Van Ess's hands; Freiburg books owned by Van Ess have characteristic bindings and are easily identified. Others were done either by Van Ess himself or by an agent contemporary with him.[9]

For someone interested in early bindings, the first group of unrestored books is obviously of major interest. But the second group, more modest, contains the more curious examples. The pamphlet bindings in this second group seem color coded: blue, yellow, black. Each of these represents a lot purchased by Van Ess, or perhaps a unit given by Van Ess to a binder. Each unit has a characteristic set of ownership marks. Books in blue pasteboard bindings were all examined and collated by Van Ess; they contain inked references to Panzer's then state-of-the-art incunable catalogue *Annales typographici* and on their final page, the note "c.V.E." (meaning that they were collated by Van Ess himself).[10] Books in yellow pamphlet bindings all contain a three-digit number on their inside cover in the form "N. 5xx." In addition, there are marks common to all Van Ess books: a Panzer reference, tags from Thomas Phillipps, who bought the lot of nine hundred early books that eventually came to the Huntington, penciled marks by A. W. Rosenbach, the dealer who sold the books to the Huntington, and finally later accession numbers of the Huntington. Some contain other numbers: either a number in red crayon on the opening leaf or other three-digit numbers that do not correspond to the numbers finally assigned by Van Ess before he sold his books to Phillipps. The various numbers, along with two extant catalogues, provide the history of Van Ess's efforts to organize his collections.

Van Ess was a much different kind of collector than was Pembroke. He was a scholar; he obtained books in large lots with the suppression of religious houses in Germany and used them for his own theological studies. At some point, Van Ess made the decision to sell off parts of his collection. The sale to Phillipps consisted of early books that were either duplicates or books of no use to Van Ess in his scholarship. To prepare for this sale, Van Ess created a catalogue of nine hundred books, organized by date.[11] Because they are numbered sequentially, Van Ess must have organized and arranged the books before assigning the final number, and he did so on the basis of Panzer's catalogue. The placement of the various color-coded pamphlets thus reflects not how they came into Van Ess's hands but rather how they were defined in Panzer's *Annales typographici*.[12] The books sold by Van Ess to Phillipps/Rosenbach and now in the Huntington have thus been what I call "Panzerized"— broken up and organized into units corresponding to the units in Panzer's contemporary incunable catalogue. Physical evidence, thus, rather than providing the material basis for scholarly abstractions, has in this case been materially rearranged to conform to those abstractions.

There should be nothing mysterious about researching the bibliographical activities of Van Ess; his catalogues exist, his books have not been sophisticated, and there are excellent records of his sales. Yet to bibliographers, Van Ess remains obscure. As far as I can tell, there is no mention of him in any bibliographical reference until his books reached the Huntington in the 1920s; the printed incunable catalogue from the Huntington by Herman R. Mead notes Van Ess ownership only for those books with his signature, a small percentage of the nine hundred books in the collection. To find the others, one must look for Phillipps provenance, check the titles in the now typed catalogue, or find his name in the library's online catalogue. The Burke Library at Union Theological Seminary is even more difficult to access, and there is presently no way of studying the twenty thousand books originally owned by Van Ess other than by calling them up one by one. Only because of the studies of Johannes Altenberend and Milton Gatch are the basic facts surrounding Van Ess in any way accessible, even though his books to a large degree define the material evidence for early books in two major American collections.

Otto Vollbehr

Otto Vollbehr was a book dealer, who in the 1920s sold thousands of incunables to the Huntington and to the Library of Congress. Although collectors such as Pembroke for the Huntington and Lessing J. Rosenwald for the Library of Congress are more visible, Vollbehr, little mentioned by bibliographers, is the most important source of fifteenth-century books now in America. Some of the earliest articles on him are little more than propaganda pieces, designed to encourage Congress to buy his books.[13] Other scholars criticized him for his mercantilism, that is, for adding an unwarranted "von" to his name and thus styling himself as an aristocratic collector (presumably a respectable thing) rather than as a dealer (something less reputable). Such criticism may be a symptom of prejudice regarding social class even among presumably disinterested scholars: even though the marks of Vollbehr's ownership are clear, and even though there are well-kept sales records of what went through his hands in the United States, there is no mention of him in standard works on provenance. His name was included on the individual catalogue cards of the several thousand books he sold to the Huntington, but in the library's first printed incunable catalogue (nearly half of the books listed came through Vollbehr's hands), his name is not included in any of the provenance notes; according to Herman R. Mead, the Huntington's first librarian, "Dr. Vollbehr's status is decidedly that of a commercial agent," a particularly strange remark from a Huntington employee.[14] Pearson's *Provenance Research* also makes no mention of major dealers such as Vollbehr or Rosenbach or H. P. Kraus.

Even without the lists of books, Vollbehr books are easy to find and their physical nature reveals how Vollbehr defined what a book was. Each contains a penciled number (five digits) on the upper right hand corner of the first flyleaf along with a clear but to me indecipherable note ("Isis"?); other marks of Vollbehr ownership are equally distinctive. Very telling is Vollbehr's apparent treatment of *Sammelbände,* that is, as single volumes containing multiple, bibliographically autonomous books, a common form in which fifteenth-century books appear (see chapter 10). Van Ess left many of his *Sammelbände* intact, but many others in his possession have been reconstructed, either by Van Ess or by those who sold the books to him, so that the physical units correspond to what is or was described as a unit in a bibliographical catalogue. Vollbehr appears to have been far more aggressive and systematic about reconstructing such volumes. There are, on the Huntington shelves, many slim incunables from Vollbehr sales bound with paper covers that were made from leaves of early printed books and, in several instances, from leaves of the same book. They look in some sense old, I suppose, but no such binding existed in the fifteenth or the sixteenth century. These pamphlets could be considered a pretentious variant of the cheaply bound pamphlets found in Van Ess's library.

Vollbehr's motives were quite different from those of Van Ess. Although Vollbehr's books contained many "treasures"—items highlighted as he tried to sell them—what he was primarily interested in were "lots," that is, individual items and the sheer numbers of such items. Vollbehr sold two large groups of books, each consisting of between two- and three-thousand lots. The first went to the Huntington; when the Huntington balked at the second group, Vollbehr peddled it to Congress. In both cases, the selling point was "lot numbers."[15] Each lot was a physical item. Composite volumes (the normal way small fifteenth-century books were bound) decreased the number of lots, so Vollbehr cut them up: five lots of paper-bound pamphlets were more valuable or looked more valuable in a checklist than the same pamphlets bound as one item in a fifteenth- or sixteenth-century binding. A congressman could hardly be expected to care much about an early Augsburg binding that might contain three different books; but that congressman could count: three was more than one. Vollbehr simply exploited that thinking. When history came in conflict with economic gain, history lost; and institutions that presumably preserve historical evidence, that is, public and private libraries, were willing accomplices. To describe Vollbehr as the villain, as many bibliographers do, is convenient but obscures a cultural and economic reality that is much more complex.

Conclusion: Provenance and the Local Library

Every library is a product of and a participant in the history of provenance, defining "what is a book" according to the often vaguely imagined needs and goals of its community. Libraries at small colleges are often the beneficiaries of donations of their graduates, many of whom have an unrealistic view of their own legacies, imagining that their contributions will stay together and continue to reflect the enthusiasms and very being of their donors. Many of these books are silently sold off, and to make this less conspicuous, small libraries often deliberately do not maintain public provenance lists.

Nonetheless, each of these libraries is a useful source in how archives are constructed. What decisions are made for the acquisition of books? How are they vetted? Do donors' libraries remain intact? How are they housed? accessed? What is the policy toward duplicates? Does the archive house books? or book-copies? and what are the implications of doing so? Just what is book history and what does a small repository have to contribute to this? Finally, is it wise to leave book history in the hands of the largest, best funded institutions and their equally wealthy benefactors?

. . .

CHAPTER TEN

Books in Books and Books from Books

The cases below deal with book combinations; these include bibliographically autonomous books bound as single book-copies (*Sammelbände*) and fragments of books bound in with other books either by accident as binding fragments or by design as illustrations. These cases are not exceptional. Yet they all pose problems for traditional bibliographical language, which often tends to idealize books and consequently the basic facts of book history.

I. Books in Books: *Sammelbände*

As we have seen in previous chapters, book-copies now on a library's bookshelf do not always correspond to or conform to the units ("books") described in bibliographies or sold to libraries by book dealers. This is especially true of early pamphlets, defined loosely and tautologically as books too small to be bound in a large conventional binding. It is also true of run-of-the-mill books; at least in the earliest period, all but the largest books were routinely bound with other books in single volumes. The most common technical term for an early composite volume is *Sammelband* (pl. *Sammelbände*), a physical, material volume consisting of two or more books deliberately bound together in an early binding. Other common English terms are *composite volume* and *tract volume*.[1]

It is obviously cheaper to bind two fifty-leaf pamphlets as one volume than as two, since the cost of the boards and construction of the spine are considerable factors in the overall cost of this binding. There also seem to be technical limitations in early binding or perhaps just conventional ones: I have never seen a fifteenth-century book bound in the slim bindings common in the eighteenth and nineteenth centuries. Books that contained fewer than about fifty leaves were either sewn as pamphlets or given limp vellum bindings.

The relationship between the texts or books in such *Sammelbände* varies. Some of these volumes have been formed by individual owners; others may well have been issued and sold in much the same state as they are found today. I define three *Sammelband* types here, but these might be thought of less as fixed types than as points on a continuous scale: (1) arbitrary combinations, that is, books bound together only by size or convenience, providing little to no evidence of how the books were intended to be distributed or read; (2) *Sammelbände* formed by owners or booksellers on the basis of literary content; (3) combinations intended by the printer.

Sammelband *Type I: Arbitrary Combinations*

The majority of early *Sammelbände* appear to be products of individual owners, formed without regard to the content of the books. Such combinations can be described as arbitrary, serendipitous, or accidental. There are scores, perhaps hundreds of such *Sämmelbande* at the Huntington Library. The books within these *Sämmelbande* are the same size; perhaps they were bought at the same time or happened to occupy the same place on a shelf. An example is the single volume with the dual accession numbers RB 102547 and 102548, two bibliographically distinct items.

Item 1 (RB 102547) is Bonaventura, *Opuscula* (Cologne: Unkel/ Koelhoff [1484]), or, more precisely, one of the many variant forms that this work takes in extant copies.[2] Item 2 (RB 102548) is a popular, much-reprinted text: Rolewinck, *Fasciculum temporum* (Strassburg: Prüss, after 6 Apr. 1490). The Huntington has over two dozen incunable editions of Rolewinck, from Cologne, Venice, and Strassburg; the Bayerische Staatsbibliothek has seven copies of this particular edition, several in *Sammelband*.³ The binding of the Huntington *Sammelband* is from Cologne (style 6 in the Kyriss catalogue, #95–101). The stamps are not recorded in the Kyriss catalogue or the Schunke-Schwenke catalogue (see chapter 8, section V above). The earliest ownership marks are dated 1554. A manuscript note in item 2 associates the book with the Carthusian monastary in Cologne.

Curiously, the opening blank of the second item in the Huntington *Sammelband,* the Rolewinck, is marked with an offset from a fresh binding nearly identical in style to that found on the front and rear panels of its present binding. This offset has implications for how this *Sammelband* was created. The unbound Rolewinck at some point was placed under a freshly bound copy of some other book before it was organized into a composite volume to be bound in the same bindery. In order for it to have this offset as the second item in a *Sammelband,* it could not have been together with what now precedes it in the present binding, the Bonaventure *Opuscula.* These two books thus went to the binder as independent items and were arranged by the binder as a *Sammelband.*

Such *Sammelbände* are a reflection of the early stages in the formation of a library. A library does not need an elaborate or even logical filing or cataloguing system as long as the number of books it owns is small. As libraries get larger and more complex and require a catalogue rather than a simple checklist, volumes such as this one become something of an irritant, since the physical nature of the book belies cataloguing conventions; these books cannot be filed by author and only in some cases by subject ("liturgical books").

Sammelband *Type II: Deliberate Compilations by Owner*

Some *Sammelbände* were deliberately created by their early owners with clear regard to content. They consist of items that are related in some way conceptually; individual items need not be contemporary. An example is a group of early eighteenth-century texts on Jane Shore in the Huntington, catalogued as PV 2187:1–5 (pamphlet volume 2187, in five parts):

1. *Tragedy of Jane Shore* (London: Lintot [1714])
2. *Life and Death of Jane Shore* (London: Roberts, 1714)

3. *Life and Character of Jane Shore* (London: J. Morphew . . . , 1714)
4. *Memoir of the Lives of Kind Edward Iv. and Jane Shore* (London: Curll, 1714)
5. *A Review of the Tragedy of Jane Shore* (London: Roberts, 1714)

The title pages of items 2–5 have printed prices (6p), suggesting that they were meant to be sold separately. This volume was thus the product of the original purchaser, the owner indicated by the stamp "M/C" on each opening page or pages. In its modern binding (ex-libris Beverly Chew), it seems to be missing part of the original *Sammelband*. Each item has an inked number (2–6) on its first leaf; no. 1 is lacking.

A nearly contemporary volume is PV 486:1–5 (RB 63093–97):

1. *Short View of the Protestant Religion* (Edinburgh, 1707)
2. *Summary of All the Religious houses in England and Wales* (London: Knapton, 1717)
3. *Scripture Politicks* (London: Senex, 1717)
4. *A Brief Enquiry into the True Nature of Schism* (London: Crutten-den, 1717)
5. *An Account of the Superstitious Ceremonies and Wicked Practices of the Church of Rome . . .* (London: Roberts, 1719)

Here, the pamphlets are not contemporary; only the title pages of items 2 and 5 have prices. This is again an owner's compilation.[4]

A more famous group consists of several pamphlet volumes printed by Caxton and de Worde now in the Cambridge University Library, all bound as pamphlets in distinctive nineteenth-century Cambridge bindings.[5] Some of these were assembled in early sixteenth century, for example, a five-part volume once owned by John Moore, Bishop of Ely (#37 in Paul Needham's *Printer and the Pardoner*). Four pamphlets are printed by Caxton (1481–90), one by de Worde, 1492, and they are individually priced. There seems little relation in subject matter, and these seem to have been bound together simply as "old books."

Such volumes can have complex histories: another *Sammelband* in Cambridge contains a Caxton item with thirteen other sixteenth-century tracts. This is really two compilations, not one. The thirteen sixteenth-century tracts, many by John Lydgate, were put together sometime in the mid-sixteenth century; they are of various dates, the latest 1554. In Seth Lerer's analysis of this volume, these medieval tracts were originally collected as examples of Catholic moral polemic; marginal notation suggests that by the late sixteenth century, well after it had been put together, the book became used pedagogically, an example of "old neglected books" of moral instruction designed for use by children. Later, in the eighteenth century, the very nature and *raison d'être* of this volume was transformed. A single Caxton volume was added at the beginning and the book rebound. What had been a moral miscellany was now a record of English printing history, with representatives of many of the earliest English printers.[6]

Sammelband *Type III: Compilations by Printer*

Occasionally, the individual items forming a *Sammelband* are from the same press and in some cases may have been issued or sold together, either by the printer or the bookseller. This may be true of several extant Caxton volumes.[7] It is certainly true of the small pamphlets printed in Cologne by Ulrich Zell often found bound together. The combinations in these *Sammelbände* are not fixed, even when they are issued by the printers themselves.

The Huntington has a number of early *Sammelbände* printed by Zell. One combines six works by Jean Gerson (PV 1111; Pr. 804, 833, 839, 805, 836, and 835). A second has Pseudo-Augustine, *De vita Christiana,* Augustine, *Homiliae* and *De agone Christiano,* and *De sermone Domini in monte habita* (Pr. 802, 826, 824); a third has four works: three by Gerson (*Conclusiones, Alphabetum divini amoris, Epistola ad Mahumetem*) and Petrarch's *Historia Griseldis* (PV 1056; Pr. 803, 801, 818.1, 846.5).[8] This last *Sammelband* is in an eighteenth-century binding and may be a later compilation: the *Alphabetum divini amoris* seems on the basis of rubrication to have been read or issued separately; the other two Gerson items may have been together originally. Some of the bibliographically autonomous items that form these collections are two separate works (Augustine's *Homiliae* and *De agone Christiano* in the second *Sammelband* described above). Neither printer nor reader seems to have distinguished the multiple works that form a single edition from the multiple editions that form a bound volume. Furthermore, later printers reprinting these volumes often incorporated the bibliographically distinct items of their copytexts in single works.[9]

If we check other library catalogues, we find many similar books: most of the British Library pamphlets of Zell are separate ("bought in 1860"); those that exist in *Sammelband* are early (1460s).[10] One of the most important is from the Bodleian (Bodl. A-543), a *Sammelband* consisting of four volumes, three by Augustine (*De vita christiana, Sermo super orationem dominicam, Enchiridion*) and one by Chrysostomos (*Sermo super psalmos L*). These texts are not strongly and obviously related by author or subject. But the volume is a product of its printer, presented to the Carthusians of St. Barbara at Cologne by Zell himself, "Printer of Books" ("Olricus pressor librorum").[11] It will not take much searching of library catalogues to discover that there is nothing unusual about these orders or combinations, and nothing definitive about the combination of texts in the book with Zell's own signature. These pamphlets were printed to be bound together and were distributed that way. The form imagined and intended by Zell is a flexible *Sammelband* of varying contents.[12]

Although the Zell *Sammelband* seems more characteristic of the earlier incunable period, there are many later examples such as the pamphlets of Savaronola, most printed in Florence. These pamphlets usually have individual title pages or initial woodcuts; they are consequently listed as separate items in standard catalogues. But in many copies, they are bound together, forming variable *Sammelbände* much like the Zell quartos. Although the copies so combined are generally by the same printer or printed in the same city, there is no consistency in the particular texts combined.[13] Such compilations were likely foreseen by the printer as one of the typical units of sale, even though the exact nature of each book-copy was not set.

A more problematic case involves folios of Cicero produced in the fifteenth century in Italy. An example is an unassigned edition of Cicero, ca. 1481 (Goff C595).[14] All catalogues consider this a single book. The catalogue of the Bayerische Staatsbibliothek (BSB-Ink) defines its "ideal copy" as containing the following four items; each consists of an autonomous set of quires with a separate and coherent signature series: *De officiis; De amicitia; De senectute; Paradoxa stoicorum*.[15] The catalogue lists four copies, each bound as a single volume (the shelfmark is shown in parentheses; the order of the four texts is shown at the end of each entry):

1: (early binding 2 Inc.s.a.315) ordered 1.4.3.2.

2: (Inc.s.a.315m) ordered 1.4.3.2.

3: (Inc.s.a.315n) ordered 2.3.4, missing 1.

4: (2 Inc.c.a. 2405 d/1) ordered 1.3.4.2.

Only the third of these copies is or was in the form of what BSB-Ink defines as its ideal or standard copy.

The British Library Catalogue (BMC) describes its copy with the following collation formula: a–t$^{8/6}$; AA–DD$^{8/4}$; aa–bb^6; a–c$^{8/6}$.[16] But its single copy does not conform to that formula: "The *Paradoxa* (quires aa, bb) are bound before the *De senectute* (quires AA–DD)." Thus BMC considers the correct order as *De officiis, De senectute, Paradoxa stoicorum; De amicitia;* in the BSB-Ink ideal-copy order, this would be 1, 3, 2, 4. If I read these descriptions correctly, and I may be mistaken, none of the four copies listed in BSB-Ink conforms to its ideal-copy description, nor does the British Library copy conform to the different ideal-copy description in BMC.

Such confusions speak more to the nature of the book than the deficiencies of these catalogues, whose various treatments are all reasonable. The works by Cicero seem to constitute a bibliographically autonomous unit, that is, a book; but the form of that book is not fixed. Perhaps as a consequence, the different *Sammelbände* created by individual owners reflect the flexible notion of a Cicero collection created by the printers. Among the various early Cicero volumes at the Huntington is one owned by Johannes Protzer, a German student who purchased books in Italy in the late fifteenth century (RB 103112–15). This volume contains the following:

1. *Orationes* (Venice: Pincius, 1493)

2. *Philippicae* (Vicenza: [Henrius de Santo ursio, Zenus], 1488)

3. *Epistolae ad brutum . . .* [Venice: Pincius, about 1495]

4. *Opera Philosophica* (Venice: Simon Bevilaqua, 1496)

Whether such combinations came into being prior to sale or at the exact moment of sale involves speculation about what went on in the minds of the seller and buyer. The various forms of these volumes suggest that printer, seller, and buyer all foresaw combinations of items that modern bibliographical descriptions keep distinct.[17]

There is no general rule that can be formulated regarding these books and book combinations. Even the classifications above and my conveniently selected examples show that the boundaries between imagined types of *Sammelbände* are porous, and categorizing them is in many cases a matter of what could be called speculative taxonomy. Book-copies are individuals.

For literary historians and critics, study of *Sammelbände* has provided what appears to be a new way to understand book reception, that is, how texts and books are read and what the conventions for historical reading might be. Perhaps the physical association of two works in a single composite volume gives us an idea of how these texts were interpreted historically or how literary genres were once constituted. As one of these literary historians, I remain skeptical of such approaches. What these volumes reveal to me are the eccentricities of individual readers and the complexities of circumstances in which those readers lived. Such complexities are interesting in themselves, but they are not generalizable and any claim that these readers and circumstances are knowable in any serious way is dubious.

II. Books from Books: The Donatus *Ars Minor* Fragments in Early Printing History

Among the Van Ess books in the Huntington Library is a physical volume shelved with fifteenth-century books printed in Strassburg (RB 96565). It contains two books in the ordinary sense, identified and catalogued as Petrus de Palude, *Sermones quadragesimales* (Strassburg: [Flach,] 1488), Goff P504; and Bernardus de Parentinis, *Expositio officii missae* ([Strassburg: Grüninger,] 1487), Goff P110. These are two separate books, printed in the same city at nearly the same time, that happen to be bound into one book-copy. That book-copy also contains in its binding materials fragments of a third book, Donatus, *Ars minor*, printed in an early Netherlands type (142G = a gothic type with a 20-line measurement of 142 mm) (fig. 10.1). Fragments like these are very common in early bindings, but they can pose serious and sometimes intractable problems for early book history and bibliography, a few of which are outlined below.

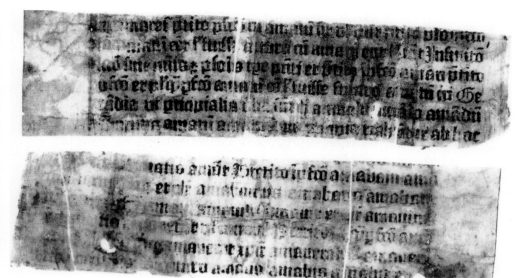

FIGURE 10.1. Donatus, *Ars minor* (before 1465). Binding fragments in RB 96565. Reproduced by permission of the Huntington Library, San Marino, California.

In the Huntington *Sammelband,* these fragments were used as reinforcing hinges, laid across the spine of the bound leaves between the cords to which the quires are sewn, and pasted onto the boards (similar vellum hinges can be seen in figure 8.1). In some bindings, but not this one, additional reinforcing strips might be glued vertically along the spine as well. Any piece of vellum could be used for these purposes, but the most plentiful source of such material is other books and manuscripts, or perhaps a Borgesian category of such books, "books whose raw material is worth more than the 'book' those materials support": unpopular and obsolete theological texts, out-of-date calendars, popular and over-used grammar books, damaged books.

In this book, there are five vellum hinges. Three of these are cut from a medieval manuscript; the other two are cut from a printed book with vellum leaves. Manuscript hinges are not rare in early bound books; they are generally ignored, and even the ones here were left undisturbed until the twentieth century. But incunabulists in the late nineteenth and early twentieth centuries realized that evidence of the earliest printing is often contained in such fragments, and a concerted effort was made to find and catalogue them.[18] Those here had been cut from the spine, but not identified, by an early Huntington librarian, probably in the 1920s.[19]

The Donatus Ars Minor

The Donatus *Ars Minor* was the most popular Latin grammar book of the fifteenth century and accounts for hundreds of entries in union catalogues of incunables. Most of the evidence for these entries consists of fragments similar to those pictured in figure 10.1 above. The Donatus grammar is a compendium of conjugations and declensions and there is no explanatory material. The following is the entry on the future and imperative of the verb *amare* (to love):

> Futuro amabo amabis amabit. et pluraliter amabimus amabitis amabunt. Imperatiuo modo tempore presenti ad secundam et terciam personam ama amet. et pluraliter amemus amate ament. Futuro amato tu amato ille. et pluraliter amamus amatote amanto vel amantote.

The student of Latin used this book to study and to look up various inflected forms, and the reasons many of them are printed on vellum rather than paper is because they were expected to receive heavy use. Many exist only in fragments because they were literally read to pieces.

The Huntington fragments are typical of this genre. The type is identifiable as one of a half-dozen types used in early Dutch printing. It is commonly called "Pontanus" type (142G = a gothic type with a 20-line measurement of 142 mm) because it is used in an early printing of Pontanus. Of the 112 Donatus editions listed in ISTC as printed in the Netherlands, 21 are printed in this type.[20] None of the extant fragments, however, contains the section of text found in the Huntington fragments, and it is thus not possible to determine whether these fragments belong to any of the editions already represented by another set of fragments (the implication of this will be discussed below). The hypothesized edition represented by these fragments would have to be included in any comprehensive list of fifteenth-century books, since it is possible that they belong to an unrecorded edition: this may be as much a "book" as any other "book," such as Caxton's first edition of Chaucer's *Canterbury Tales* or the Gutenberg Bible.

Printer's Waste vs. Binder's Waste

In the late nineteenth century, Henry Bradshaw promoted a distinction between printer's waste and binder's waste. The above fragments are rubricated: that is, they come from a book that was read and used. Bradshaw described such fragments as *binder's waste,* meaning fragments from previously used books that ended up in a bindery. *Printer's waste,* by contrast, includes waste from a printer that was never used in an actual book: proofsheets, trial sheets, or damaged or excess leaves. A second set of early grammatical fragments from the Huntington will illustrate this distinction. Figure 10.2 shows one sheet of a set of ten paper bifolia, printed by Zainer, a prolific late-fifteenth-century printer from Augsburg: pseudo-Donatus, *Rudimenta grammatices,* [Augsburg: Johann Zainer, 1480–90], Goff D342. Some of the pages have been overprinted; others have pages upside down. These are clearly proofsheets of some kind, although the page and formes as set here could not have been combined in any way to form a book. Two of the pages contain the same text, but they are not printed in the same page format. This is printer's waste; it was never in an actual book.

Both printer's waste and binder's waste are indications of the corporate nature of book production. Book-copies are products of a number of institutions and individuals—a paper mill, a printing press, a distributor, a binder, and an owner. Traditional bibliography tends to privilege the printing house, an institution that is the dominant one for most of the book-copies handled by modern readers. But historical book-copies only rarely show such dominance.

Early Grammar Books and the Notion of Edition

There is no clear record of how early grammars like the Donatus *Ars Minor* were printed, how many were printed, or how they were distributed. When they appear in early book lists or catalogues, the references indicate little more than that such books are in the inventory of a

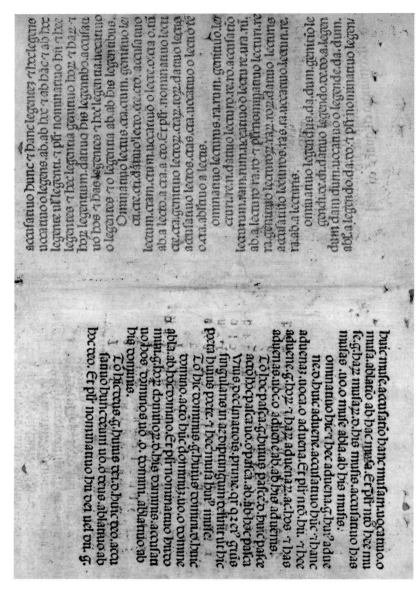

FIGURE 10.2. Proofsheet. Ps.-Donatus, *Rudimenta grammatices* (Ulm: Joannes Zainer, 1480–90). Reproduced by permission of the Huntington Library, San Marino, California.

distributor. Thus, despite the large numbers of fragments, it is difficult to know what percentage of early printing these books represent.[21] Of the thirty thousand entries in *Gesamtkatalog der Wiegendrucke* (GW) and the comparable number in ISTC, nearly four hundred are for the Donatus. Most catalogues consider an entry equivalent to an edition. For the Donatus *Ars minor,* however, an entry means "a set of fragments that cannot with certainty be collated with another set of fragments unambiguously from the same edition." The four hundred plus entries for the *Ars Minor* in ISTC or GW, thus, represent (or do they?) a much smaller number of editions and consequently book-copies than do other entries in the same catalogue.[22]

Because the demand for grammar books in the fifteenth century was constant, it is possible individual books or editions were printed almost continuously, and not according to the procedures described by Moxon in the seventeenth century (see chapter 4 above). Pages were small, and in the process of printing individual sheets, type could have been broken up, used for other projects, then reset to complete the edition. To reset a small quarto page of a Donatus would not have required the same effort as to reset a large folio page, and this may explain why in those cases where surviving leaves match and thus are assumed to be from the same edition, they show many variants. Books like this in constant demand could also have been used as fill-in jobs by printers between more expensive work. And halting, sporadic printing could then account for the hundreds of entries in modern incunable catalogues: what we are seeing is not a list of autonomous editions but rather variants of the same printing project—not quite the same as a bibliographical edition—carried on over a long period of time.

III. Books from Fragments: Leaf Books and Their Bibliographical Status

In the late nineteenth century and early twentieth century, fragments similar to those described in the first part of this chapter were commonly removed from books and even used as gifts by some book dealers.[23] While removing such book material from an early binding may seem to a modern bibliographer an act of vandalism, it was only a variation of bookselling and bibliographical practices common in all periods. In the book trade, when individual parts of a book-copy are more valuable taken singly than the book-copy as a whole, the larger unit is sacrificed.

In the nineteenth century, loose leaves created a new genre of book: the leaf book. One of the first was Francis Fry, *A Description of the Great Bible* (1865).[24] Each copy contained fourteen leaves from the various Bibles described: they were thus both exemplars of the thing described as well as part of the description itself. Other notable examples of early leaf books are E. Gordon Duff's *William Caxton* (Chicago: Caxton Club, 1905) and what are known as the Noble Fragments of the Gutenberg Bible. The first 148 copies of Duff's *Caxton* included a leaf from Caxton's *Canterbury Tales*, taken from the incomplete Ashburnham copy. The Noble Fragments were produced in 1921: each lavishly bound book contains a single leaf of the Gutenberg Bible, and copies of this book today sell for tens of thousands of dollars. Figure 6.6 above is taken from one of these copies.[25]

Many leaf books are belletristic: the leaf is ornamental, as in Duff's *Caxton*, or a collectible, as seems to be the case with the Noble Fragments. But leaf books are not simply products of the book trade; their production involves bibliographers as well, those who presumably have a greater interest in the historical unit of the book or the individual book-copy than does a book dealer.

One of the most eccentric and much denigrated bibliographers of the eighteenth century was John Bagford, who amassed a collection of title pages in preparation for a never completed history of printing. Although Bagford has been much criticized for vandalizing early books, his instincts were in accord with modern bibliographical theory: a book's bibliographical identity, that is, how it will be listed and evaluated in a union catalogue, is in large part determined by its title page, not by whether it happens to be exemplified by a complete copy; we speak of such a unit as the 1598 edition of Chaucer because there is a title page claiming such a thing exists, not because we have carefully evaluated and collated the individual printed sheets that constitute such a book. Title pages have a privilege in bibliographical history greater than that accorded to any other book section.[26] Bagford's collection of title pages was to him a portable history of printing, at least for a certain period of printing history, providing evidence not only for early printers, many of whom were identified on that page, but for the history of type often shown on those pages.

Leaf Books of Incunabula and the Notion of Typographical Value

In the late nineteenth and early twentieth centuries, the primary task of scholars of fifteenth-century books was associating books with their printers, and the basis for such identification was typography. Konrad Burger included original leaves of incunables as specimens in *Monumenta Germaniae et Italiae Typographica* (1892–1913), and in 1927–28, Konrad Haebler published a series of leaf books: *German Incunabula: 110 Original Leaves; Italian Incunabula: 110 Original Leaves; West-European Incunabula: 60 Original Leaves.*[27] All were designed as bibliographical aids; they supplemented facsimile collections of leaves illustrating early type such as VGT.[28] Though expensive, they were cheaper than even a modest collection of incunables, and libraries that own them provide their readers with a large sampling of fifteenth-century typographic and paper evidence.

As noted in chapter 6, Henry Bradshaw had suggested in the late nineteenth century that the history of printing was to be understood as a history of typefonts.[29] These could be organized much as an evolutionary biologist organizes biological specimens. This understanding of the history of early printed books as a history of type made the production of such volumes as Haebler's inevitable. Through such productions, books were transformed from "things to be read" to "art objects," suitable for viewing but not reading, and "examples of printing history," useful for determining the history of typography.

How important these books were to early scholars of incunables can be seen by looking at the 1937 catalogue of Huntington incunabula by Herman R. Mead. Mead's catalogue includes entries for all of the over five thousand fifteenth-century books in the Huntington, and among these are included entries for many fragments, including some of the leaves in the Haebler collections, the criteria being whenever the fragment is "of typographical value."[30]

Mead arranged incunables in Proctor order (see chapter 6 above). Under this system, books are identified and organized largely according to the history of fonts used to print them. The Haebler leaf books could have been useful in two ways: (1) for identifying books and typefonts in the collection, and (2) for providing examples of typefonts not represented in the Huntington collections. Since incunables at the Huntington had already been assigned Proctor numbers, and Haebler included Proctor type numbers in his collection, it would have been fairly straightforward to determine which typefonts in Haebler's collection were not represented by books at the Huntington. In this way, the Huntington incunables, along with the Haebler leaves, could have constituted the "history of typefonts" that many bibliographers at this time considered the primary scholarly purpose of collecting such books.

But the precise status of these fragments was never clearly defined. Huntington bibliographers never organized or referenced them in any systematic way, nor did they cross-reference the types represented in their collection with those in VGT, even though in some of the earliest correspondence, there are statements that for the purposes of the library, facsimile representatives of each typefont are as good as real ones.[31] The existence of Haebler's leaf books, and the sporadic and unsystematic reference to them in the catalogue published in 1937, are signs of a once imagined history—a *grand récit* of typography for which the books themselves are not individual objects of textual or aesthetic interest but rather repositories of evidence of a much more coherent cultural narrative.

Conclusion

The subject of fragments bring us back to a question that has been under consideration throughout this study: what is a book?

Most book histories are organized around the monumental book: the Gutenberg Bible, early editions of Caxton, books by Aldus, Etienne, etc. This was the working assumption even by those makers of leaf books who systematically destroyed books in order to write portions of this history. But the actual history these written histories allude to and document is made up of run-of-the-mill books—books like the Donatus grammars that are much more valuable evidence of, say, the rise of literacy than is a high-end production like the Gutenberg Bible. It is one of the many paradoxes of book history that fragments of the books best documenting that history have been so thoroughly dissociated from their own history: trashed and rebound as binding material in the fifteenth and sixteenth centuries, removed from those bindings with no note or documentation and sold separately or simply given away by professional bibliographers in later centuries. We find with these fragments what we have found with other books: when the evidence does not accord with our theories of what books are or should be (why do book-copies not promote the typographical history that is the basis of book history?), our reaction is not to revise our theories of what books are but rather to manipulate the evidence to make it more congenial.

CHAPTER ELEVEN

Ideal Copy and the Goals of Enumerative and Descriptive Bibliography

A fundamental problem for the book historian, book collector, or bibliographer involves what might seem an overly fastidious and technical issue—what bibliographers refer to as "ideal copy" description, that is, the description and characterization of an idealized representative copy of any edition. For the 1623 First Folio of Shakespeare, this standard description of title page, quire structure, and other details of printing might not correspond to any one of the more than two hundred extant copies of this book but would be the basis for describing any of them. Abstruse as the technicalities and theory of such description may seem, the notion of ideal copy is one of the most basic principles in book history, for it concerns what we finally consider the identity of any book or book-copy: how do we know that a book is a copy of the 1623 Shakespeare? how do we distinguish the first edition of Chaucer's *Canterbury Tales* by Caxton from the second edition or from any other edition?

These are things book collectors have always wanted to know, and they invest heavily in the results. The abstract notion of ideal copy is consequently firmly grounded in very practical and economic questions. I own a Caxton Gower; a Caxton Gower comes up for sale. Do I buy it? Or is it a duplicate of what I already own? Does the value of this copy lie in its copy-specific characteristics such as its binding or its history of ownership, or does the copy have bibliographical or bibliophilic "points," such as an interesting printing variant? The answer to these questions can then be the basis for an entire series of related questions: what about a radically sophisticated item? if a copy of what is claimed to be the 1623 First Folio of Shakespeare is made up of leaves from a hundred different book-copies, then how should that be described and what is that finally worth? what about cancelled editions? remains of aborted editions?

These questions can be asked in terms of general cataloguing problems as well. Library X has a *Canterbury Tales* printed by Caxton; so does Library Y. Are these the same? or do they represent two editions? Library X has three copies of the 1623 Shakespeare; Library Y has two copies. If these are the same in a bibliographical sense, they can receive one entry in my catalogue. But are they the same? And in what bibliographical sense? Do I need one entry? Or should I have five? To answer such questions requires not only an examination of the extant copies but some thought concerning the language chosen to describe them and some accepted standard or set of standards for such language. Part of my focus here will be on the evolving language used by A. W. Pollard and G. R. Redgrave in the *Short-Title Catalogue* (1926), revised in 1976, and now the basis of the online ESTC.[1]

I. Enumerative vs. Descriptive Bibliography

Pollard and Redgrave's *Short-Title Catalogue* (STC) is an *enumerative bibliography:* a list of books and book-copies that does not include a detailed description of them. An enumerative catalogue defines an area and attempts to include all books within that field in its catalogue. In the case of STC, the area is "all books printed in England or printed in English from the beginnings of printing to 1640"; for an individual library catalogue, the area would be "all books owned by Library X."

There is no set rule for the amount of information contained in an enumerative catalogue other than that it be brief. Catalogue entries in the 1926 STC provide only author, title, publication data, basic format, and a brief holdings list:

5068 Chaucer, Geoffrey. The workes of Geffray Chaucer newly printed, with dyuers workes neuer in print before [*Ed.* W. Thynne.] fol. *T. Godfray*, 1532. L.O.C.; HN.CH

The entry means that STC 5068 is a book by Chaucer, whose title is roughly "The workes . . ."; both Chaucer's name and a version of the title appear on the title page or colophon. It is edited by William Thynne, whose name is bracketed because it does not appear on the title page. It is in folio, and it is printed by Thomas Godfray in 1532; both the printer's name and the date of printing appear in the book. There are copies at the British Library (L, for London), Oxford, and Cambridge. There are copies in the United States at the Huntington (HN) and the Chapin Library.

Descriptive bibliography is the classification of books according to editions, issues, and variants. An entry for a book in a descriptive bibliography includes more information than what is found in an enumerative catalogue such as STC: it generally includes a collation formula or statement of pagination, a precisely transcribed title page, and a transcription or summary of the colophon; it might include a table of contents or an analysis of contents and book structure; a description of a fifteenth-century book would contain a description of the type.

The following is an entry from W. W. Greg's *A Bibliography of the English Printed Drama to the Restoration.*[2] Greg's bibliography is designed to help identify any play text from the period; it is thus organized by title, each arranged according to the date of the first printed edition: item 379 includes all editions of *Othello*, beginning with the first quarto edition. Greg item 379 (1622) *Othello:*

THE | Tragoedy of Othello, | The Moore of Venice. | *As it hath beene diuerse times acted at the* | Globe, and at the Black-Friers, by | *his Maiesties Seruants.* | *Written by* VVilliam Shakespeare. | [device 316] | Printed by *N. O.* for *Thomas Walkley*, and are to be sold at his | shop, at the Eagle and Child, in Brittans Bursse. | 1622. . . .

Collation: 4°, A² B–M⁴ N² [fully signed except F; misprinting I3 as I5 or I4], 48 leaves, paged (B1) 1–99 [misprinting 74 as 78 or 84, 75 as 77 or 85, 78–9 as 80–1, and omitting 81–8].

Title, A1 (verso blank). Address by 'The Stationer to the Reader' signed 'Thomas Walkley', A2 (verso blank) ['the Author being dead': see appendix]. Text with HT and initial, B1 (N2v blank). . . .

Greg lists twelve copies in England and the United States. Minimal notes are given on these.

The object of this description is not a single copy but an abstraction or ideal: the standard used to identify and define individual book-copies as copies of the same edition or book. Only a few of the printing variants of individual copies are mentioned, such as the missing quires in some copies and defective title pages in others, and there is no copy-specific detail as to binding or provenance. Nor does Greg group copies by their various states, that is, by the way certain sections are misnumbered.

What bibliographers call the abstract standard that defines this bibliographical entry is *ideal copy*. And this standard is in turn presumed to reflect actual historical events and ideas in a printing house. It is the description that applies to all extant copies of a particular book or edition; by consulting Greg's description of the 1622 *Othello*, we can determine whether our copy, however fragmentary, belongs to this edition (Greg item 379a) or to those listed immediately following (Greg item 379b, the copy in the First Folio, and item 379c, the 1630 quarto).

Unlike manuscripts, printed books exist at least potentially in series, that is, in what are called editions. What each printer intended was the production of objects that were indistinguishable from each other. Only differences that involve type or printed illustrations are considered in ideal-copy description. There could be several subgroups within an edition that are clear products of a printer's intentions. Some of these are recognized in ideal-copy description: a printer produced half of the edition with one colophon and half with another. Others would not be: a printer intended to produce 990 copies on paper and 10 on vellum.[3] In this case, the paper and vellum copies are typographically identical, and most descriptive bibliographers would note such differences only in the notes.

Variants and Ideal Copy

For books such as the 1622 *Othello*, the main form of the book is not in question and the bibliographical problems are matters of *degressive bibliography*—how much detail is to be included in ideal-copy description. Other books pose problems in terms of defining the form of ideal copy. Typical cases involve books with systematic variants to which the printers themselves might be indifferent. Printers might find, at the end of a printing project, that they had printed too few copies of an individual sheet or set of sheets. To avoid waste, it might be economically feasible to reset and print a few copies of these sheets rather than scrap those sheets that were printed in greater numbers.[4] Reset sheets will thus have two variants in the final copies, one produced during the initial print-run, and one produced when the sheet was reset and printed at the end of the print-run. Any given copy of the book will thus show either one or the other of these variants. If there were more than one sheet reset (say sheets B and C have variants), book-copies can combine these sheets in many ways—four if there are two reset sheets, eight if three sheets are involved. But unless the printer intended these variant sheets to be bound as a unit or recognized as a unit, there is no reason to speak of variant editions or issues. The printer regarded the reset sheets as interchangeable with the original sheets. And unless such sheets involve the defining features of a book, that is, the title page and colophon, they pose little difficulty for bibliographers.

A more complex case involves what bibliographers often interpret as expanded editions: a printer prints a certain number of the initial quires and then decides to increase the size of the edition, printing more copies of later quires than these early quires. This entails resetting those early quires, and individual copies will thus show systematic variation in initial quires, with invariant final quires. Note that the evidence here is merely variation in initial quires and no variation in later quires; an increase in edition size is only one way to account for this.[5]

Determining how to deal with these variations is a central problem for descriptive bibliography. Descriptive bibliography is the system of explicit rules and implied rules distinguishing how differences in book-copies are to be considered or, more strongly, how those differences can be ignored and the book-copies considered "the same"—that is, how they are transformed from book-copies into books.

Editions and Printers' Intentions

Questions as to what constitutes an edition and significant variation within an edition are often decided by the notion of "printers' intentions."[6] An ideal copy is what the printer intended to print. But the term is full of difficulties: all of us intend greater things than we can reasonably produce, and what "intend" means here is only "what a printer's product implies about that printer's reasonable intentions," that is, what that printer could realistically expect to produce. No book is error-free; the notion "printer's intentions" refers to the real forms of a book the printer foresaw and would distinguish, for example, two different prologues as opposed to a single prologue that happens to be reset. These intended forms are distinguished from accidental forms, however inevitable and predictable they may be, for example, variant forms of a single sheet reset due to ordinary mechanics of printing (see chapter 4).

If the actions of a printing house were completely logical and systematic, the task of descriptive bibliography would be to create a language that reflects this coherence. Two colophons in one edition? two variant editions? two title pages? Then two editions. But printers' intentions are neither consistent nor necessarily coherent. At times printers produce variants accidentally; at times, they do it to divvy up copies among printers and publishers in a shared-printing project;[7] at times, they do it to dress up old editions as new. And there is not enough bibliographical language available to describe the myriad situations printers face and printers create.

II. Edition, Issue, State, Variant

I have already referred to the most general notion of a "printer's project": Caxton printed the *Canterbury Tales* in 1476; he printed it again in 1483. The books are different, and their differences indicate two printing projects. These are what are generally referred to as editions. To describe smaller units within these larger projects, bibliographers have developed a series of technical terms.

No two copies of any edition are absolutely identical, but they will show various degrees of identity. Nearly every edition will show *stop-press* variation (deliberate corrections requiring stopping the operation of the press) or accidental variation. In the first quarto of *Lear*, collated extensively by Greg, the variant *ausrent/miscreant* appears, that is, copies read variously "you stubburne miscreant knaue, . . ." or the nonsensical "you stubburne ausrent knaue."[8] These variants are likely the result of a conscious decision at press to correct an apparent error in a forme while it was being printed. Others might involve the mechanical movement of type as sheets are printed, and the printer might well be unaware of this disturbance. Still others might involve wholesale reprinting of complete quires. The 1561 Chaucer shows two systematic sets of initial quires before sig. B1 (these consist of preliminaries and the text to the General Prologue); one includes a set of woodcuts illustrating the characters in the General Prologue; the other has no woodcuts. All such differences, whether substantive or accidental, whether consciously or mechanically produced (the chance movement of a piece of type, for example) are "variants."

Four major terms are used to describe such variations: *edition, issue, state, variant.* These seem to constitute a hierarchy, and are usefully discussed that way in Fredson Bowers's classic *Principles of Descriptive Bibliography.* Variants can be significant enough to rise to the level of *states,* which if extensive enough can constitute *issues;* issues are major subgroups within *editions.* But there are ambiguities throughout; one can use the term *variant* as a noun, referring to different readings on a forme, or as an adjective applicable to any level in the above hierarchy.

The most important of these terms is *edition,* which is the basic unit of any descriptive catalogue or enumerative catalogue based on such bibliographical description. An edition is the set of book-copies intended to be sold by a printer as part of the same printing project. The book-copies will bear the same imprint, that is, the statement of publisher, place, and date, and they will be textually and visually identical as far as the printer is concerned. Sheets of any two of these copies can be interchanged. There may be a subset of an edition distinguished only by material, for example, copies on large paper, copies printed on vellum. A bibliographical edition in the hand press period is thus a single setting of type for an entire book. If a book is reprinted, even if that reprint is line-for-line, such an act involves resetting of type for each page, and the result is as much an autonomous edition as any other book printed by any other printer.[9]

Each edition, or any subset of editions, will include variants; using the term as an adjective will describe the nature of the variation: variant state, variant edition, variant reading. A *variant* is any textual difference involving reset type, or any significant visual difference such as the placement of illustrations, between copies of the same edition. It may involve as little as a single letter; or there may be a set of variants that allow one to speak of a "variant edition," whereby a set of copies differs in a definable way from other copies within the same edition. How significant, extensive, or systematic these variants are will determine how we speak of them: are they local, with only different literal readings? or are they found grouped systematically on, say, a sheet or forme, or in entire sections of the completed book?

The two terms, *edition* and *variant,* are generally sufficient to describe most basic printing projects. Together with the two additional technical terms *state* and *issue,* these imply the hierarchy noted above: edition > issue > state > variant (in the sense of "local printing variant"). Other terms are also found: *re-edition, re-issue,* etc. These are somewhat misleading as technical terms, since what is called a re-issue of an edition is identical to what would be defined as an issue of that edition.

The most important of these additional terms is *state.* As shown in chapter 4, printing according to the methods described by Moxon proceeds by the forme, that is, a single side of a single sheet, not by the page or by the sheet. Everything on that forme, exists as a unit, and for bibliography, it is useful to have a term to describe the complex of variants associated with this unit. *State,* in the strict bibliographical sense, thus refers to the complex of variants found on the basic unit of printing, which in most cases is a forme. In those cases where printing can be demonstrated to have proceeded page by page, state would refer to the complex of variants on the page. The term *state* is used loosely in other senses; for example, a book-copy might be said to have two states; but strictly speaking only the side of the sheet as printed can exist in a state. During printing, each case of stop-press correction will produce an additional state for that forme.

When such states have significant implications for the entire edition, that is, when they involve a title page or colophon page, or when they are extensive and related in some systematic way, a bibliographer will speak of a variant edition or even a separate issue of an edition, although the neutral term *variant edition* is in most cases preferable. Variant title pages are generally enough to constitute a variant edition or issue for the bibliographer, whereas a single variant sheet of the text portion of the book would not. Variant sections of a book, for example, two completely different sets of preliminaries, might also result in variation

significant enough to constitute a different edition. The practical implications are simple: a variant edition or issue receives a separate entry in
a catalogue. That is, a bibliographer must decide when a complex of variants involving larger sections of a book is significant and systematic
enough to speak of a printing project as involving two books or editions
rather than one. Suppose there are one hundred extant copies of a book;
minor variants may exist on every page, such that no two of these copies
are exactly the same. Yet ten of these copies contain a preliminary quire
with an introduction; ninety have only a title page. It is reasonable to
speak here of an edition and a variant edition (= issue), meaning, a variant of this same edition: one has the preliminary introduction, the other
does not. All other leaves of the two variants are essentially the same,
even though they may exist in variant states. And these two variant
forms of the single edition are what the printer intended.

Of the terms used in these contexts, *issue* was once a very common
one. But this is a tricky word. In the nineteenth century, it might refer
to a printer's attempt to sell off unsold copies of a previously printed
edition. That hypothetical printer printed a new title page, with a new
date, and sold leftover copies of an earlier edition as new; the new issue
had a title page with a more recent date. Thus, for some bibliographers,
a variant that involves a title page is sufficient to trigger the notion of
issue. Issue has also been used to describe significant variation within
an edition, such as large differences in preliminaries. In this case, issue
means only a "consciously planned subset of a single edition." Such
subsets can be defined in whatever language the bibliographer might
choose; the word *issue* is an unfortunate choice, since in most of these
cases, there is no evidence that printers intended to "issue" these subsets
of editions separately. And in some cases, the bibliographer may distinguish subsets of editions to which the printers themselves were indifferent.

III. Evolving Conventions of Bibliographical Description

Modern bibliographers are more sparing in the use of the term *issue*.
The changing conventions can be traced in the two editions of Pollard
and Redgrave's *Short-Title Catalogue* (STC). The word *issue,* used frequently in the 1926 edition, is now generally reserved for documented

cases of historical re-issue or for cases involving the resetting of a title page. The definitions by Katharine F. Pantzer, in the introduction to the revised STC (1976–91), p. xli, are as follows:

> *Variant.* A major change in title, imprint, or colophon produced in the course of printing off the relevant sheet . . .

> *Issue.* The addition, deletion, and/or substitution of leaves or sheets constituting up to half of a book's original sheets . . .

> *Edition.* An item having a majority of sheets (usually all) from reset type is introduced as '[Anr. ed.]'[10]

What earlier bibliographers casually described as a separate issue, modern bibliographers might describe as a variant or edition: we do not always know why extant copies of a particular book might have variants in their title pages and colophons; cases of shared printing marked by variant colophons, for example, are not well-described as cases of re-issue. And it is desirable to have a bibliographical language that accurately reflects this ignorance. Thus a series of closely related editions might be described: edition X, variant edition, another edition.

The conventions used by STC in 1926 (STC1) were less clearly defined than those in the revised edition (STC2) and its occasional vagaries reflected the then standard descriptions found in other bibliographies and even in sale catalogues. Nonetheless, simplifying and clarifying the language does not mean it more easily fits complex cases. I take as my example the series of folio Chaucer editions produced in the sixteenth century. These editions have been well studied: they all have title pages and colophons; there are numerous copies; and, with the exception of the precise date of one of them, there is no serious dispute about how they came to be. The difficulty lies in how to express in bibliographical terms what we already know.

The first of these editions with significant variants is the 1542 edition: the original STC numbers were 5069 and 5070, defined on the basis of title pages. Ideally, 5069 and 5070 have variant title pages and variant colophons, identifying two different printers, Bonham and Reynes; the two books are otherwise identical. In most, but not all extant copies, the information on the title page matches that in the colophon.

STC1 calls these separate issues; STC2, perhaps recognizing that this may be a case of shared printing rather than "re-issue," calls 5070 a "var. ed.":[11]

	Title Page	Colophon	STC1	STC2
5069	Bonham	Bonham	edition	edition
5070	Reynes	Reynes	issue	var.

The next, undated edition (ca. 1550) is assigned four STC numbers, 5071–74; all copies are identical, except for the colophon. STC1 calls these four "issues"; STC2 again calls them "variant editions," implying as in the 1542 edition that this is for all intents and purposes a case of shared printing: no one of the variants has historical priority over the others.

A more complex case involves the next edition of 1561, edited by John Stow. STC1 recognized two issues (STC 5075 and 5076) and defined them on the basis of their variant title pages and variant preliminaries: the General Prologue in one variant includes a series of woodcuts representing the *Canterbury Tales* pilgrims. In 1926, there were two variant title pages, two sets of preliminaries, and one colophon. A second colophon had surfaced by 1975, and STC2 assigned three numbers to this edition: 5075, 5076, and 5076.3. STC2 here invokes the word *issue*: 5076 is "another issue" (title page reset, and without woodcuts; colophon same as 5075); 5076.3 is a "variant" (title page same as 5076, with woodcuts and the variant colophon). I think 5076.3 is considered a variant of 5075, even though the sole exemplar of this variant combines features of 5075 and 5076:[12]

	Title Page	Gen. Prol.	Colophon	STC1	STC2
5075	1	woodcuts	Wight	[edition]	[edition]
5076	2	no woodcuts	Wight	issue	anr. issue
5076.3	2	woodcuts	Brasha		var.

What triggers the term *issue* in STC2 is "the resetting of a title page . . . coupled with significant changes." Thus the second colophon alone, defining 5076.3, is not enough to constitute a third issue. But the three bibliographical forms and even their descriptions do not accurately indicate the forms in which extant copies appear nor do they predict the forms in which subsequent copies may appear. The sole extant copy of 5076.3 has the woodcuts characteristic of 5075 but the title page of 5076. It is unlikely that the three forms described in STC2 are those imagined by the printers, although it is difficult to see what better options STC bibliographers have here.

The 1475 Terence

A second example is the 1475 Terence and the treatment by the Incunable Short Title Catalogue (ISTC)—an enumerative catalogue comparable to STC. There are several known copies, which are distinguished according to two entries in ISTC; the second has more elaborate preliminaries than the first:

> it00070600 [= IGI 9422]: Terentius Afer, Publius
>   Comoediae. Add: Vita Terentii
>   [Venice: Adam de Ambergau?], 21 July 1475
> it00070800 [= IGI 9723]: Terentius Afer, Publius
>   Comoediae. Add: Vita Terentii; Epitaphium Terentii
>   [Venice: Adam de Ambergau?], 21 July 1475

There are copies of the first at Florence, with Politian's notes, and at Copenhagen. There are copies of the second at Milan and Vincenza. The copy at Milan has notes by Bembo. A survey of Terence editions by Dennis Rhodes in 1988 lists another copy at St. Paul's School in London.[13] Rhodes follows ISTC and calls them two editions. That they should have the same date, Rhodes finds "inexplicable" and adds with a flurry of qualifications: "Il ne faut peut-être pas toujours trop ajouter foi à la date d'impression" [It is perhaps not always necessary to put too much faith in the printed date].[14] This marvelously evasive statement likely means that he assumes that the printed date in one of these copies (or group of copies) is a re-impression of the other. In fact, the final quires of these two editions are invariant, that is, they are from the same setting of type.

The distinguishing feature of these editions, noted even in the brief description of ISTC, involves the preliminaries. The first (IGI 9422) contains three pages of excerpts from the vita of Terence by Donatus beginning on the verso of leaf 1; the second (IGI 9423) contains a two-page vita following a blank leaf and adds a brief *Epitaphion Terentii* preceding the prologue to *Andria*.[15] Elsewhere, the books are more or less the same. They are printed in the same type and show only slight differences in the conventions of printing speaker names and in a few textual variants. The nature of these variants shows that pages were set from the same copytext and that they are not copied one from the other. By constructing a list of the variant settings, you can produce, at least for some quires, two coherent and idealized "books"—one with a setting I will call A; the other with a distinguishable and consistent setting I will call B. The page breaks in the two variant settings do not always correspond. Yet in the extant copies, these settings are mixed: the two coherent and distinguishable sets of variants are not distributed in the copies in consistent ways. However these variants were produced, whether simultaneously on two separate presses, immediately upon the completion of each separate quire, or at the end of the first print-run, the printer seems unconcerned about their differences.

The copies of the 1475 Terence constitute two editions in a bibliographical sense because the variants in the preliminaries are textual and obvious. But the case also shows the limitations of an ideal-copy notion of edition: these variants are part of the same printing project; that they are bound indifferently together suggests that while the printer may have distinguished the two preliminaries, he did not distinguish the two autonomous and coherent sets of variants that could be associated with these preliminaries. Nor, significantly, did Bembo and Politian, who, in looking for an edition to use in collating the Bembo manuscript, chose this one: they too considered the two copies "the same." As bibliographers, however, we cannot follow them, even though, in this case, we must violate what seems to be clear evidence of printers' intentions. The ideal-copy solution must define two self-consistent entities: one in the distinguishable setting A, the other with the variant quires associated with setting B. Depending on our preliminary definitions, we can call these editions, issues, or variants. This has the unfortunate but perhaps inevitable result that none of the extant copies so far collated actually takes either of these forms. The descriptive bibliographer can only conclude: so much the worse for the extant copies.[16]

Conclusion

Printing procedures were not the same from the fifteenth through the eighteenth centuries, and they varied from project to project. Individual cases will thus often challenge the technical terminology of descriptive bibliography. Different terms are used in bibliographical descriptions, and no single set of technical terms can be expected to apply efficiently to all cases: in English, we might hear of "printing," "impression," "setting," meaning a setting of type (for a forme? for an entire book?); in German we hear of *Auflag* (printed edition); *Ausgabe* (editorial edition); *Druck* (impression); *Satz* (setting of type); in French, *tirage, état, impression, édition*. The boundaries between these terms can never be exactly set because the situations to which they apply are various, and intentions of human beings are often incoherently developed and inaccurately realized. Bibliographical language is simply an example of human language, which is incapable of adequately describing any of the extra-linguistic objects to which it applies.

Coda: The Emphasis on Preliminary Leaves

Several of the rules of descriptive bibliography privilege the early leaves of a book: a change in title page is enough to trigger the notion of issue; for books with identical title pages, extensive changes elsewhere would be required to constitute issue. This emphasis on early leaves in bibliography has had consequences; books documented as having variant preliminary quires have given rise to several theories, chief among them, the notion that editions were routinely increased during production, necessitating the reprinting of the deficient early sheets.[17]

What bibliographers detect, however, is not an inherent quality of discernibility or detectability in books themselves. Bibliographers will only discern what is within the focus of their attention. Preliminaries of books are usually more closely examined than later quires, and thus cases involving variant preliminaries are more often documented than cases of variant quires in later sections of books. Variants in title pages and preliminaries will show up in the ordinary transcriptions that descriptive bibliography requires of these leaves; variants elsewhere are less well recorded, simply because few bibliographers take the time to look for them. In the case of the 1475 Terence, bibliographers were not able to see that the settings of the two colophons were the same, since that could only be determined by optical collation of microfilm copies or by physically taking microfilm impressions of one copy to a library holding another copy.

Getting two copies of a book together is often impractical; even libraries engaged in digitization do not routinely digitize all copies. The Bayerische Staatsbibliothek, now in the process of digitizing their incunabula, has a policy of digitizing only one copy of multiple copies for BSB-Ink. Equally important, not all bibliographers are comfortable with the various procedures of optical collation. This must be done either on a large, cumbersome, and cantankerous machine, such as the Hinman collator, of which there are fewer functioning examples each year, or by a process of optical superimposition that can make otherwise healthy bibliographers physically ill.[18] Since what constitutes bibliographical issue or edition involves textual differences in the preliminary pages, there is a disproportionate number of books recorded whose only variant quires seem to be preliminary sheets. But until far more books are systematically collated, and until scholars take the time to test the results of other scholars' collations, it is impossible to know how representative or even significant these cases are.

CHAPTER TWELVE

The Ersatz Book I

Facsimiles and Forgeries

What I call ersatz books come in many varieties: electronic pictures of books, photostat reproductions, scholarly editions, verbal descriptions, textual reproductions. The discussion in this chapter is limited to material facsimiles; the de-materialized, electronic facsimile and associated databases is the subject of chapter 13.

I. Facsimile Types

What most bibliographers consider a facsimile is a photographic one, picturing individual pages of a book. But there are other forms of bibliographic facsimile, historical and modern, and many of these can be facsimilized electronically. Some hybrid forms serve the same functions as a textual, scholarly edition. A *diplomatic edition* is one that reproduces, according to a set of variable conventions, the physical line structure and appearance of a book or manuscript. Diplomatic editions were common in the late nineteenth century, and many of the early editions in the Early English Text Society founded in 1864 are examples. A second form of the facsimile is the type facsimile. A *type facsimile* is a typeset version of an earlier printed book that uses a closely related typeface. Such editions differ from diplomatic editions in that they are designed to look like their originals. Textual and editorial matters are secondary, even though some are line-for-line reproductions of their original and may serve the same editorial functions as diplomatic editions.[1]

It is difficult for a modern reader, accustomed to photographic reproductions, to judge the extent to which such facsimiles reproduce or represent the original for early nineteenth-century readers, or even what reproduction means. In some cases, a type facsimile might give an accurate idea of the original. But "accurate idea" is not the same thing as an accurate image. Several type facsimile editions from the Malone Society reproduce the original book in a modern typeface that is only vaguely like that of the original (a modern textura is used in place of the original bastard).[2]

Bibliographical and Textual-Critical Implications of the Modern Photographic Facsimile

Type facsimiles have been largely replaced by photographic facsimiles. We are most accustomed to facsimiles whose pages appear to be photographs, that is, collotypes, relief half-tones, or lithographic offsets. But any process used in illustration (intaglio, relief, and planographic) can be combined with photography to produce facsimiles.[3] The functions of such photographic facsimiles are various: some are expensive and essentially collectors' items; others seem designed as research tools.[4] Early photographic facsimile editions of Shakespeare's First Folio served many purposes and in turn justified the production of facsimile editions of Shakespeare quartos. The facsimiles produced by the Shakespeare-Quarto Facsimile Series in the late nineteenth century (publ. C. Praetorius) were largely editorial: they replaced or supplemented earlier diplomatic editions of these same quartos.[5] But the books that were reproduced by these facsimiles existed in variant copies (copies of the first quarto of *King Lear* are not the same); and as ordinary press-variation became a standard topic in editorial studies,[6] the production of photographic facsimiles raised a bibliographical problem we have been looking at throughout this study. What is the object of a facsimile? should a facsimile, particularly one designed for editorial purposes, reproduce a particular copy? or should it reproduce something like an ideal copy, that is, a composite copy selected from portions of all available copies? Is the facsimile a reproduction of a book-copy? or a book?

The Facsimile and the Question of Ideal Copy: The Shakespeare First Folio

Photographic facsimiles of the Shakespeare First Folio include the photo-lithographic facsimile of Howard Staunton (1866); the reduced facsimile of J. O. Halliwell-Phillipps (1876); the Oxford facsimile (collotype) by Sidney Lee (1902); and the Methuen photo-zincographic facsimile (1910). These were followed by two more major projects in the mid-twentieth century: the Yale facsimile (photo offset, reduced) and the full-size Norton facsimile. As noted by Charlton Hinman in his edition of the Norton facsimile, all of the early facsimiles were expensive with the exception of the reduced facsimile associated with Halliwell-Phillipps. They were thus art objects rather than research tools. The inexpensive Halliwell-Phillipps facsimile, even though doctored with pen and ink, thus became paradoxically the most often used for editorial purposes.[7]

Not until the mid-twentieth century did the notion that *a* facsimile of the First Folio represented *the* First Folio of Shakespeare come under critical review.[8] Images in all facsimile projects were necessarily and inevitably altered; in addition, the production of a facsimile involved the selection of an original copy, in editorial terms, a copytext. In some cases, original copies were combined, as in the Halliwell-Phillipps facsimile; in others, the original was itself a facsimile. The 1998 Routledge facsimile (ed. Doug Moston) is a reproduction of the Halliwell-Phillipps facsimile. Assuming that a facsimile is an editorial tool and not simply an art object, what do these facsimiles represent and what should they represent?[9]

The Halliwell-Phillipps facsimile was based on two copies: one of the Folger Library copies (Folg 33) and for texts following *Henry IV, Part One,* the Staunton facsimile; Fredson Bowers thus refers to it as "an arbitrarily mongrel copy";[10] the Oxford facsimile reproduced the First Folio now in the Huntington; the Yale facsimile was taken from the copy of the Elizabethan Club at Yale. In all cases, the principle of selection seems mere expedience. That any one copy could be superior to another in terms of text rather than appearance was not raised and probably not seriously considered.

What could be called the first critical facsimile was the Norton facsimile by Charlton Hinman. Hinman created his facsimile on the basis of his study of press-variants (see chapter 4); the pages he selected were those that contained the "corrected" readings. And in his introduction, Hinman described the edition as the facsimile equivalent of the bibliographical "ideal copy," although "ideal" in this context had a slightly different meaning from what it has in descriptive bibliography. Bowers, who was responsible for the notion of ideal copy, argued in his review of the Yale facsimile for the reverse solution: a facsimile, insofar as it was to be an editorial tool, should not include the final corrections of the printer, those representing the printer's final intentions; it should rather reproduce the first, uncorrected variant, the variant more likely to represent the manuscript or printed source of the facsimile, and one presumably closer to the author. That is, a facsimile should not present what the printer might have intended but the version of the printed pages with the least editorial intervention by that printer.

Michael Warren, in his facsimile edition of *King Lear,* following up on the critical discussion by Bowers and Hinman, seems to have accepted Hinman's argument, but goes even further and chooses not the best page for reproduction, but the best forme, that is, a two-page unit.[11] Both Hinman and Bowers selected the original to be reproduced on a page-by-page basis; they thus implicitly defined the page as the basic unit of printing. But the basic unit of printing is the forme (see chapter 4), as Bowers himself pointed out in many of his editorial projects. Thus, a facsimile reproducing anything like the printer's ideal should produce the best possible edition the printer could produce: this, paradoxically, cannot be as perfect an edition as Hinman's claimed to be, since Hinman chose his page images without regard to the quality of the facing page image originally printed on the same sheet.

The arguments by Bowers and Hinman were built on the assumption that the facsimile was primarily an editorial tool. Warren's claim, by contrast, amounts to de-editorialization of the facsimile: a facsimile is an image of a book. Although equally interested in editorial matters, Warren redefines the facsimile as the image of a product of a printing press, more specifically, an image of a possible rather than ideal product of that press.

These facsimile projects by the late twentieth century combined the best thinking of analytical bibliography and textual criticism. The production of facsimile editions gave material and economic form to what to most scholars was the abstruse and purely abstract question of ideal copy. Questions of ideal copy arose in large part due to developments in technology; and it is perhaps fitting that just when such questions reached their maximum sophistication, they were abandoned in the face of new technology. Any library that owns a First Folio can now fairly cheaply produce easily accessible electronic images of it, and many have done so. What I have called ersatz books will in the twenty-first century exist in a nonmaterial form.

Physical, material facsimiles, that is to say, things one can put on one's bookshelf, came to be the very thing that Bowers warned against—objects of merely antiquarian interest.[12] Book owners, antiquarians, or book displayers of any kind might well want a Shakespeare First Folio or a physical version of it on their shelves, but why would a scholar bother with such a thing if a searchable version is available online?

II. Facsimiles and Forgeries

What we think of as facsimiles are generally reproductions of entire books. But an important class of facsimile production involves only parts of books, that is, copies of sections of books used to complete damaged copies circulating in the book trade. Such sections can be supplied in various ways: one is by cannibalizing what dealers call "hospital copies" of the same book.[13] In extreme cases, book parts necessary to complete a copy have been stolen outright from otherwise autonomous copies. Thomas J. Wise famously completed books he was selling with leaves taken from British Museum copies; some of these are now in the Wrenn Library in Texas.[14] Missing parts of valuable book-copies can also be created by hand. The best known of the many artists and owners who completed books this way is Joseph Harris in the mid-nineteenth century.[15] To the modern eye, such hand-drawn pages are not deceptive: they are clearly drawings and do no more than describe, allude to, or identify the original that they replace. It is not so clear how they looked to their contemporaries. The Huntington Library copy of a 1542 Chaucer edition once owned by Robert Hoe (RB 99596) contains a title page that to a modern bibliographer is obviously hand drawn or traced. Yet the nineteenth-century description included in the book describes it as "so good as to escape detection"; this description does not seem to imply that there was ever an intention to deceive or defraud anyone by completing the book this way.

By the mid-nineteenth century, special type was occasionally cast for the purpose of completing early books; a version of Caxton's type 2 was cast by Vincent Figgins and used to reprint Caxton's *Game of Chess*.[16] Lithography provided a new method of reproduction, although prior to photography, there were limits to the ways in which it could be used. The ink of an original document, whether an autograph or a printed page of an early book, must substitute somehow for the image an artist would draw directly on the stone in ordinary lithographic methods. The original ink thus is involved chemically in the lithographic process.

In one technique, the original is dampened, then charged with ink that sticks only to the ink of the original (see chapter 2; this process can only be used with grease-based ink). The new ink is then transferred to the stone. The process of lithography then proceeds.[17] This method could be used for reproducing original drawings, engravings, or pages of printed editions; but in these processes, the original is destroyed or at least compromised. For an owner of a Caxton copy missing, say, the final leaves, there would be little point in attempting a lithographic copy from another book-copy; Caxton copies are not accessible, and even if they were, one original would have to be destroyed in order to provide the needed facsimile. But where multiple copies or potential multiple copies are involved, the sacrifice might be worthwhile, and this is the case with illustrations and title pages of semi-valuable and relatively common sixteenth- or seventeenth-century books. Thus, when one finds an early lithographed page in an otherwise original early book, it is likely that there will be other copies of that page as well.[18]

The development of photolithography solved several problems: the original was not compromised, and the chemical composition of the ink, whether grease based or water based, was irrelevant. No originals were damaged in Staunton's 1866 photolithographic facsimile of Shakespeare First Folio. Photolithography changed both the basic methods of forgery and the methods required to detect them.

Engravings are easily lithographed; the resultant lithographed copies are usually easily detected by the absence of the characteristic plate mark associated with engravings, although this plate mark, of course, can itself be faked. For moderately priced books destined to receive limited if any bibliographical scrutiny, such forgeries are seldom documented, and neither owner nor seller has a stake in uncovering them.[19]

Typeset pages sometimes require an additional step. Since lithographs are planographic, it is not likely that one would be mistaken for an original typeset page if the book happened to be valuable enough to inspect. There is thus an even more accurate and pernicious variation, whereby the planographic print such as a photograph is reworked as a relief print. A photograph is taken of an original page. That photograph is then transferred to a metal plate, which, by a process of etching and cutting, is cut as a relief plate. A copy is then printed from this plate on paper as close to that of the original book as possible. The usual tests of originality will not work: I look at the paper and judge it contemporary with the book; if the leaf is a title page, I do not expect it to be of the exact same paper as the original. I examine the reverse side of the leaf and feel the impression made by the block; I can see under a glass the characteristic squash of relief printing. Since this process does not result in the destruction or even possession of an original, which can be in the vault of a rare books library, it can be used to copy any leaf of any book-copy that can be photographed.

This is the method used in E. Gordon Duff's *Fifteenth-Century English Books* of 1917, where the illustrative facsimile pages of early English type are printed in letterpress. It is also the method used by certain book dealers to provide prominent missing leaves of incomplete early book-copies (although I cannot publicly identify them here). Such forged leaves are difficult to detect unless one first suspects them and is willing to spend the time to examine the books for them. For extravagantly expensive books, Caxtons for example, it is worthwhile for a skeptical buyer or bibliographer to do so. But for books of moderate value, such as early Chaucer folios, which sold for less than £50 in the nineteenth century, there is little incentive for anyone to examine them in detail. All parties have a stake in the authenticity of such books and their parts, and it is in these books where the workings of facsimilists and forgers are likely the most prevalent.[20]

III. The Question of Accuracy

In the 1860s, in preparing for the Caxton sesquicentennial, a catalogue of Caxton books and a detailed study of types was planned by William Blades.[21] Illustrations of the various types were to be done by G. I. F.

Tupper. Tupper made two kinds of illustrations, one called "facsimiles," the other called "imitations." The facsimiles used a process of lithography, beginning with tracings from the original page; the imitations used hand-cut relief blocks. To us, the differences seem obvious: the facsimiles, being closer in appearance to photolithography (a process available to Tupper but one he rejected), seem clearly superior. But the dialogue between Blades and Tupper shows a more sophisticated view of what accuracy means, a view that bears on the processes of reproduction. Blades, discussing the lithographic versions, clearly shares our naïve view:

> I have just seen the progress made with the facsimile illustration of No. 1 Type and am delighted with it. . . . Given a paper similar in appearance to Caxton's and I would defy Old Caxton himself to have repudiated it as one of his own offspring.[22]

Tupper, the artist and technician, was far less certain about the object of reproduction:

> Ye object has been to show ye true face of ye type as nearly as possible from a printed example . . . without idealizing—but I confess I am by no means satisfied with this plan and trust that if any one should ever go over ye ground again (which there is no chance of my doing—once in a lifetime being sufficient) he will, as I at first intended, give 2 representations of each character—one showing ye true face of ye type—discarding ye surplus ink round ye edges—ye other an exact facsimile of an *average* impression as it appears.[23]

Note that the word "true" is used of a tracing/lithographic reprint, incorporating the very idealizing Tupper specifically rejects ("discarding the surplus ink"); such truth is opposed to "an exact facsimile of an average impression as it appears." It is difficult to translate this: the *appearance* of an *average* impression is to be facsimilized exactly! But since both "appearance" and "average" are abstractions, it is equally difficult to see how the notion of exactitude can be applied.

CHAPTER THIRTEEN

· · ·

The Ersatz Book II

Electronic Books and Databases

Electronic books come in various forms; essentially facsimiles, most provide images combined with some form of searchable text. When designed for scholarly purposes, digital versions of individual works are often related to editorial projects; the results of these projects are, I think, mixed, and they are not my concern here.[1] The present chapter looks at two primarily bibliographical projects, which can serve as examples of the digitization of images and cataloguing data. The first, the Incunabula Short Title Catalogue (ISTC), is primarily a database; it provides, in some of its versions, selected and largely illustrative images. The second is a consortium of databases on early English books: the English Short Title Catalogue (ESTC), Early English Books Online (EEBO) and Eighteenth-Century Collections Online (ECCO). The combination of these will eventually combine information from enumerative bibliographies (ESTC) with the images and searchable text from EEBO and ECCO.

I am assuming the problems I have found here are not unique; they are rather variants of those that would be found in any other bibliographical database, although I will let my own readers test that statement. I should note also that I am writing and revising this book in 2011; but much of my material comes from research earlier than that. By the time most readers get to this chapter, every specific bit of information I cite here will likely be out of date: databases will have been revised, corrected, improved. They will rely on different platforms. New and improved databases will be available. I could of course wait until the last minute, performing all my searches on whatever version of these databases is available the week before final proof is due. But that only obscures the basic problem of obsolescence and currency I address here: that every statement can be revised means that none can be critiqued.

I. Incunabula Short Title Catalogue

The Incunabula Short Title Catalogue (ISTC) is an electronic catalogue listing every recorded fifteenth-century book (www.bl.uk/catalogues/istc/). The first attempt to provide what could be called a comprehensive catalogue of fifteenth-century books is Michael Maittaire's *Annales typographici* of 1719; several major catalogues followed, including most notably Georg Wolfgang Panzer's *Annales typographici* and Ludwig Hain's *Repertorium Bibliographicum,* and in the twentieth century, the British Museum Catalogue (BMC) and the *Gesamtkatalog der Wiegendrucke* (GW).[2] ISTC makes at least some of the information in these catalogues easily searchable.

ISTC is an enumerative bibliography, not a descriptive one. The only information given for each book is format (folio, quarto, etc.), author, title, place of publication, printer, and date. The database lists individual copies, and occasional copy-specific detail is provided when copies are incomplete or differ from ideal copy. The goal is comprehensiveness, or at least some form of comprehensiveness: ideally, all fifteenth-century books in accessible libraries could be listed. A typical entry in ISTC is as follows:

> Catullus, Gaius Valerius
> Carmina. Add: Statius: Sylvae. Ed: Franciscus Puteolanus
> Parma: Stephanus Corallus, 31 Aug. 1473
> > Also recorded as 2 Sept. 1473?
> 4°

A list of locations and copy-specific notes follow.[3]

By comparison, I list the entry of the same book in the *Gesamtkata-log der Wiegendrucke;* this is an ideal-copy description and includes details of structure, type, and some indication of the relation of the book structure to text.

6386 Catullus, C. Valerius: Carmina.—P. Papinius Statius: Silvae. Hrsg. Franciscus Puteolanus. Parma: Stephanus Corallus, II. Kal. Sept. [31. August] 1473. 2°.

96 Bl. Lagen: [a⁸–m⁸] 34 Z. Type: I: 112R. Min. f. Init.

. . .

That final line needs translation: "there are 96 leaves; the quires are un-signed (thus the brackets); the twelve quires (a–m, not counting j; see chapter 2) are of 8 leaves each. Each page has 34 printed lines. The type is Proctor #1, which is a roman measuring 112 mm for twenty lines. Lowercase letters are used for initials." A twenty-seven-line transcription of the opening and closing leaves of each section follows, itself followed by notes, and, as in ISTC, reference to other catalogues and a location list.

ISTC was originally produced commercially in a CD-ROM version, entitled *Illustrated Incunable Short Title Catalogue.* There were two editions, then abbreviated I-ISTC1 (two discs) and I-ISTC2 (four discs).[4] They contained select images of the books catalogued on the basic database. These images were illustrative only: no book is illustrated completely nor is any particular group of books illustrated systematically. The two versions of this database contained in I-ISTC1 and I-ISTC2 mark two "states" of the evolving database known as ISTC.[5]

The Corpus of Information

The ISTC database, and others like it, will never be complete. There is no final publication date for the project, and no entry needs to be written or corrected today or ever. The corpus is thus an evolving one; even though fifteenth-century books are not being created physically, those books continue to surface in the process of recording them. Because of the evolving corpus and the evolving nature of the database describing them, there is no editorial or bibliographical standard that is enforced at one moment in time. When we use the database in its online versions, we do not know, for example, which entries have been verified by ISTC bibliographers in the field and which rely on individual library catalogs and descriptions. Even if we could determine that from the ISTC database, we could not use such evidence in a systematic way, since the distinction between what might be called verified and unverified books is arbitrary and has little to do with the actual history of the books or book-copies. Because the database is not fixed, and because entries cannot be constructed according to consistent principles, it is impractical to proofread the entire database to produce a quasi-definitive state. This is advantageous to the creators of the database; but it poses problems for users, particularly critical users interested in the implied parameters of the database.

Database Uses and Searches

The basic search routines in the ISTC database allow a user to pose and answer many questions in a quantitative manner, although questions are limited to those imagined in some form by the designers: how many book titles were printed between 1486 and 1488? how many incunable editions exist of an author?[6]

Searches such as these have not been possible before, and figures regarding numbers of books have been wildly uncritical.[7] Union catalogues and catalogues of individual libraries have either alphabetized their incunables by author (e.g., Hain, GW, Goff, BSB-Ink, CIBN) or organized them by printer in some version of Proctor order (e.g., BMC and the incunable catalogue from the Huntington).[8] The order determines what questions can be asked; it is difficult to ask a question concerning the popularity of an author by consulting a catalogue in Proctor order unless there is a supplementary index.

There are many ways of conducting searches in ISTC; but there can be no definitive instructions on how to do them, since the means of doing them are evolving. The examples below are thus necessarily and deliberately disjointed. The results depend on whether one is using the database contained in the earlier published versions of the databases

(I-ISTC1 or 2 and their associated platform) or the version now available online. It is worth noting that the prohibitively expensive CD-
ROMs from I-ISTC will no longer function in the operating systems
of many recent computers.

Standard Questions

I begin with a question of a type clearly foreseen by the designers of the
database: "How many folio editions of Cicero are recorded as printed in
the fifteenth century in Venice?" The online version of ISTC strangely
tells me there are no folio Ciceros printed in Venice. I know this is incorrect (but how do I know this? does this suggest I am searching for
information I already possess?). I realize that "Cicero" is not an exact
author match. I try again with Marcus Tullius Cicero. Now I get 103 for
Cicero/Venice, and 88 for Cicero/Venice/f. This is odd: my notes say
that two hours earlier, the result was 87, but of course, there is no way to
check that. Theoretically, I should be able to compare this result with
results for other dates or printing towns and find something of interest.
But there are many practical problems involved.[9]

The Question of Dates

The answer to questions such as the above depends on the assignment
of dates. And to understand the nature and quality of the information
in the database requires understanding the rationale behind these dates.
The means of dating books are various and the dates in the database are
consequently assigned variously: in addition to specific dates (the dates
in the colophon), there are phrases such as "1484–86"; "before 1487";
"not after 1488." In earlier versions of ISTC, the entry "1484–86" would
show up in searches for 1484, 1486, but not 1485. In the present platform,
these problems seem to have been corrected. Now each book is assigned
one date and one date only. A date listed in its ISTC entry as "about
1471–72" comes up only in a search for 1471. A date 24 Jan. 1481/82
(which refers to the same historical day under two calendars) is interpreted as 1482; "not after 9 Nov. 1471" is interpreted as 1471. The dates
"[14]78," "not before Aug. 1479," "between Apr. 1484 and 1486," "15 Feb.
1499/1500," "after 1500"—these are standardized for searching as 1478,

1479, 1484, 1500, and 1501. This is an improvement over the earlier search platform, although the assignment of date for searching purposes misrepresents the assignment of date by bibliographers. Somewhat curiously, the discussion of dating in the ISTC's introduction (one that gives some idea of the complexity involved) has not changed.[10] Standardizing these dates enables rough searches to be conducted; yet the results are based on an oversimplification of the date assigned each book, and the apparent precision is specious.[11]

Furthermore, the ISTC database in its present platform has introduced a difficulty not found in the earlier versions. It is no longer possible to use a fourth search term, and even in the examples above, I have had to reformulate certain questions: I can still ask "how many folio editions of Cicero were printed in Venice?" but I can no longer ask "how many folio editions of Cicero were printed in Venice in 1480?"[12] At least, when I wrote this sentence I could not.

Nonstandard Questions

Questions such as the above ("how many incunables were printed in year X?") are those foreseen by the catalogue designers. My second example is of a question not foreseen by the designers. Such nonstandard questions cannot be answered and at times they cannot even be formulated by using this tool. Suppose I wanted to know how many English incunable editions there are in the USA besides those at the Huntington Library (HEHL). I do not know why anyone would want the answer to this question—could the Huntington purchases somehow skew the basic patterns of American book acquisition?—but despite the apparent simplicity of the question, there is no obvious way of asking it of ISTC.

My first difficulty involved the discovery that the database did not see "USA" (or "not USA") as an acceptable term. To get around this, I tried "Goff" in the "Bibliographical key-word" search ("Goff" refers to Frederick Goff's comprehensive census of incunables in American libraries, and a Goff number cannot be assigned unless that book is, or was, recorded in America). I got the number 12919, which I accepted because I knew this was roughly correct. Limiting that with the query "not HEHL" gave me 7727. Since I know the number of incunables at the Huntington, this seemed correct, even though it leads to the unnerving realization that the best way to conduct a search is to know the answer beforehand. I then try to add one more limit, "language: English," but this will not work. This gave 12869 for one search, 12902 on a second attempt. The database has a tendency, when frustrated, to return the answer 0 or a wildly inflated number. I tried to work around this problem in a number of ways, with no success.

I gave up and turned to the CD-ROMs. Or rather, I turned instead to my notes of previous searches on these CD-ROMs, because they will not run on the operating system of my new computer, now almost five years old. The database yields the following:

> How many editions are in English? 231
> Of those, in American libraries? 104
> Excluding those at the Huntington? 51

This seems correct, since there are fifty-three editions at the Huntington and 53 + 51 = 104. But of course it is not correct. This is not what I wish to know.

What I want is "how many English incunable editions are there in America if we disregard those at the Huntington Library?" What the above search gives me (51) is the number of incunable editions in America that are not found in the Huntington. This is not it. I obviously want to include editions that are both in the Huntington and in other libraries, that is, I want to know not "how many English incunable (titles) are there in American libraries that are not in the Huntington?" but "how many would still be in America if those in the Huntington were shipped overseas tomorrow?" The basic searches require statements such as the following: it is either in HEHL or it is NOT in HEHL. To find a book in America excluding those in HEHL seems to require an expression such as "in America, NOT at HEHL." The way to express what I want seems to be IN America, NOT at HEHL, plus IN America, AT HEHL, and IN another American library. Searches like this are possible, as long as you can remember what they mean, and perhaps as long as you know the answer beforehand so that you can be sure the result is correct.[13]

This illustrates what should now be a familiar problem: the difference between books and book-copies. Most of the searches in ISTC deal with books; but some of the fields deal with copies (the exemplars of that book that appear in specific locations). As the above simple example shows, these cannot be easily combined.

Conclusion

Any use of a catalogue is restricted by the principles built into it: it is possible to search ISTC for "quartos printed in Augsburg" or "books written by Augustine," but because ISTC contains no information about typeface, it says nothing about "the number of books printed in roman type" nor is it possible to find candidates for a printer of a fragment printed in, say, 94G. The value of searches is restricted further by the changing quality and currency of the information in the database. I cannot update in any systematic way my own descriptions to enable the reader of this book to use this or other databases more efficiently. The problems I encounter today are not the same problems I encountered a year ago, and a perfect description of how to use that database now might not help someone trying to use it a year from today. This means that there can be no sustained critique of the database, nothing comparable to Paul Needham's critique of the CD-ROM versions in 1999 or Peter Blayney's comparable critique of the printed version of STC in 1994.[14] Paradoxically, because those in charge of the database can and have responded to criticisms, there can be no independent critique and counter-critique by bibliographical scholars, since the object of criticism will no longer stay in place.

II. Early English Books (ESTC, EEBO, and ECCO)

The second part of this chapter involves early English books. At present, there are three relevant projects: (1) ESTC (now English Short Title Catalogue) (2) EEBO (Early English Books Online); (3) ECCO (Eighteenth Century Collections Online).[15]

Basic Definitions and Goals

The goal of these ambitious projects is to make available online an enumerative and I believe descriptive catalogue of all early English books, defined according to the three catalogues at the origins of these projects: STC = < 1641; Wing = 1641–1700; ESTC* = 1701–1800. Eventually, or ideally, these databases will provide images of all the books they catalogue, as well as a searchable version of the texts.

The three major databases are outgrowths of several independent projects. STC is the enumerative *Short-Title Catalogue* of Pollard and Redgrave (1926), revised in three-volume form in 1976–91. This included a holdings list limited largely to public libraries in Great Britain and the United States. Wing is a three-volume continuation of STC, constructed on slightly different principles.[16] The original ESTC was a microfiche extension of these two catalogues and was known as the *Eighteenth-Century Short Title Catalogue*. The three (STC, Wing, and the original ESTC) were combined electronically to form the ESTC, now an acronym for the English Short Title Catalogue.[17] In its online form, the original enumerative catalogue is developing into a descriptive one, although individual entries vary in the amount of information they contain. Brief statements of structure (pagination or foliation) are now included, although not always in a consistent form. Neither STC nor Wing contains collation formulae of any kind.[18]

STC (1926):

> Chaucer, Geoffrey. The workes of Geffray Chaucer newly printed, with dyuers workes neuer in print before. [*Ed.* W. Thynne.] *T. Godfray*, 1532. L. O. C. HN. CH.

STC (1976–91):

> Chaucer, Geoffrey. The workes of Geffray Chaucer newly printed, with dyuers workes neuer in print before. [Ed.] (W. Thynne.) fol. (*T. Godfray*, 1532). L.O.C(imp.). E. G2 +; F. HN.HD(imp.). N. PML. +

> In most copies Qq3 is cancelled and replaced by 4 leaves including The testament of Creseyde [by R. Henryson], also pr. sep. as 13316; a few (NY, Robert Taylor) also retain orig. Qq3.

Wing entries for a comparable book are more laconic; Wing provides 21 locations following the brief entry here:

3736. Chaucer, Geoffrey. The works of. Printed, 1687. fol.

The online ESTC entry gives a full-title transcription:

> The workes of Geffray Chaucer newly printed, with dyuers workes whiche were neuer in print before: as in the table more playnly dothe appere. Cum priuilegio. [Printed at Lo[n]don: By Thomas Godfray. The yere of our lorde. M.D.xxxii. [1532]]
>
> [10] CC.xix. [3] CC.xx–CCC,CCC–CCC.lxxxiii leaves: ill.; 2°.
>
> Notes: Edited by William Thynne, who is named on A2v.
>
> Mostly in verse.
>
> Includes a number of spurious works.
>
> Imprint from colophon.

The statement of foliation in the above ESTC entry is an example of the now conventional way of describing book structure.[19] Transcriptions of half-title pages follow what is quoted above. This record (nearly the same as the record in EEBO) is followed by what is called an "Uncontrolled note" concerning the copy filmed in University Microfilms International; a list of libraries holding copies is then followed by a section "Surrogates" (that is, on microfilm facsimiles). In earlier public forms of ESTC, the list of copies led directly to copy-specific information for some of the listed libraries (Huntington and Folger). In the British Library version available online, the path to this information is less direct.

Early English Books Online is based on *Early English Books*, a microfilm collection of those books recorded in STC (that is, to 1640), begun in 1938.[20] That year Eugene B. Power formed his company University Microfilms International (UMI) and began two projects: one on filming dissertations, essentially enabling "editions of one"; the second, in response to the wartime destruction of books, on the early English books in the British Library.[21] Power's concern was preservation, not bibliography. The reels are of indifferent quality, and there are many errors in photography. Power provided what amounted to a pictorial record of perishable objects in an existing collection. According to Pro-

Quest, the number of customers in 1938 for UMI was eleven, enough to meet the major goal of preservation. The function of the project then expanded. *Early English Books* became a bibliographical project as more copies of the microfilm were sold to individual libraries. The images reproduce the entire book-copy (or theoretically they do). Thus, these images complete rather than simply illustrate the ideal-copy descriptions in ESTC.

These microfilm images are the basis of EEBO—Early English Books Online. In addition to disseminating these images, EEBO intends to make all these records searchable through what is called the Text Creation Partnership. According to EEBO, some 100,000 of 125,000 titles have been scanned in as images; some 25,000 have been transcribed as texts (neither number is of course current for anyone reading this sentence). ECCO (Eighteenth-Century Collections Online) has the same goals as ESTC and EEBO: although it is far less complete, it intends to provide images of all eighteenth-century English books along with a searchable textual database.

The Image: From Book-Copy to Book and the Creation of the Standard Edition

One of the effects of EEBO is to canonize individual copies of books rather than promote those copies as unique exemplars of an edition. In other words, EEBO has returned the question of what the object of a facsimile should be to the state it was in before the critical discussion of Shakespeare facsimiles in the 1950s, producing in its images a standard edition rather than pictures of an individual book-copy. Just as a scholar can cite the Norton facsimile of Shakespeare as *the* First Folio (even though it is no such thing), scholars can now consult or cite an image in EEBO not as an example of, say, sig. IV of a particular book, but as sig. IV itself. EEBO has inadvertently reproduced a basic goal of the technology of print—the production of an exactly repeatable copy of a text. Book historians concentrating on the materiality of books have shown that this repeatability is illusory: book-copies obstinately retain their singularity in history. The electronic book, however, turns the argument on its head by beginning with the singular book-copy and promoting it as endlessly repeatable.

The easiest critique of this situation could focus on the quality of the images, which are not good by modern standards; compare, for example, the detailed color images of bindings and pages in the BSB-Ink collection. Yet considered bibliographically, an excellent image of a book-copy masquerading as a book is no better than an execrable one. Neither one is the book itself. In addition, the transformation is done in what could be called bibliographical bad faith, in that the images are stripped of nearly all that would make them book-copies. There are only incidental signs of provenance and binding in an EEBO image. There are no notes on sections tipped in or even faked, and no notes on condition. The implication now, but probably not to Power when he initiated this project, is that these are not the British Library copies, those objects that were exposed to possible destruction in wartime bombing, but representatives of all copies, as the reproducibility of the microfilm attests.

Searchability: The Text Creation Partnership

The Text Creation Partnership (TCP), which is the branch providing searchable texts for EEBO, claims to have 25,000 of 125,000 copies in the "first phase" of its operation. These are scanned with a claimed accuracy rate of 99.995 percent. I assume this unexplained figure means that of one hundred thousand characters (or am I miscalculating this dizzying figure?), only five will be mistranscribed, that is, one of every twenty thousand characters. That is about one per ten pages. That error rate for seventeenth-century books seems unreasonably precise; but I am not certain what "error" means—whether it refers to transcription (if the machine transcriptions are proofread, should it be this high?) or the tagging, which would be the organization of individually spelled words into searchable terms (why would it be this low?).[22]

I know that searching the database can provide me with much information that I don't know, as can reading any book at random or looking through the pages of the *Oxford English Dictionary*. The only way to critique this information, however, is to look for information I do know, for example, the words from a common text in Chaucer; but this proved more difficult than I imagined.[23]

Searching the EEBO database gives the citation and one-line context. Thus, if you search "retraction," you get "Caxton, *Canterbury Tales*"; if you click on that, you should get the one-line context, although you need to search a bit to find the word *retraction* itself. Since I know from this search that Caxton's version of Chaucer's Retraction is in the database, I conduct a new search for words I know are from Caxton's version. Inexplicably, for the first word I choose, "default," I do not get a reference to the Caxton edition. Instead, I get the 1542 and 1687 editions, although neither actually contains a version of the Retraction; the references are to a different text.

The only way to find a word that I know is in a text included in EEBO is to know how it is spelled in the text included in EEBO. I assumed I had a transcription of Caxton's *Canterbury Tales* ready to hand, but of course, I do not, so I had to go to the text in EEBO. Now I discover the source of my difficulty: the EEBO text is apparently taken from the image in EEBO (from the British Library copy). But this copy appears to have an ink blot (?) on the word for "default," leaving the nonsensical "defa . . . ."

Perhaps I should try *unconnynge,* although I do not know whether the Text Creation Partnership transcribers or transcription program interpret that final flourish as a terminal *-e* or simply ignore it. I can get around this problem by searching for *unconnyng**. I get 0 results. Instead, and somewhat desperately, I try the absurd *vnconnyng**. Finally, I find not only *vnconnyng* (transcribed with an initial *v-* and no terminal *-e*), but I also confirm my suspicions of *defaute,* which is transcribed without comment "defa," and now, I suppose, a canonized entry in the database.[24] I will try *herkene* (the spelling in the Caxton text).

I first try *harken:* I get nothing.
I next try *herken:* I do not get the Retraction citation.
I try *herken*:* the Caxton Retraction appears.

I tried a different term from the opening lines of the *Canterbury Tales:*

April*: no
Appril*: yes
Ap*ril*: no

As these examples show, I need to know both what is in this database (which I do not and cannot possibly divine) as well as what variant spellings are possible. To find these, I use the EEBO's word index. This will help, but I still must conduct all searches with a fairly clear idea of what the results will be.

Searching Eighteenth Century Collections Online (ECCO)

Searching in ECCO is slightly different. Here, searches can be performed using various levels of "fuzziness." But exactly how these levels work is not entirely clear, at least not to civilian users. I again use the text of the Retraction as printed in one of the books included in this database: figure 13.1 is the version from the 1721 edition of Chaucer by John Urry. This is on p. 214 or Image #361 of the edition in this database. Here, I am facing a major problem as I revise and proofread this section—a problem I make no effort to disguise below: each time I conduct the searches I describe here, I get different results. The following is what I wrote in late 2010; my corrections in 2011 are in brackets.

I chose several key words: *tretise, sounen, synne, defawte.* If I search for these words as they appear, I get nothing—no matches. That is, the database does not search character combinations; it searches what it calls "terms." I thus tried "treatise" limited to 1721, and the Urry edition again did not seem to come up until I searched "Chaucer" in the "Search within these Results" (I do not know where it was hidden, but I could not find it under C, U, or even W). [When I performed the same search later, the edition came up immediately, as it should have.] To find the actual citations, I then had to search the edition, since only one reference seems to come up otherwise (in EEBO's TCP, by contrast, all text references are listed with the item).

The database contains three levels of "fuzzy" searches: low, medium, and high. I believe that in the EEBO database this function is served by the word index. So I search, somewhat mischievously, for the words as spelled in Urry, along with their modern spellings (essentially a term search). I perform all these searches from within the entry for the Urry edition. My results are below; they refer not to whether the word appears in the edition, but whether the citations are to the text of the Retraction:[25]

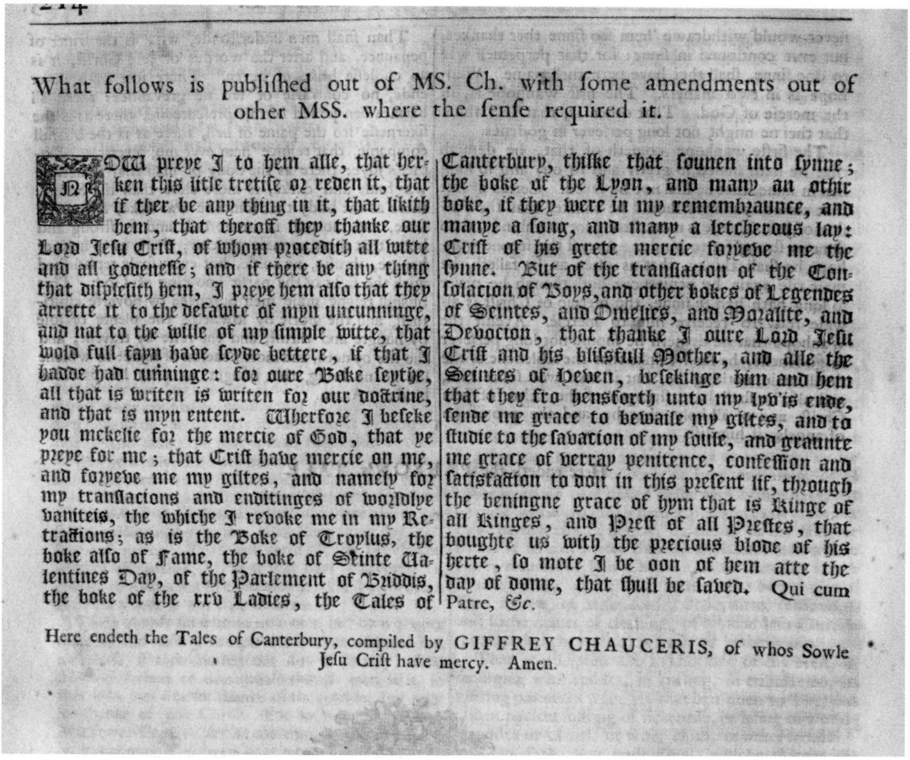

214

What follows is publiſhed out of MS. Ch. with ſome amendments out of other MSS. where the ſenſe required it.

NOW preye I to hem alle, that herken this litle tretiſe or reden it, that if ther be any thing in it, that likith hem, that theroff they thanke our Lord Jeſu Criſt, of whom procedith all witte and all godeneſſe; and if there be any thing that diſpleſith hem, I preye hem alſo that they arrette it to the defawte of myn uncunninge, and nat to the wille of my ſimple witte, that wold full fayn have ſeyde bettere, if that I hadde had cunninge: for oure Boke ſeythe, all that is writen is writen for our doctrine, and that is myn entent. Wherfore I beſeke you mekelie for the mercie of God, that ye preye for me; that Criſt have mercie on me, and foryeve me my giltes, and namely for my tranſlacions and enditinges of worldlye vaniteis, the whiche I revoke me in my Retractions; as is the Boke of Troylus, the boke alſo of Fame, the boke of Seinte Valentines Day, of the Parlement of Briddis, the boke of the xxv Ladies, the Tales of Canterbury, thilke that ſounen into ſynne; the boke of the Lyon, and many an othir boke, if they were in my remembraunce, and manye a ſong, and many a letcherous lay: Criſt of his grete mercie foryeve me the ſynne. But of the tranſlacion of the Conſolacion of Boys, and other bokes of Legendes of Seintes, and Omelies, and Moralite, and Devocion, that thanke I oure Lord Jeſu Criſt and his bliſsfull Mother, and alle the Seintes of Heven, beſekinge him and hem that they fro hensforth unto my lyv'is ende, ſende me grace to bewaile my giltes, and to ſtudie to the ſavacion of my ſoule, and graunte me grace of verray penitence, confeſſion and ſatisfaction to don in this preſent lif, through the beningne grace of hym that is Kinge of all Kinges, and Preſt of all Preſtes, that boughte us with the precious blode of his herte, ſo mote I be oon of hem atte the day of dome, that ſhull be ſaved. Qui cum Patre, &c.

Here endeth the Tales of Canterbury, compiled by GIFFREY CHAUCERIS, of whos Sowle Jeſu Criſt have mercy. Amen.

FIGURE 13.1. Geoffrey Chaucer, Retraction, from *Works,* ed. J. Urry (London, 1721).

treatise: no

fuzzy search: low-high: no

tretise (the spelling in Urry): no

fuzzy search low: no

medium: no

high: yes

[I am somewhat disturbed by these results, since when I did the same search in February 2011, my results were different: the word did not appear even with fuzzy search set at "high"]

default: no

fuzzy searches: no

defawte: no
> fuzzy search low: yes [in February 2011, no hits on any fuzzy search, although *defawt,* not the spelling in Urry, did show up; I am not sure whether this was there in 2010]

sounen: no
> low: no
>
> medium: no
>
> high: yes [in February 2011, the word did not appear, even with fuzzy search set at high]
>
> (I am not certain how this word would be normalized)

sjn: no
> fuzzy searches: no

synne: no
> low: yes [in February 2011, no "fuzzy search" found the term]

Among various keywords I tried as spelled in the Urry text, the only one that produced a match at all was *letcherous,* but the reference was to p. 26. This page is from the Urry preface, quoting the very text at issue, the Retraction. The text on p. 214 was not identified under any level of fuzzy search (*letcherous*), nor could I come up with that text by searching for the term *lecherous.*

The only explanation I can imagine for this result is that the black-letter text *letcherous* on p. 214 (the Retraction text) was omitted from the database altogether, even though other words like *preye, defawte, sounen, synne* were included in some form [at least, they were in 2010]. Is it really possible that whatever reader or optical reader transcribed this text simply copied, without comment, what it could read and omitted what it could not? And that no human editor checked the results? I have no other explanation for what I found.

I am not certain whether better results are generally achieved by beginning with the normalized(?) term and searching for specific text or by beginning with the original text spelling. Nor am I certain what "better" would even mean in this case.

Writing now in 2011, it is difficult for me to ignore the fact that I obtained different results a few months ago and, if my notes are accurate, different results when I tried these searches originally. And of course I cannot today verify my transcription of results I got in the past, whether two months or two years ago. I realize I often make mistakes in transcribing things of this nature. Many good scholars do. But if I can't make sense of the results I get, and I am unable to get consistent results, then just who can? I have revised this section now three times, and I am not going to do it again.

The searches I performed in EEBO and in ECCO produce the kind of information once available in concordances. But concordances too can only answer a limited range of questions: for example, does the word X appear in the corpus of material Y with the meaning Z? And these questions can only lead to a significant answer if the answer is yes. A negative answer is difficult to evaluate and must be considered in terms of the corpus of information ("Shakespeare does not use the word X in these texts of these particular plays"). Negative results are meaningful only when the corpus of evidence is clearly and coherently defined. In ECCO, it is difficult to evaluate the quality or even the nature of the information one finds.

Conclusion: Implications for Rare Book Use

The increased access to rare materials through digital catalogues and digitized versions of rare books, along with increased pressure on academics to produce printed scholarship has changed the culture of rare book rooms. The objects housed in those collections are no longer things owned and controlled by small groups of librarians, collectors, scholars, and dealers. Scenes of exclusion such as described by Virginia Woolf in *A Room of One's Own* are rare. The creation of online cataloguing has led paradoxically to increased pressure on some rare book collections—more visits and more use; at others, use of the library is up, but the use of rare books is down.[26] No one misses the old days, which were bad for scholars, young scholars in particular, and bad for scholarship as well. Rare books are no longer accessible only to a small club of scholars. "Heaps of evidence" are available in databases like EEBO, at least, for those scholars with access to a major university library, and ESTC references now abound in the footnotes of mainstream literary journals. Opportunities to challenge old ideologies and canons seem never to have been greater: the texts of Jasper Heywood are as accessible as those of Shakespeare. Yet does this readily accessible evidence in EEBO or increased access to early printed books in any way lead to a change in basic attitudes, opinions, or theories?

That demonstration seems to me an important one. It is not enough to note in an analysis of Hamlet's "To be or not to be" that Q1 has a different version of this soliloquy. Nor enough to note that the watermark on sheet C of a particular book-copy may well be contemporary with the date in the colophon. Material books and expensive databases are a waste of library resources and limited public resources if the only purpose they serve is decorative ("as the layout of the material book reminds us . . . ," "Whitchurch, it should be noted, also published . . ."). Material books must reveal to us more than things we already know or only what we want to know; they should be able to reveal to us things we do not know, or even more significantly, things we do not want to know. If those heaps of books provide nothing more than supporting evidence for familiar arguments, whether bibliographical, historical, or literary, they may as well be returned to the hands of the preservationists.

Conclusion

I am sitting in a small rare book library. I could say that I have selected a book at random, but that is not the case. The book before me has a history. The difference between this book and most others is that I know part of its history in advance. I would like to know more.

The book is the 1594 edition of Camden's *Britannia.* And as I write up some of its features, I realize that later I will doubtless refer to EEBO to complete the details that I neglect to note now—publication data, details from a different copy. Although I try to maintain as strictly as I can the difference between books and book-copies, I know that the two will be blurred when I sort this information out. This copy of *Britannia* is the fourth edition (STC 4506, "nunc quarto recognita"; the first edition is dated 1586, STC 4503). Like all book-copies, this one combines many histories; unlike most book-copies, some of these histories intersect with my own.

I was never a serious scholar of early modern English literature and history; I did not know until recently the importance of this book or why anyone would want to own a copy. The binding is undistinguished, perhaps contemporary. I reflect not on the history of bindings but rather on the history of my own awareness of them. I owe that to a rare book librarian, who once walked me through the library shelves discoursing on varieties of bindings and the innumerable mistakes I have made on the subject. This willingness to correct is a kindness many bibliographers and librarians have shown me. I am surprised that I feel the gratitude I do.

The previous ownership of the book is well noted: "Pescall Forster" (seventeenth century?); "Hen. Mellor"; a longer inscription "E Libris Rob[erti] Hutchinson Dunelm[ensis]" (a Durham cleric?); a "Smith"

(J H?) of 1809, from a town I cannot identify; "P. Studer 1910" (fig. C.1). There is a book plate (eighteenth-century?) with the common motto "Dum Spiro Spero." Perhaps it belongs to one of these owners. I believe there are a few notes by this Hutchinson in the early portions of the book.

These names might be traceable. But I have not found reference to any of them in the more obvious indexes of provenance. Even the extensive list in Hazlitt's *Roll of Honour* provides no names that match, and I am frankly not certain I would be any the wiser if it did (see chapter 9 above). There is no pattern I can find here, no obvious reason this book-copy should have passed through the hands of these unknown owners rather than other owners, through these locations rather than other ones. Its history appears to be a series of accidents; but all the word *accidents* means is that the historical events that have occurred cannot be described in any of the essentialist language I have at my disposal. Since these early owners were obscure (at least to me), this book provides a nexus not of known histories but of unknown ones. I can trace the book and its text; the owner, the ink, the structure. But there will be no coherence to this history, because the histories recorded in the sourcebooks I have available and which I am competent to use do not include any of these histories.

This book has several corresponding call slips; these were produced under old cataloguing conventions, when each book-copy in a rare book library was matched to one or more such cards. Some of these cards are arranged in the same order as the books on the shelf and such cards constitute a shelf list, something rarely seen by ordinary users of libraries. Others are alphabetized in some way to form the public catalogue, and others are arranged by date. All that is on the public catalogue slip (or was on it when I first saw this book) is "Camden. Britannia. 1594." There is more information than this on the corresponding card in the shelf list. The information on these various cards is rarely conventional enough to guarantee to a user that any of it is reliable. There is no electronic record of this book, even in the present library. The copy here is not yet registered in ESTC, although some books in this particular library are.

I remember having seen the detailed shelf-list card earlier, and that is why I am looking for this book in the public card file. A librarian passing through that library had directed me to the shelf list. And it is through her that I have even as much of the story as I do.

My father taught in the institution that owns this library; when we moved during a period in my life when I did not much care about familial house moving, this book and dozens of others slipped out of his possession into the institution. After forty years, some remain uncatalogued, essentially lost and quite lost to me, since this library has no provenance index. What would be the point of such a thing? Provenance lists, with their records of donations and losses, can be embarrassing for small college libraries to maintain if early donors decide to find out what has happened to their gifts. The books that were once nearly mine are not especially valuable; there are far more valuable ones on adjacent shelves of this library. Eventually, through a combination of grants, librarian interest, and chance, the books my father donated will be officially found, either to be catalogued or perhaps to be sold on the open market.

I think of these books being sold. Libraries are discreet, and if these books are converted to cash, I will never know when this happens. Yet I realize too that my uneasiness is ridiculous. The books of Robert Hoe, one of the greatest American collectors, are scattered now over the world. Hoe wanted his books to go to those who would love them; and the best place to find such people was on the open market. I try to remember that whenever I hold one of his books in the Huntington.

I return to the name "Hen. Mellor." A year after handing back to the librarian that Camden (so nearly *my* Camden), I will encounter that name again. I happen to own a 1602 Chaucer, bought ten years ago in Los Angeles. As rare books go, it's not much. I use it in classes, and I have used it for several illustrations here. And there, on the title page: "Michael Hall, 1755," and an earlier name "Henry Mellor" (fig. C.2). And once again, histories have bizarrely crossed—Henry Mellor, a *Britannia* purchased by my father somewhere on the East Coast, my own Chaucer, somehow finding its way fifty years later to Los Angeles.

And I think back to that Camden *Britannia,* thinking now about what I do not know: all that early modern history; all those deaths catalogued here (why do I know only one of them?); the binding; the print. And I look for a characteristic "N. Dane" that should be inked in the upper right corner of the first flyleaf. I have seen that many times in the books now on my shelves—books of so little value that even when offered to the institutional library they were refused. But this one has no such marking; rather, an institutional "Gift of . . ." slip with his name typed in. Not a valuable gift. Doubtless my father purchased this book, among many others, for almost nothing. I wonder why; what possible interest did such things have for a classicist with a specialty in Aeschylus? And I wonder too why when I became obsessed with books myself, why he never apologized for the egregious mistake of so charitably donating so many of his own books to that library. Why the librarian who accepted these donations never mentioned this to me in all my many dealings with him later. Was it some peculiar discretion of librarians? Had he himself forgotten? How convenient it would have been to start my own collection with these books. Did my father think that this obsession of mine would pass before I had the chance to discover what he had done? Did he think that my mother would make no casual reference to "oh, you know, those little Latin books with the white covers," referring, I think, to early Aldine editions? those books, I am told, that filled the bookshelves of an early childhood home?

It is something else I will never know, and as I hold this book, I am reminded of the most important bibliographical principle of them all: that for the most important things, no amount of methodological study will finally do any good.

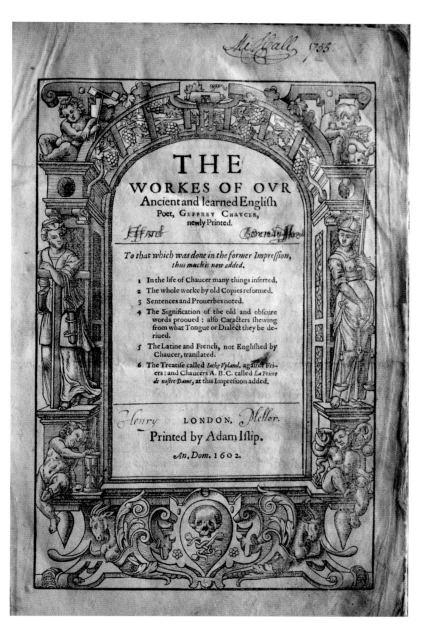

FIGURE C.2. Geoffrey Chaucer, *Works* (London, 1602), title page.

N O T E S

· · ·

Introduction

1. The seminal essays are in Gary Taylor and Michael Warren, eds., *The Division of the Kingdoms: Shakespeare's Two Versions of King Lear* (Oxford: Clarendon Press, 1986).

2. The Huntington Library copy is available from Early English Books Online (EEBO), eebo.chadwyck.com, STC 22292. The Norton facsimile is Charlton Hinman, *The First Folio of Shakespeare: The Norton Facsimile* (New York: W. W. Norton, 1968). The nature and reliability of these sources is discussed in chapters 11–12 below.

3. Among the more useful introductory works, each defining the field in a different way, are the following: Ronald B. McKerrow, *An Introduction to Bibliography for Literary Students* (Oxford: Clarendon Press, 1927) (focus is on seventeenth-century English books); Philip Gaskell, *A New Introduction to Bibliography* (New York: Oxford University Press, 1972) (emphasis on eighteenth-century books); Mark Bland, *A Guide to Early Printed Books and Manuscripts* (Chichester: Blackwell, 2010); and William Proctor Williams and Craig S. Abbot, *Introduction to Bibliographical and Textual Studies,* 4th rev. ed. (New York: Modern Language Association, 2009). Those that define the same field as roughly the history of printing itself include S. H. Steinberg, *Five Hundred Years of Printing,* new ed., ed. John Trevitt (New Castle, DE: Oak Knoll, 1996; orig. pub. 1955); and Lucien Febvre and Henri-Jean Martin, *The Coming of the Book: The Impact of Printing 1460–1800,* trans. David Gerard (London: Verso, 1976; orig. pub. 1958 as *L'apparition du livre*). One of the most useful visual introductions is Michael Olmert, *The Smithsonian Book of Books* (Washington, DC: Smithsonian Books, 2003). With the exception of the last work here, it can be very difficult to use these books as introductions—that is, as basic guides to material more complex than what they themselves are.

4. Quoted as "vigorously" by Bradshaw's biographer G. W. Prothero, *A Memoir of Henry Bradshaw* (London: Kegan, Paul, 1888), 349, and produc-

tively misread as such by later scholars; see Paul Needham, *The Bradshaw Method: Henry Bradshaw's Contribution to Bibliography* (Chapel Hill, NC: Hanes Foundation, 1998).

5. See my critique in *The Myth of Print Culture: Essays on Evidence, Textuality, and Bibliographical Method* (Toronto: University of Toronto Press, 2003), 21–31.

6. Basic though the notion of a print-run or edition may be, like a number of other basic notions (moral ones, for example) it is not always easy to define. I do not know how to avoid the invocation of "printer's intentions" in the definition, although I do not think the intentions of any human being, even one's own, can ever be known.

7. Frank Isaac, *English and Scottish Printing Types, 1501–58, 1508–58*, 2 vols. (Oxford: Bibliographical Society, 1930–1932), vol. 1, fig. 63.

8. Unfortunately for this appealing cliché, the mechanics of the fifteenth-century press are much less well known than those of the sixteenth century, and it would perhaps be better to teleport our fantastic eighteenth-century printer to the printing house of Wynkyn de Worde. See my *Out of Sorts: On Typography and Print Culture* (Philadelphia: University of Pennsylvania Press, 2010), chap. 1.

9. The most convenient single source for this period is Richard-Gabriel Rummonds, *Nineteenth-Century Printing Practices and the Iron Handpress*, 2 vols. (New Castle, DE: Oak Knoll, 2004).

Chapter One   Terminology

1. The most useful of many guides to bibliographical terminology is any of the many editions of John Carter's *ABC for Book Collectors*, 8th ed., ed. Nicolas Barker (Newcastle, DE: Oak Knoll, 2004; orig. pub. 1951).

2. Dane, *Out of Sorts*, 105–17; William Sherman, *Used Books: Marking Readers in Renaissance England* (Philadelphia: University of Pennsylvania Press, 2008), 25–52.

3. A somewhat more circuitous definition by G. Thomas Tanselle is, "the number of page-units that the printer decided upon to fill each side of an unfolded sheet." *Bibliographical Analysis: A Historical Introduction* (Cambridge: Cambridge University Press, 2009), 38.

4. See chapter 2. These foldings were of course second nature to printers but often less obvious to researchers, who can use the tables in Gaskell, *New Introduction to Bibliography*, or in any of the printing manuals listed in chapter 3, n. 10.

5. The only way this language can be unambiguous is if the terms *folio, quarto, octavo,* etc., refer to the size of the leaf in relation to a full sheet, but this is often counter-intuitive. If one allows the description "folio in half sheets"

(which is perfectly intelligible), the phrase "quarto in half sheets" is necessarily ambiguous. Seventeenth-century books correctly described as 16° are very often books made from half sheets folded into quires of eight leaves.

6. Discussion can be found in any of the introductory manuals listed above in the introduction, n. 5. The most detailed discussion of such formulae remains Fredson Bowers, *Principles of Bibliographical Description* (Princeton: Princeton University Press, 1949).

7. Many early books begin their text portions with signature B, saving A and its variants for preliminaries. Books whose text does not begin with signature A or B are often reprints, set up from a printed copytext.

Chapter Two   The Matter of Size

1. Febvre and Martin, *Coming of the Book,* 109–15, state that paper equals all other costs of printing, and their conclusions are often cited. So James Raven, "The Economic Context," in *The Cambridge History of the Book in Britain,* vol. 4, *1558–1695,* ed. John Barnard and D. F. McKenzie (Cambridge: Cambridge University Press, 2002), 587. Binding costs were additional; early records of booksellers who sold books both bound and unbound show binding costs could add another 50 percent. Ferdinand Geldner, "Das Rechnungsbuch des Speyrer Druckherrn, Verlegers und Grossbuchhandlers Peter Drach," *Archiv für Geschichte des Buchwesens* 5 (1962): 1–196.

2. Giovanni Andrea Bussi, *Prefazioni alle Edizioni dei Sweynheym e Pannartz, Prototipografi Romani,* ed. Massimo Miglio (Milan: Polifilo, 1978), 5.

3. E. P. Goldschmidt, *Gothic and Renaissance Bookbindings,* 2 vols. (London: Benn, 1928), 1:36–37.

4. On basic units of distribution, see Paul Needham, "The Customs Rolls as Documents for the Printed-book Trade in England," in *Cambridge History of the Book,* vol. 3, *1400–1557,* ed. Lotte Hellinga and J. B. Trapp (Cambridge: Cambridge University Press, 1999), 148–73.

5. The best introduction to liturgical books is Christopher de Hamel, *A History of Illuminated Manuscripts,* 2nd ed. (London: Phaidon, 1994).

6. James McLaverty, *Pope, Print, and Meaning* (Oxford: Oxford University Press, 2001), 46–48.

7. See Joseph A. Dane, *Who Is Buried in Chaucer's Tomb: Studies in the Reception of Chaucer's Book* (East Lansing: Michigan State University Press, 1998).

8. See Robert Steele, "What Fifteenth-Century Books Are About, IV," *The Library,* ser. 2, 8 (1907): 125–38.

9. Bettina Wagner, "The Bodleian Incunables from Bavarian Monasteries," *Bodleian Library Record* 15 (1995): 90–107.

10. For details, see Joseph A. Dane and Alexandra Gillespie, "The Myth of the Cheap Quarto," in *Tudor Books and Readers,* ed. John King (Cambridge: Cambridge University Press, 2009), 25–45.

Chapter Three   Materials

1. Joseph Moxon, *Mechanick Exercises on the Whole Art of Printing (1683–4)*, ed. Herbert Davis and Harry Carter, 2nd ed. (New York: Oxford University Press, 1962), 82. In 1841, William Savage claims he himself is "the only person who has written a practical work on the subject." *A Dictionary of the Art of Printing* (1841; repr., London: Longman, 1941), 417, s.v. "ink."

2. A well-known case involves disputes on the dating of the Vinland Map, where scientific studies of the ink produced quite different results in the twentieth century; see among many histories, the review by Paul Saenger, "Vinland Re-read," *Imago Mundi* 50 (1998): 199–202. For general discussion, see Joe Nickell, *Pen, Ink, and Evidence: A Study of Writing and Writing Materials for the Penman, Collector, and Document Detective* (1990; repr., New Castle, DE: Oak Knoll, 2000), 33ff. For the Gutenberg Bible, studies on ink tend to confirm rather than challenge theories from other fields of analytical bibliography; Paul Needham, "Division of Copy in the Gutenberg Bible: Three Glosses on the Ink Evidence," *PBSA* 79 (1985): 411–26.

3. The process of ink manufacture is described in detail in the twelfth-century manual by Theophilus, *On Divers Arts*, trans. J. G. Hawthorne and C. S. Smith (Chicago: University of Chicago Press, 1963), chap. 38.

4. See further chapter 7, section III; and discussion in Richard S. Field, "The Early Woodcut: The Known and the Unknown," in *Origins of European Printmaking*, ed. Peter W. Parshall, Rainer Schoch et al. (New Haven: Yale University Press, 2005), esp. 25–26.

5. N. F. Blake, "Manuscript to Print: Caxton Prints for Which a Copytext Survives or Which Were Used as a Copytext," in *Book Production and Publishing in Britain, 1375–1475*, ed. Jeremy Griffiths and Derek Pearsall (Cambridge: Cambridge University Press, 1989), 403–8.

6. The printer generally given credit for this is John Baskerville, using paper manufactured by James Whatman; see J. N. Balston, *The Elder James Whatman: England's Greatest Paper Maker (1702–1759)*, 3 vols. (West Farleigh, Kent: J. Balston, 1992). The first book printed by Baskerville to use wove paper is the 1757 edition of Virgil; the 1759 edition of Milton's *Paradise Regained* is entirely in wove paper. Baskerville is an important and eccentric figure in English printing history and often credited with a number of other developments in typography, page layout, and the technology of paper. For Baskerville's place in typographical history, see Daniel Berkeley Updike, *Printing Types: Their History, Forms, and Use: A Study in Survivals*, 2nd ed., 2 vols. (Cambridge: Harvard University Press, 1937); and chapter 6 below.

7. The most basic and readable history remains Dard Hunter, *Papermaking: The History and Technique of an Ancient Craft*, 2nd ed. (New York: Dover, 1978; orig. pub. 1947); for documents, see Joel Munsell, *Chronology of the Origin and Progress of Paper and Paper-Making* (Albany: J. Munsell, 1876). See also

John Bidwell, "The Study of Paper as Evidence, Artefact, and Commodity," in *The Book Encompassed: Studies in Twentieth-Century Bibliography*, ed. Peter Davison (Cambridge: Cambridge University Press, 1992), 69–82; and the section on paper in Gaskell, *New Introduction to Bibliography*, 57–108.

8. My view is that this is urban mythology; Dane, *Myth of Print Culture*, chap. 7.1, "The Curse of the Mummy Paper," 170–85; others, unaccountably, disagree: Nicolson Baker, *Double Fold: Libraries and the Assault on Paper* (New York: Random House, 2001), 58–64.

9. Febvre and Martin, *Coming of the Book*, chap. 1, "The Introduction of Paper into Europe," 29–44.

10. See chapter 2; and the tables of imposition in Gaskell, *New Introduction to Bibliography*, 88–105, condensing the more complete tables in such publications as C. Stower, *The Printers' Grammar: or Introduction to the Art of Printing* (1808; repr., London: Gregg Press, 1965), chap. 7, "Of Imposing," 170–98; and Savage, *Dictionary of the Art of Printing* (1841), "Tables of Imposition," 335–410.

11. Hunter, *Papermaking*, 103.

12. These sizes are described variously: Haebler defines *forma regalis* as 70 × 50 cm (I believe this is imperial!); *forma mediana* as 50 × 30 cm (or 35); Briquet defines *realle* as 60 × 41.5 cm; chancery as 43 × 30.5 cm; see Parshall, Schoch et al., *Origins of European Printing*, 124n.4. Paul Needham expands these sizes into what he calls a *Scala sapientiae;* his figures below are for the trimmed page, which is the unit one would actually measure:

1. mezzo-median 25 × 18 cm
2. CHANCERY—reçute 29/30 × 21 cm (commonest; all of Caxton)
3. super-Chancery 32 × 21 cm (Aldine Greek folios; Augsburg folios)
4. MEDIAN—mezzana 34 × 24 cm
5. super-median 36 × 24 cm
6. ROYAL—reale 40/41 × 28/29 cm (Gutenberg Bible; Schoeffer Aquinas)
7. super-royal 43/44 × 28/29 cm
8. IMPERIAL 47/48 × 33 cm (Nuremberg Chronicle)
9. papal 55 × 40 cm

(from Paul Needham, Seminar notes, Rare Book School, University of Virginia, 1996)

See further Paul Needham, *Incunabula from the Court Library of Donaueschingen, Sale LN4389* (London: Sotheby's, 1994).

13. Gaskell, *New Introduction to Bibliography*, 72–75.

14. An example is Curt Bühler, "Watermarks and the Dates of Fifteenth-century Books," *Studies in Bibliography* 9 (1957): 217–24.

15. Joseph Ames, *Typographical Antiquities, being an Historical Account of Printing in England* (London, 1749), 73. New plates of these watermarks are made for the revision of Ames's book by Thomas Frognall Dibdin, *Typo-*

graphical Antiquities: or The History of Printing in England, Scotland, and Ireland, 4 vols. (London, 1810–19), 1:cxxv–vi, but Dibdin includes only scattered remarks on paper, 1:cxxv–vi.

16. C. M. Briquet, *Les Filigranes,* ed. Allan Stevenson, 4 vols. (Amsterdam: Paper Publications Society, 1968; orig. pub. 1907).

17. Gerhard Piccard, *Wasserzeichen: Findbücher,* 17 vols. (Stuttgart: Kohlhammer, 1961–96), http://www.piccard-online.de/.

18. On ongoing or in-progress databases, see chapter 13. An example of a limited corpus database is the collection of watermarks in Ben Jonson folios by David Gants, *A Digital Catalogue of Watermarks and Type Ornaments Used by William Stansby in the Printing of* The Workes of Beniamin Jonson *(London, 1616),* Institute for Advanced Study in the Humanities, http://www2.iath .virginia.edu/gants/; or Daniel W. Mosser and Ernest W. Sullivan, II, comp., *The Thomas L. Gravell Watermark Archive,* http://www.gravell.org/. See further "Survey of Known Databases of Paper Structure Reproductions," Bernstein— The Memory of Paper, http://www.bernstein.oeaw.ac.at/twiki/bin/view/Main/ PaperDatabases.

19. Bibliothèque Nationale, *Catalogue des Incunables* (Paris: Bibliothèque Nationale, 1981), vol. 1 (= CIBN). See the detailed descriptions of blockbooks by Nigel F. Palmer, "Blockbooks, Woodcut and Metalcut Single Sheets," in *A Catalogue of Books Printed in the Fifteenth Century Now in the Bodleian Library,* ed. Alan Coates et al. (Oxford: Oxford University Press, 2005), 1–50 (esp. description of *Apocalypse,* BB-1).

20. Allan Stevenson, "Watermarks Are Twins," *Studies in Bibliography* 4 (1951): 57–91.

21. See Paul Needham, review of *On-line Illustrated Database of Watermarks Printed in the Low Countries,* by Gerard van Thienen, *Quaerendo* 36 (2006): 3–24.

22. Allan Stevenson, *The Problem of the Missale Speciale* (London: Bibliographical Society, 1967); see also Stevenson, "Paper as Bibliographical Evidence," *The Library,* ser. 5, 17 (1962): 197–202; and Stevenson, "Watermarks Are Twins." An example of the growing interest in paper among descriptive bibliographers is the most recent volume of BMC: for the first time in this project since its first volume of 1908, paper evidence is included in the description of editions. See BMC XI: *England* (The Netherlands: Hes & de Graaf, 2007).

23. Nancy Ash, "Recording Watermarks by Beta-Radiography and Other Means," *The Book and Paper Group Annual,* vol. 1 (Washington, DC: American Institute for Conservation, 1982), http://aic.stanford.edu/sg/bpg/annual/v01/. Back-lighting paper can be done with any light; the best, although not cheapest way is with a Nouvir Illuminator—a fiber optic light with a flat light panel that can be placed between the leaves of a book.

24. David Vander Meulen, "The Identification of Paper without Watermarks: The Example of Pope's *Dunciad,*" *Studies in Bibliography* 37 (1984): 58–81, formula above modified from p. 64.

25. For details, see my "'Wanting the First Blank': The Frontispiece to the Huntington Library Copy of Caxton's *Recuyell of the Historyes of Troye*," in *Manuscript, Print, and Early Tudor Literature,* ed. Alexandria Gillespie, special issue, *Huntington Library Quarterly* 67 (2004): 315–25.

26. For engravings and title pages, which are often missing in early book-copies, the problem is complicated by the fact that engravings are generally printed separately from the book itself, and even authentic title pages are often printed on paper distinct from that used in the text. See chapter 4.

Chapter Four   Mechanics of the Press

1. Joseph Moxon, *Mechanick Exercises on the Whole Art of Printing (1683–4),* ed. Herbert Davis and Harry Carter, 2nd ed. (London: Oxford University Press, 1962); see Savage, *Dictionary of the Art of Printing,* 417.

2. The term *copytext* has technical meanings in editing history; in the context of printing history, the term has the simpler, more obvious meaning above.

3. It is likely that the composing stick is a late development (sixteenth or seventeenth century?), although it is rarely described that way, and that the earliest printers set type directly. See Benjamin Franklin's description of Keimer's printing house in *Autobiography:* "Keimer made Verses, too, ... He could not be said to write them, for his Manner was to compose them in the Types directly out of his Head; so there being no Copy, but one Pair of Cases, and the Elegy likely to require all the Letter." Franklin, *Autobiography, Poor Richard, and Later Writings,* ed. J. A. Leo Lemay (New York: Library of America, 1987), 1331.

4. See Moxon, *Mechanick Exercises,* 28n., 249. The first reference to a galley proof is in Savage, *Dictionary of the Art of Printing* (1841).

5. For patterns of imposition, see Moxon, *Mechanick Exercises,* sec. 7, pp. 223–33; and imposition tables in Gaskell, *New Introduction to Bibliography,* 88–105.

6. If the leaves of a book have not been trimmed, these points should be visible. It is also possible to position pins initially so that they do not have to be moved prior to perfection, but this is not absolutely necessary.

7. The term *blind impression* is generally attributed to Roger E. Stoddard, *Marks in Books* (Cambridge: Harvard University Press, 1985), where numerous examples can be found.

8. Among the editorial implications for early printing is that any authorial corrections to be made once the printing process begins must be made during the printing process. An author/editor (for example, Erasmus working for Aldus Manutius) must be in the immediate vicinity of the shop.

9. On stereotyping, see Rummonds, *Nineteenth-Century Printing Practices,* chap. 25, "Stereotype and Electrotype Printing," 2:715–59.

10. Seriatim printing was used by Ulrich Zell, an early and prolific printer from Cologne. Zell printed from half sheets, rather than full sheets, and page by page. In addition, many pages and sections seem to have been set up and printed twice, sometimes from different presses, and individual copies mix these settings indifferently. See Francis Jenkinson, "Ulrich Zell's Early Quartos," *The Library,* ser. 4, 7 (1926): 46–66; and Severin Corsten, "Ulrich Zells früheste Produktion," *Gutenberg Jahrbuch* (2007): 68–76.

11. The term *two-pull printing* can refer also to a different process in two-color printing, whereby the two colors are printed in two separate "pulls"—one to print red, the other to print black. See chapter 7.

12. Fifteenth-century classical editions from Italy provide many examples of page-for-page, line-for-line reprinting of earlier editions. These can be easily found by looking at collation formulae in catalogues of fifteenth-century books.

13. For the two methods of setting, see Peter W. M. Blayney, *The Texts of King Lear and Their Origins,* vol. 1, *Nicholas Okes and the First Quarto* (Cambridge: Cambridge University Press, 1982), 90–91.

14. Adrian Weiss, "Font Analysis as a Bibliographical Method: The Elizabethan Play-Quarto Printers and Compositors," *Studies in Bibliography* 43 (1989): 95–164.

15. Fredson Bowers, "Note on Running-Titles as Bibliographical Evidence," *The Library,* ser. 4, 19 (1938): 315–38.

16. On the meaning of the word *state* in descriptive bibliography and in the definition of editions, see chapter 11.

17. Randall McLeod, "McLeod Portable Collator," *Newsletter,* Humanities Association of Canada (1988).

18. See my discussion in *Myth of Print Culture,* chap. 4, "The Notion of Variant and the Zen of Collation," 88–113.

19. Gaskell, *New Introduction to Bibliography,* 131; McKerrow, *Introduction to Bibliography,* 210–11; Bowers, *Principles of Bibliographical Description,* 46.

20. On these issues, see further my "Perfect Order and Perfected Order: The Evidence from Press Variants of Early Seventeenth-Century Quartos," *PBSA* 90 (1996): 272–320, and, on the difficulty of finding unmediated evidence, *Myth of Print Culture,* chap. 4, "The Notion of Variant and the Zen of Collation," 88–113.

21. McKerrow, *Introduction to Bibliography,* 1; for changing relation of textual criticism to bibliography, see Peter W. M. Blayney, *The Texts of King Lear and Their Origins,* vol. 1, introd.

22. See the more expansive definition of Tanselle, *Bibliographical Analysis:* "[analytical bibliography] concentrates on using physical details to learn something about the manufacturing processes that produced a given book and its

text, the historical influences underlying its physical appearance, and the responses that its design engendered" (3).

23. Jerome J. McGann, *A Critique of Modern Textual Criticism* (Chicago: University of Chicago Press, 1983).

24. See, for example, Randall McLeod, "Un-Editing Shakespeare," *Substance* 33 (1982): 26–55.

25. Analytical bibliography assumes necessarily a logical relation between extant evidence (material books) and the historical processes that produced them. A now classic essay by D. F. McKenzie shows the pitfalls of such an apparently innocent assumption: D. F. McKenzie, "Printers of the Mind: Some Notes on Bibliographical Theories and Printing-House Practices," *Studies in Bibliography* 22 (1969): 1–75; repr., *Making Meaning: Printers of the Mind and Other Essays,* ed. Peter D. McDonald and Michael F. Suarez (Amherst: University of Massachusetts Press, 2002), 13–85.

26. Compare the discussion of error-types, based on types of scribal errors, in Bland, *Guide to Early Printed Books and Manuscripts,* 159–77.

27. Brian Vickers, "Hamlet by Dogberry," review of *Shakespearean Originals: First Editions: The Tragicall Historie of Hamlet, Prince of Denmarke (1603),* by Graham Holderness and Bryan Loughrey, eds., *Times Literary Supplement,* December 24, 1993, 5–6.

28. Conventional type, and some of the earliest type, contained a "nick" of some sort on one side that prevented the compositor from incorrectly orienting a typesort on a composing stick or tray. This, however, would not prevent a typesort from being misfiled in the distribution process (named by McKerrow, *Introduction to Bibliography,* 255, as "foul case"). A compositor would know by means of the nick whether a particular letter was properly set but would not know in the case of *w* and *m* whether the *correct* letter was properly set.

29. Ibid., 255–56. For the examples below, William Blades, *Shakspere and Typography: Being an attempt to show Shakspere's personal connection with, and technical knowledge of, The Art of Printing. Also, remarks upon some common typographical errors, with especial reference to the text of Shakspere* (1872; repr., New York: Burt Franklin, 1969), 73–78.

30. Randall McLeod, "Unemending Shakespeare's Sonnet 111," *Studies in English Literature, 1500–1900* 21 (1981): 75–96.

31. Percy Simpson, *Proof-Reading in the Sixteenth, Seventeenth, and Eighteenth Centuries* (London: Oxford University Press, 1935).

32. All quarto editions (1622, 1630, 1655, and 1695) read "Like the base *Indian.*" The later folios, all copied from earlier folios, here revert to the quarto reading.

33. Richard S. Veit, "Like the Base Judean": A Defense of an Oft-rejected Reading in Othello," *Shakespeare Quarterly* 26 (1975): 466–69; Julia Reinhard Lupton, *Citizen Saints: Shakespeare and Political Theology* (Chicago: University of Chicago Press, 2005), 235n.27. Only some seventeenth-century typefonts

contain a *j*. What modern typesetters set as *J* is represented as *I* (or in italics as the swash *J* seen in the Second Folio).

34. Collations of various copies show that those containing the reading "mocking" tend in other quires to contain "uncorrected" readings. The likelihood, thus, is that this was a reading "corrected" at press, which may have required the competence in Middle English possessed only by the editor John Stow himself; Joseph A. Dane and Seth Lerer, "Press-Variants in John Stow's Chaucer (1561) and the Text of *Adam Scriveyn*," *Transactions of the Cambridge Bibliographical Society* 11 (1999): 468–79.

35. See further my "'Which is the Iustice, which is the theef': Variants of Transposition in the Text(s) of *King Lear*," *Notes and Queries* 42 (1995): 322–27.

Chapter Five   Page Format and Layout

1. Lotte Hellinga, in BMC XI, 24, sees this process of right justification as a "matter of skill, not of style" distinguishing two compositors, although the evidence for this involves not Caxton books but contemporary books printed at Oxford.

2. For some of the conventions of handling run-on lines in early printing, see Margaret M. Smith, "Space-Saving Practices in Early Printed Books," *Journal of the Printing Historical Society* 6 (2003): 19–39.

3. Because manuscripts are ruled separately from writing, some attempts to quantify page formats have been made in manuscript studies, for example, Albert Derolez, *Codicologie des manuscrits en écriture humanistique sur parchemin,* 2 vols. (Turnhout: Brepols, 1984). Nothing similar has been attempted for printed books.

4. Harry Carter and Christopher Ricks, eds., introduction to *A Dissertation upon English Typographical Founders and Founderies (1778),* by Edward Rowe Mores (Oxford: Bibliographical Society, 1961), call English typography before Caslon "a weak and fitful accompaniment to the continental" (lxvi; see also p. lxvii).

5. See John M. Kemble, *The Anglo-Saxon Poems of Beowulf, the Traveler's Song, and the Battle of Finnesburh,* 2nd ed. (London: Pickering, 1835).

6. *The Owl and the Nightingale Reproduced in Facsimile from the Surviving Manuscripts Jesus College, Oxford 29 and British Museum Cotton Caligula A.IX,* ed. N. R. Ker, EETS OS 251 (London: Oxford University Press, 1963).

7. Nicolas Udall, *Floures for Latin speking selected and gathered out of Terence* (1538), STC 23900, is one of many examples; the Latin as transcribed and presumably committed to memory will not scan metrically.

8. Goff T64; the ISTC dates as "not after 1470."

9. For examples, see my "On Metrical Confusion and Consensus in Early Editions of Terence," *Humanistica Lovaniensia* 48 (1999): 103–31.

10. See the essays in Taylor and Warren, *Division of the Kingdoms.*

11. Stanley W. Wells and Gary Taylor, eds., *William Shakespeare: The Complete Works* (Oxford: Clarendon Press, 1986).

12. W. W. Greg, "The Rationale of Copy-Text," *Studies in Bibliography* 3 (1950–51): 19–36; repr., *Collected Papers,* ed. J. C. Maxwell (Oxford: Clarendon Press, 1966), 374–91.

Chapter Six   *Typography*

1. Febvre and Martin, *Coming of the Book,* 30.

2. Hans Peter Willberg, "Fraktur and Nationalism," in *Blackletter: Type and National Identity,* ed. Peter Bain and Paul Shaw (New York: Cooper Union, 1998), 40–49; Bormann's typescript edict reproduced on p. 48.

3. An extremely useful source for the history of type is James Mosley, *Typefoundry: Documents for the History of Type and Letterforms* (blog), http://typefoundry.blogspot.com/.

4. The language used to describe type is often ambiguous and one will find words such as *typeface, typefont,* and *type* used to refer to the same thing. Hendrik D. L. Vervliet, "Robert Estienne's Printing Types," *The Library,* ser. 5, 2 (2004): 107–79, n. 4, regards these terms as typographical synonyms. Vervliet's articles on this subject are usefully collected in *The Palaeo-typography of the French Renaissance: Selected Papers on Sixteenth-Century Typefaces* (Leiden: Brill, 2008).

5. A typeface is then roughly equivalent to a computer font, which can be created or reproduced in any size. A typographer or bibliographer, however, uses font and typefont as synonyms, since these would be the sorts cast by particular physical matrices.

6. Albert Derolez, *The Palaeography of Gothic Manuscript Books, from the Twelfth to the Early Sixteenth Century* (Cambridge: Cambridge University Press, 2003); Paul Needham, "Palaeography and the Earliest Printing Types," in *Johannes Gutenberg—Regionale Aspekte des frühen Buchdrucks,* ed. Holger Nickel and Lothar Gillner (Berlin: Staatsbibliothek zu Berlin, 1993), 19–27.

7. The classic work on type is Updike, *Printing Types;* see also A. J. Johnson, *Type Designs: Their History and Development,* 3rd ed. (Norwich: Andre Deutsch, 1966; orig. pub. 1934).

8. The word *hybrida* is now more commonly used of mixed styles; see Derolez, *Palaeography of Gothic Manuscript Books,* 20, on the system of Lieftinck, and discussion of these terms on p. 124.

9. Ibid., 124.

10. See my discussion in *Myth of Print Culture,* 22–28.

11. Needham, *Bradshaw Method;* Henry Bradshaw, *Collected Papers* (Cambridge: Cambridge University Press, 1889).

12. Robert Proctor, *Index to Early Printed Books in the British Museum . . . to the Year 1500* (London: Kegan Paul, 1898). Irritatingly, BMC does not provide the Proctor number that is the basis for the order of entries in the catalogue.

13. Proctor, *Index to Early Printed Books,* 13.

14. Konrad Haebler, *Typenrepertorium der Wiegendrucke,* 5 vols. (Leipzig, 1905–24); Konrad Burger, *Monumenta Germaniae et Italiae Typographica: Deutsche und italienische Inkunabeln in getreuen Nachbildungen,* 10 vols. (Berlin, 1892–1913).

15. www.bsb-muenchen.de/inkunabel.181.0.html (=BSB-Ink).

16. See my discussion in *Out of Sorts,* 20–24.

17. See William Blades, *The Life and Typography of William Caxton, England's First Printer,* 2 vols. (London: J. Lilly, 1861–63), pl. XVI and XIII comparing types 3 and 5. There are seventeen varieties of *s* and twelve varieties of *e* in type 3, eleven and four respectively in type 5 (many of these of course would have been considered identical by Caxton).

18. George Painter, *William Caxton: A Quincentenary Biography of England's First Printer* (London: Chatto & Windus, 1976), 95. On Veldener, see Wytze Hellinga and Lotte Hellinga, *The Fifteenth-Century Printing Types of the Low Countries,* trans. D. A. S. Reid, 2 vols. (Amsterdam: Hertzberger, 1966).

19. Paul Needham and Blaise Agüera y Arcas, "Temporary Matrices and Elemental Punches in Gutenberg's DK Type," in *Incunabula and Their Readers: Printing, Selling and Using Books in the Fifteenth Century,* ed. Kristian Jensen (London: British Library, 2003), 1–12; see also my "Note on Some Fifteenth-Century Types of Johannes Koelhoff," *PBSA* 97 (2003): 167–82, and *Out of Sorts,* chap. 2.

20. See the discussion of this problem in Mores, *Dissertation upon English Typographical Founders and Founderies (1778),* 17–23, and, in the same volume, the facsimile reproduction of "A Catalogue and Specimen of the Typefoundry of John James" (1782). See also the type-specimen book of the Bodoni Press: *Fregi e majuscole incise e fuse da Giambattista Bodoni, direttore della Stamperia reale* (1771; facs. ed., Cambridge, MA: Friends of the Harvard College Library, 1982).

21. Johnson, *Type Designs,* chap. 3, "Roman: The Development of Modern Face"; Updike, *Printing Types,* 2:188–219; Warren Chappell, *A Short History of the Printed Word* (New York: Knopf, 1970), 143–45. See also Martin Antonetti, "Typographic Ekphrasis: The Description of Typographic Forms in the Nineteenth Century," *Word and Image* 15 (1999): 44–45.

22. John Carter and Graham Pollard, *An Enquiry into the Nature of Certain Nineteenth Century Pamphlets,* 2nd ed., ed. Nicolas Barker and John Collins (London: Scolar Press, 1983; orig. pub. 1934), chap. 5, "The Typographical Evidence," 56–70.

23. William Morris, "On the Artistic Qualities of the Woodcut Books of Ulm and Augsburg in the Fifteenth Century," *Bibliographica* 1 (1895): 437–55;

William S. Peterson, *The Kelmscott Press: A History of William Morris's Typographical Adventure* (Berkeley: University of California Press, 1991), esp. chaps. 2 and 3, pp. 41–104.

24. The term persists in typography, although its meaning varies: I cannot determine what the word *gothic* means in the twentieth century Blackfriars Type Foundery "Jobbing Series" specimen book, where it is used to refer to a number of bold, sans serif typefaces of various styles.

25. B. L. Ullman, *The Origin and Development of Humanistic Script* (Rome: Edizioni di storia e letteratura, 1960); Stanley Morison, "Early Humanistic Script and the First Roman Type," *The Library*, ser. 4, 24 (1943): 1–29.

26. Lucien Febvre, *Le Problème de l'incroyance au xvie siècle: La religion de Rabelais* (Paris: Michel, 1947); the date of *L'Apparition du livre* is 1958. See above, n. 1.

27. Similar attempts to write a narrative of "gothic" typography in the eighteenth century also are a case of petitio principii. See Nick Groom, *The Making of Percy's "Reliques"* (Oxford: Clarendon Press, 1999), 202; Joseph A. Dane and Svetlana Djananova, "The Typographical Gothic: A Cautionary Note on the Title Page to Percy's *Reliques of Ancient English Poetry*," *Eighteenth-Century Life* 29 (2005): 76–96, repr., Dane, *Out of Sorts*, chap. 4.

28. An example is Talbot Baines Reed, *A History of the Old English Letter Founderies,* ed. by A. F. Johnson (1887; London: Faber & Faber, 1952), 45 (on the efficiency of Aldine italics): "Aldus intended to use it for printing his projected small editions of the classics, which would have been bulky volumes if printed either in the roman or gothic character" (45n.2). See my critique of this notion of economy in *Out of Sorts,* chap. 3.

29. On the economics of such presumed efficiency, see Dane and Gillespie, "Myth of the Cheap Quarto," 25–45; Aldine editions were not cheap.

30. I believe Martin Lowry argues both sides of this question on the same page; Lowry, *The World of Aldus Manutius: Business and Scholarship in Renaissance Venice* (Ithaca: Cornell University Press, 1979), 135. See also Brian Richardson, "The Diffusion of Literature in Renaissance Italy," conflating the "portability" of Aldine books with an undefined "readability," in *Literary Cultures and the Material Book,* ed. Simon Eliot, Andrew Nash, and Ian Willison (London: British Library, 2007), 175–89.

Chapter Seven   Illustrations

1. Arthur M. Hind, *An Introduction to a History of Woodcut,* 2 vols. (1935; repr., New York: Dover, 1963), chap. 3, "The Origin of Woodcut, with a Survey of Single Cuts before the Period of Book-Illustration," 1:64–206; and Hind, *A History of Engraving and Etching from the 15th Century to the Year 1914* (1923; repr., New York: Dover, 1963), chap. 1, pp. 19–70.

2. Edward Hodnett, *English Woodcuts, 1480–1532,* 2nd ed. (Oxford: University Press, 1973; orig. pub. 1935), nos. 214–36 (*Canterbury Tales*); the often-used scholar cuts are nos. 926 and 927. David Carlson, "The Woodcut Illustrations of the Canterbury Tales, 1483–1602," *The Library,* ser. 6, 19 (1997): 25–67.

3. Such factotum images also appear in early English printing; Martha W. Driver, *The Image in Print: Book Illustration in Late Medieval England and its Sources* (London: British Library, 2004), chap. 2.

4. Among comprehensive catalogues of images is Albert Schramm, *Der Bilderschmuck der Frühdrucke,* 23 vols. (Leipzig: Hiersemann, 1921–83); and Hodnett, *English Woodcuts.* Large uppercase letters are included in facsimile leaves of VGT.

5. The best guide to these processes is Bamber Gascoigne, *How to Identify Prints: A Complete Guide to Manual and Mechanical Processes from Woodcut to Ink-Jet* (New York: Thames and Hudson, 1986); for mezzotint and aquatint, see secs. 16–17.

6. See ibid., sec. 47b.

7. Dante, *Divina Commedia* (Florence: Nicolaus Laurentii, Alamanus, 1477), BMC VI, 628; see also Antonius Bettini de Senis, *Monte santo di Dio* (Florence: Nicolaus Laurentii, Alamanus, 1477), BMC VI, 626.

8. See my *Abstractions of Evidence in the Study of Manuscripts and Early Printed Books* (Aldershot: Ashgate, 2009), chap. 7, "Formal Perfection and Historical Perfection in the 1476 Boccaccio by Colard Mansion: Note on a Note by Seymour De Ricci," 119–27.

9. The best history is Michael Twyman, *Early Lithographed Books: A Study of the Design and Production of Improper Books in the Age of the Hand Press* (London: Farrand Press, 1990).

10. Gascoigne, *How to Identify Prints,* sec. 34.

11. See ibid., secs. 38–39; for differences in appearance, see sec. 55r.

12. Ibid., sec. 41.

13. There was theoretically another way to do this: that is to mask first the black portions and print red, then mask the red portions and print black. But this process means that if there are "islands" of one color (that is, a red word surrounded by black) there can be no "islands" of the other (black surrounded by red). More elaborate uses of this same process could be used to print in three colors, as in the color-printing of arms in *The Book of Hawking, Hunting, and Heraldry* (St. Albans, not before 1486), Goff B1030.

14. See Irving Masson, *The Mainz Psalters and Canon Missae, 1457–1459* (London: Bibliographical Society, 1954).

15. See, among many studies by Robert N. Essick, *William Blake at the Huntington: An Introduction to the William Blake Collection in the Henry E. Huntington Library* (San Marino, CA: Huntington Library, 1994); and for the most concise description of Blake's technique, Robert N. Essick, ed., *William Blake:*

Visions of the Daughters of Albion (San Marino, CA: Huntington Library, 2002), 21–24. See also William Blake Archive, www.blakearchive.org.

16. Most incunable catalogues provide special sections for these books: the British Museum Catalogue (BMC), the catalogue of the Bibliothèque Nationale (CIBN), and the incunable catalogue from the Huntington Library include blockbooks; the Incunable Short Title Catalogue (ISTC), a union catalogue produced by the British Library, omits them.

17. Text in Gottfried Zedler, *Von Coster zu Gutenberg: Der holländische Frühdruck und die Erfindung des Buchdrucks* (Leipsiz: Hiersemann, 1921), 132–34, English translation available in J. H. Hessels, trans., *The Haarlem Legend of the Invention of Printing by Lourens Janszoon Coster, critically examined by A. Van der Linde* (London, 1871).

18. Stevenson dates the earliest extant blockbooks four or five years earlier than the earliest extant printed books, and only these support the myth of the transitional. The earliest (Schreiber *Apo.* I) is dated by Stevenson on the basis of paper evidence as 1450–51. Allan Stevenson, "The Problem of the Blockbooks," in *Blockbücher des Mittelalters: Bilderfolgen als Lektüre,* ed. Elke Purpus (Mainz: Gutenberg Gesellschaft, 1991), 229–62. Elke Purpus argues for an earlier date; "Die Blockbücher der Apokalpyse," in *Blockbücher des Mittelalters,* 81–97. For early woodcut history, see the catalogue for the 2005 exhibition at the National Gallery, Parshall and Schoch, *Origins of European Printmaking;* and for blockbooks generally, the many studies of Palmer, for example, "Blockbooks, Woodcut and Metalcut Single Sheets."

19. Stevenson, "Problem of the Blockbooks."

20. Joseph A. Dane, "The Huntington Blockbook Apocalypse (Schreiber, IV/V), with a note on Terminology," *Printing History* 42 (2001): 3–15.

21. Stevenson, "Problem of the Blockbooks," so defines editions as the set of plates and refers to units within these editions as "impressions"; see further chapter 11 below.

Chapter Eight   Bindings

1. Among many studies, Nicholas Pickwoad, "The Interpretation of Bookbinding Structure: An Examination of the Sixteenth-Century Bindings in the Ramey Collection in the Pierpont Morgan Library," *The Library,* ser. 17, 3 (1995): 209–49.

2. E. P. Goldschmidt, *Gothic and Renaissance Bookbindings,* 1:36. The same notion can be found in many brief surveys of binding, for example, P. J. M. Marks, *The British Library Guide to Bookbinding: History and Techniques* (London: British Library, 1998).

3. Stuart Bennett, *Trade Bookbinding in the British Isles, 1660–1800* (New Castle, DE: Oak Knoll Press, 2004).

4. The figure 80 percent, although only an estimate, is ambiguous: it could apply to titles, but if 80 percent of the titles published between 1520 and

1800 were printed after 1700, this would mean that 0 percent of those printed before 1700 were trade bindings, which is clearly not what Bennett means. If the figure applies to raw numbers of books, and print-runs in the eighteenth century are significantly greater than print-runs in sixteenth century, again, the meaning of the figure is murky. See ibid., 7.

5. See Edith Diehl, *Bookbinding: Its Background and Technique* (1946; repr., New York: Dover, 1980), 1:80, on unfounded statements by the forger Guglielmo Libri on Grolier, Canevari, and Maioli.

6. David Pearson, *English Bookbinding Styles, 1450–1800* (New Castle, DE: Oak Knoll Press, 1995). On binding structures in general, see the excellent study by J. A. Szirmai, *The Archaeology of Medieval Bookbinding* (Aldershot: Ashgate, 1999).

7. See, for example, Phillip J. Pirages, *Catalogue 54* (McMinnville, OR: Phillip J. Pirages Fine Books & Manuscripts, n.d.).

8. Needham, *Incunabula from the Court Library at Donaueschingen;* or *The Nakles Collection of Incunabula: Auction Monday, 17 April 2000* (New York: Christies, 2000).

9. Wagner, "Bodleian Incunables from Bavarian Monasteries"; and Bettina Wagner, "Venetian Incunabula in Bavaria: Early Evidence for Monastic Book Purchases," in *The Books of Venice,* ed. Lisa Pon and Craig Kallendorf, Miscellanea Marciana 20 (Venice, 2007), 153–78.

10. Pearson, *English Bookbinding Styles,* appendix 1, "Diagrammatic Summary of the Chronological Progression of Binding Styles," 178–82.

11. Diehl, *Bookbinding,* 65, with reference to J. Basil Oldham, *Shrewsbury School Library Bindings: Catalogue Raisonné* (Oxford: University Press, 1943).

12. Ernst Kyriss, *Verzierte gotische Einbände im alten deutschen Sprachgebiet* (Stuttgart: Hettler, 1951–58); *Die Schwenke-Sammlung gotischer Stempel- und Einbanddurchreibungen, nach Motiven geordnet und nach Werkstatten bestimmt und beschrieben von Ilse Schunke,* Beiträge zur Inkunabelkunde, 3, 7 (Berlin: Akademie Verlag, 1979), and 3, 10 (Berlin: Akademie Verlag, 1996). See also Michael Laird and Paul Needham, "Unofficial Index to Ilse Schunke's *Die Schwenke-Sammlung,*" BibSite, http://www.bibsocamer.org/BibSite/Laird -Needham/schwenke.html. Works on English binding include Strickland Gibson, *Early Oxford Bindings* (Oxford: Oxford University Press, 1903); among many works by J. Basil Oldham, *English Blind-Stamped Bindings* (Cambridge: Cambridge University Press, 1952); G. D. Hobson, *English Binding before 1500* (Cambridge: Cambridge University Press, 1929). See also Mirjam M. Foot, *History of Book Binding as Mirror of Society* (London: British Library, 1999); Staffan Fogelmark, *Flemish and Related Panel-Stamped Binding, Evidence and Principles* (New York: Bibliographical Society of America, 1990).

13. An excellent and often reproduced example is Jan van der Heyden's painting "Library Interior with Still Life" (1712) from the Norton Simon Museum in Pasadena, CA.

14. Jeff Weber, *The Fore-Edge Paintings of John T. Beer: A Biographical and Historical Essay Followed by a Catalogue Raisonné Based on the Sale of His Library. With a Prologue: The ABC's of Fore-Edge Painting* (Los Angeles: Jeff Weber Rare Books, 2006).

Chapter Nine Marks in Books

1. Seymour De Ricci, *English Collectors of Books and Manuscripts (1530–1930) and Their Marks of Ownership* (Cambridge: Cambridge University Press, 1930); David Pearson, *Provenance Research in Book History* (New Castle, DE: Oak Knoll, 1998). See also the online bibliography by William Hamlin, "Important Works and Web Sites for the Study of Early Modern English Libraries," *Early Modern English Library Catalogues: A Working Bibliography*, http://www.wsu.edu/~whamlin/important.html.

2. See Nicolas Barker, *Bibliotheca Lindesiana: The Lives and Collections of Alexander William, 25th Earl of Crawford and 8th Earl of Balcarres, and James Ludovic, 26th Earl of Crawford and 9th Earl of Balcarres* (London: Quaritch, 1977), for the influence of T. F. Dibdin on nineteenth-century English collecting.

3. W. Carew Hazlitt, *A Roll of Honour: A Calendar of the names of over 17,000 men and women who throughout the British Isles and in our Early Colonies have collected MSS. and printed books from the xivth to the xix century* (New York, 1908).

4. Anthony Grafton, "Gabriel Harvey's Marginalia: New Light on the Cultural History of Elizabethan England," *Princeton University Library Chronicle* 52 (1990): 21–24.

5. See my "'Si vis archetypas habere nugas': Authorial Subscriptions in Politian, *Miscellanea* (Florence: Miscomini 1489)," *Harvard Library Bulletin*, n.s., 10 (1999): 12–22.

6. See Paul Needham "Copy Description in Incunable Catalogues," *PBSA* 95 (2001): 173–239; Ursula Baurmeister, "The Recording of Marks of Provenance in the Bibliothèque Nationale de France and Other French Libraries," *PBSA* 91 (1997): 525–38. Paul Needham's *Index Possessorum Incunabulorum* (IPI) is now available online from the Consortium of European Research Libraries, http://ipi.cerl.org/cgi-bin/search.pl.

7. For example, Ida Maïer, *Les Manuscrits d'Ange Politien: catalogue descriptif* (Geneva: Droz, 1965), "Les annotations, les collations, et les ex-libris," 329ff.

8. BSB-Ink (online); Vera Sack, *Die Inkunabeln der Universitätsbibliothek und anderer öffentlicher Sammlungen in Freiberg und Umgebung* (Freiburg im Breisgau: Harrassowitz, 1985), vol. 3.

9. On Van Ess's books, see Milton McC. Gatch, ed., *"So precious a foundation": The Library of Leander van Ess at the Burke Library of Union Theological*

Seminary in the City of New York (New York: Grolier Club, 1996); Gatch, *The Library of Leander van Ess and the Earliest American Collections of Reformation Pamphlets* (New York: Bibliographical Society of America, 2007; and related materials on his website www.miltongatch.us. For a book-length biography, see Johannes Altenberend, *Leander van Ess: Bibelübersetzer und Bibelverbreiter zwischen katholischer Aufklärung und evangelikaler Erweckungsbewegung* (Paderborn: Bonafatius, 2001).

10. Georg Wolfgang Panzer, *Annales typographici ab artis inventae origine ad annum MD; Annales typographici ab anno MDI ad annum MDXXXVI continuati,* 11 vols. (Nuremberg: J. E. Zeh, 1793–1803).

11. Privately printed by Phillipps as *Catalogus Incunabulorum Professoris et Doctoris Theol. L. Van Ess, Darmstaedt, nunc in Bibliothecâ deposit* [1825?]; see Milton McC. Gatch, "The Book Collections of Leander van Ess, " www .miltongatch.us.

12. For an example, see my *Abstractions of Evidence,* chap. 9, "Leander van Ess and the Panzerization of Early Books and History," 139–54.

13. See the lecture, variously titled, by Frederick W. Ashley, "The Story of the Vollbehr Collection of Incunabula," Eleventh Annual Conference on Printing Education, Library of Congress, Washington, DC, June 27, 1932; and House Committee on the Library, *Vollbehr Collection of Incunabula: Hearing Before the Committee on the Library on H.R. 6147,* 71st Cong., 2nd sess., 10 March 1930.

14. Herman Ralph Mead, *Incunabula in the Huntington Library* (San Marino, CA: Huntington Library Press, 1937). By contrast, the only Van Ess books included in the Huntington's online catalogue are those with his name; sales records, however, clearly identify books of his ownership. The Huntington online catalogue was generated from the card catalogue—a process that is responsible for some of these discrepancies.

15. The Huntington Library and the Library of Congress are still competitors in their collections of incunables, a direct result of Van Ess's manipulation of the book trade; the Huntington claims the larger number of titles, the Library of Congress claims the larger number of book-copies, due to their retention of duplicates.

Chapter Ten   Books in Books and Books from Books

1. Paul Needham, *The Printer and the Pardoner* (Washington, DC: Library of Congress, 1986).

2. What is contained in RB 102547 is only part of the bibliographical book—the *Opuscula* printed by Koelhoff. The second part of the bibliographical book is Bonaventure's *Apologia* printed by Unkel, a book that Koelhoff added to many copies of his *Opuscula.* In some of these, Koelhoff printed a

single title page for both parts; others have a manuscript title page. Others, such as this copy with only the quires printed by Koelhoff (not the Unkel *Apologia*), must have been issued alone. On this book, see my *Abstractions of Evidence,* chap. 9, "Leander van Ess and the Panzerization of Early Books and History," 139–54.

3. *Inkunabelkatalog der Bayerischen Staatsbibliothek* (BSB-Ink) (http://www.bsb-muenchen.de/inkunabeln.181.0.html), see main entry.

4. Such volumes can be found, somewhat unsystematically, by searching for "PV" (Pamphlet Volume) as a keyword search in the HEHL online catalogue. But only volumes with three or more items receive this cataloguing mark.

5. Many are described by Needham, *Printer and Pardoner,* appendix B, "Caxton Tract Volumes."

6. Seth Lerer, "Medieval Literature and Early Modern Readers: Cambridge University Library Sel. 5.51–5.63," *PBSA* 97 (2003): 311–32; Alexandra Gillespie, "Caxton's Chaucer and Lydgate Quartos: Miscellanies from Manuscript to Print," *Transactions of the Cambridge Bibliographical Society* 12 (2000): 1–25. Lotte Hellinga, "A Note on Caxton's Edition," in *Table Manners for Children: "Stans Puer ad Mensam" by John Lydgate,* ed. Nicholas Orme (Salisbury: Wynkyn de Worde Society, 1990), 17–21, argues that such pamphlets were intended by their printers to be sold as miscellanies. Alexandra Gillespie, "Poets, Printers and Early English Sammelbände," *Huntington Library Quarterly* 67 (2004): 189–214, argues that de Worde and retailers may have made up composite volumes in house, as well as selling separate pamphlets.

7. See Needham, *Printer and Pardoner,* 65, and item #3.

8. Corsten, "Ulrich Zells früheste Produktion," 68–76, notes that libraries are full of these. See also Jenkinson, "Ulrich Zell's Early Quartos." Proctor numbers above are those assigned by the Huntington.

9. BSB-Ink, item G-140 (Cologne: Unkel 1480) prints as a single edition Gerson's *Conclusiones de diversis materiis moralibus; Opusculum tripartitum de praeceptis decalogi; De confessione; De arte moriendi;* these works are published as separate pamphlets by Zell (see following note).

10. Gerson, *Conclusiones de diversis materiis, Alphabetum divini amoris, Opus tripartitum,* BMC I, 179–80 (shelfmarks IA 2709, 2718, and 1722). Two of these works are together in the HEHL copy described above.

11. Coates et al., *Catalogue of Books Printed in the Fifteenth Century Now in the Bodleian Library,* 313.

12. See chapter 4, n. 11 on further bibliographical inconveniences of these Zell volumes.

13. See, for example, the thirteen Savaronola pamphlets, by various Florentine printers, in the Huntington pamphlet volume PV 1105:1–13.

14. BSB-Ink, item C-358; BMC VII, 1145. BSB-Ink assigns this to Padua 1481–82; ISTC lists as Venice, based on Hain 5268*.

15. This is the same order of texts given in the descriptions of ISTC and GW 6948.

16. Superscripts in this formula refer to the alternating number of leaves in each section of quires; that is, the section signed aa–tt consists of quires of six or eight leaves.

17. Further examples can be easily seen by leafing through any incunable catalogue listing works by author and title. In CIBN, the four texts, *De officiis, De amicitia, De senectute,* and *Paradoxa stoicorum,* are often found together in editions beginning with Sweynhem and Pannartz (1469) and continuing through the 1480s (examples from Rome, Milan, Venice, Paris, and Lyons).

18. Early incunabulists saw such fragments as evidence of early printing and ignored their context; more recent bibliographers are more interested in the evidence they provide about a book's provenance. See Paul Needham, "Fragments in Books: Dutch Prototypography in the Van Ess Library," in Gatch, *"So precious a foundation,"* 85–110.

19. The sale records make no mention of the fragments bound in to this volume and there is no reference to them in the Van Ess catalogue printed by Thomas Phillipps in 1825, even though such fragments are, from a bibliographical point of view, more interesting than either of the two books that form this *Sammelband;* see *Catalogus Incunabulorum,* #388a.

20. GW 8723–42; two more are added by Lotte Hellinga, "Further Fragments of Dutch Prototypography. A List of Findings since 1938," *Quaerendo* 2 (1972): 182–99. Only one other Donatus in Pontanus type is presently in an American library; Zoltan Haraszti, "Two Donatus Fragments," *More Books: Bulletin of the Boston Public Library* 20 (1945): 9–26. See the catalogue and plates by Hellinga and Hellinga, *Fifteenth-Century Printing Types,* 1:4–9 (prototypography), and plates 9–10. See also the earlier, and in many respects more satisfactory, photographic reproductions in Zedler, *Von Coster zu Gutenberg,* Tafeln I–IV. A reference edition for early printed Donatus texts is in Paul Schwenke, *Die Donat- und Kalender-Type: Nachtrag und Übersicht* (Mainz, 1903), 37–49. For a caveat on measurement, see my *Myth of Print Culture,* 75–82.

21. Included in an early edition of the *Postilla* by Sweynheim and Pannartz is a letter of Giovanni Andrea Bussi to Pope Sixtus IV asking for support for printing. This includes a list of books, each of which is given an edition size of 275 or 300. Among these books are Donatus grammars: "Donati pro puerulis ut inde principium dicendi sumamus: unde imprimendi initium sumpsimus: numero trecenti CCC." Rudolf Hirsch is skeptical of this figure, suggesting that it is only one that "seemed about right" to those who gave it; Hirsch, "The Size of Editions of Books Produced by Sweynheim and Pannartz between 1465 and 1471," *Gutenberg Jahrbuch* (1957): 46–47.

22. See my *Myth of Print Culture,* chap. 2, "Twenty Million Incunables Can't Be Wrong," 32–56, on some of the consequences of imagining that these entries represent typical cases.

23. See Needham, "Fragments in Books."

24. Francis Fry, *A Description of the Great Bible, 1539 and the six editions of Cranmer's Bible; also of the editions, in large folio, of the Authorized Version of the*

Holy Scriptures, printed in the years 1611, 1613, 1617, 1634, 1640 . . . (London: Willis and Sotheran, 1865).

25. *A Noble Fragment: Being a Leaf of the Gutenberg Bible (1453–1455), with a Bibliographical Essay by A. Edward Newton* (New York: Gabriel Wells, 1921). See further Christopher de Hamel and Joel Silver, *Disbound and Dispersed: The Leaf Book Considered* (Chicago: Caxton Club, 2005).

26. T. A. Birrell, "Anthony Wood, John Bagford, and Thomas Hearne as Bibliographers," in *Pioneers in Bibliography,* ed. Robin Myers and Michael Harris (Winchester, Hampshire: St. Paul's Bibliographies, 1988), 25–39. See further, Arthur Freeman, "*Everyman* and Others, Part I: Some Fragments of Early English Printing, and their Preservers," *The Library,* ser. 7, 9 (2008): 267–305. See also chapter 11 below on ideal copy.

27. Konrad Haebler, *German Incunabula: 111 Original Leaves,* trans. André Barbey, 2 vols. (Munich: Weiss & Co., 1927); Haebler, *Italian Incunabula: 110 Original Leaves,* trans. André Barbey (Munich: Weiss & Co., 1927); Haebler, *West-European Incunabula: 60 Original Leaves from the Presses of the Netherlands, France, Iberia, and Great Britain,* trans. André Barbey (Munich: Weiss & Co., 1928).

28. VGT (*Veröffentlichungen der Gesellschaft für Typenkunde*) was designed to illustrate Haebler's *Typenrepertorium der Wiegendrucke.*

29. Henry Bradshaw, "List of the Founts of Type and Woodcut Devices Used by Printers in Holland in the Fifteenth Century" (Memorandum 3, June 1871), in *Collected Papers,* 258–79; Needham, *Bradshaw Method.*

30. Mead, *Incunabula in the Huntington Library;* the fragments receive a modified "starred" entry. See further my "Herman R. Mead's *Incunabula in the Huntington Library* and the Notion of 'Typographical Value,'" *Bulletin of the Bibliographical Society of Australia and New Zealand* 28 (2004): 24–40.

31. HEHL, Inst. Arch. 34.22.4.2, "Report on Incunables for 1927," 9.

Chapter Eleven   Goals of Enumerative and Descriptive Bibliography

1. A. W. Pollard and G. R. Redgrave, *A Short-Title Catalogue of Books Printed in England, Scotland, and Ireland, and of English Books Printed Abroad (1475–1640)* (1926) [= STC1], 2nd ed., 3 vols., revised and enlarged by W. A. Jackson, F. S. Ferguson, and Katharine F. Pantzer (London: Bibliographical Society, 1976–91) [= STC2]. See David McKitterick, "'Not in STC': Opportunities and Challenges in the ESTC," *The Library,* ser. 6, 2 (2005): 178–94.

2. W. W. Greg, *A Bibliography of the English Printed Drama to the Restoration,* 4 vols. (London: Bibliographical Society, 1939–59).

3. To include description of paper stocks requires a limited number of copies and extensive resources of space: see for an example the entries on Caxton by Paul Needham in the recent BMC volume (XI): *England* (2007).

4. This obviously occurs only when a small number of quires has *too few* sheets. If only one or two quires has *too many*, it is unlikely to make economic sense to reset all remaining quires to even out the numbers.

5. The same procedure might be used to get copies on the market more quickly: a printer prints off one hundred copies of initial quires, three hundred of later quires. There are now one hundred copies ready to be marketed; the printer then completes the remaining two hundred copies of the initial quires while the first one hundred copies are being sold. For critique, see Martin Boghardt, "Partial Duplicate Setting: Means of Rationalization or Complicating Factor in Textual Transmission," *The Library,* ser. 6, 15 (1993): 306–31.

6. The standard discussion remains Bowers, *Principles of Bibliographical Description,* esp. 113–23.

7. The term *shared printing* as commonly used in bibliography is misleading; it refers to cases where printers or publishers share in what could be called the publishing or distribution of a book and are named on the title page or in the colophon. In most of these cases, the actual printing is done by only one of those printers.

8. See W. W. Greg, *The Variants in the First Quarto of "King Lear": A Bibliographical and Critical Inquiry* (Oxford: University Press, 1940), variant #13. In this case neither the error nor its apparent correction is correct; the correct reading may well be Folio's "ancient."

9. In the nineteenth century, with the development of stereotyping, this definition of edition will have to change. After a forme is set, a paper mold is taken of the standing type, and that forme can be stored and used to create a new plate of type at any future time. In the context of literary history and textual history, edition refers of course to something else entirely—an act of an editor (e.g., Erasmus edited Terence, and each subsequent printing is still the same "Erasmus edition").

10. The word *state* is reserved by Pantzer for engravings.

11. I assume there is no sense of priority in STC's numbering of 5069 and 5070; it would be just as accurate to refer to 5069 as the "var. ed."

12. The decimal is used only because a third variant was discovered after the numbers were assigned in STC1. The number 5076.3 has no more relation to 5076 than the next sequential number would, but the language and conventions of STC does not indicate to me whether STC considers 5076.3 a variant of 5076 or a variant of the combined edition/issue 5075–76. For further discussion, see my *Who Is Buried in Chaucer's Tomb,* 5–8.

13. Dennis E. Rhodes, "La Publication des comédies de Térence au xve siècle," in *Le Livre dans l'Europe de la Renaissance, Actes du XXVIIIe Colloque international d'études humanistes de Tours,* ed. Pierre Aquilon and Henri-Jean Martin (Paris, 1988), checklist on p. 295.

14. Ibid., 286.

15. *Indice generale degli incunaboli delle bibliotheche d'Italia,* 6 vols. (Rome: Libreria dello Stato, 1943–81) (= IGI).

16. See my "A Ghostly Twin Terence, 21 July 1475; IGI 9422, 9423," *The Library,* ser. 6, 21 (1999): 99–107, where I believe I come to the opposite conclusion. For similar cases, see my *Abstractions of Evidence,* 190–200; and on early Zell quartos, Jenkinson, "Ulrich Zell's Early Quartos," and above, chapter 4, n. 11.

17. See Boghardt, "Partial Duplicate Setting"; and n. 5 above.

18. See my *Myth of Print Culture,* chap. 4, "The Notion of Variant and the Zen of Collation," 88–113.

Chapter Twelve   The Ersatz Book I

1. "Such recreations became not so much a substitute for the original, but, in the eyes of many, the original itself." David McKitterick, "Old Faces and New Acquaintances: Typography and the Association of Ideas," *PBSA* 87 (1993): 170.

2. See, for example, John Heywood, *A Mery play betwene the pardoner and the frere* (1533), Malone Society Reprints (Oxford: University Press 1984).

3. Gascoigne, *How to Identify Prints,* sec. 36, photogalvanographs; sec. 41, photolithographs; sec. 42, relief. See further chapter 7 above.

4. The facsimile of the Ellesmere manuscript produced by the Huntington Library is in two forms: some are in full color; others are monochrome. The monochrome edition is easily within the budget of even the casual Chaucer scholar; Geoffrey Chaucer, *The Canterbury Tales: The New Ellesmere Chaucer Monochromatic Facsimile,* ed. Daniel Woodward and Martin Stevens (San Marino, CA: Huntington Library, 1997).

5. For a list of these early facsimiles, see John Stephen Farmer, *A Handlist to the Tudor facsimile texts; old English plays printed & ms. rarities, exact collotype reproductions in folio & quarto* (issued for subscribers) (1914).

6. For example, Greg, *Variants in the First Quarto of "King Lear."*

7. Helge Kökeritz, ed., *Mr. William Shakespeares Comedies, Histories, and Tragedies: A Facsimile Edition* (New Haven: Yale University Press, 1954); Hinman, *First Folio of Shakespeare.* For a survey of earlier facsimile projects, see Charlton Hinman, "The Halliwell-Phillipps Facsimile of the First Folio of Shakespeare," *Shakespeare Quarterly* 5 (1954): 395–401; see also T. H. Hubeart, Jr., "Of Folios and Facsimiles: Photoreprints of the First Folio of Shakespeare," Pennuto.com, the website of T. H. Hubeart, Jr., 1998, http://www.pennuto.com/lit/wsfacs.htm.

8. Fredson Bowers, "The Problem of the Variant Forme in a Facsimile Edition," *The Library,* ser. 5, 7 (1952): 262–72; Bowers, "The Yale Folio Facsimile and Scholarship," *Modern Philology* 53 (1955): 50–57.

9. Facsimile editors had cleaned up what were considered illegible readings. For the relation of this to the photographic process, see Bowers's review, "Yale Folio Facsimile."

10. Ibid., 55.

11. Michael Warren, *The Complete King Lear (1608–1623)* (Berkeley: University of California Press, 1989).

12. The point is made by Ralph Hanna in a review of late-twentieth-century manuscript facsimile projects. See Hanna, review of *Facsimile of Oxford, Bodleian Library, MS Digby 86,* and *The Works of Geoffrey Chaucer and The Kingis Quair: A Facsimile of Bodleian Library, Oxford, MS Arch. Selden, B.24, Huntington Library Quarterly* 61 (1998): 107–14.

13. For examples, see Arthur Freeman, "*Everyman* and Others, Part I," esp. 279–80.

14. John Collins, *The Two Forgers: A Biography of Harry Buxton Forman and Thomas James Wise* (New Castle, DE: Oak Knoll, 1992).

15. See notes on Harris in Barker, *Bibliotheca Lindesiana.* See also Nicolas Barker, "The Forgery of Printed Documents," in *Fakes and Frauds: Varieties of Deception in Print and Manuscript,* ed. Robin Myers and Michael Harris (Winchester: St. Paul's Bibliographies, 1989), 109–20.

16. Peterson, *Kelmscott Press,* 73 and fig. 23.

17. The method, developed in the 1830s and 1840s, is described as typolithography in Twyman, *Early Lithographed Books,* 212. For early experiments in lithographing parts of early printed books, and particularly the competition organized in 1839 by Jurors of the Exposition des Produits de l'Industrie, see pp. 212–25.

18. See my *Abstractions of Evidence,* 101–18, on title pages for the 1542 Chaucer.

19. My copy of the 1602 Chaucer has a lithographic copy of the engraving of Chaucer's genealogy, one taken from the 1687 version instead of the 1598 version. The engraving (either the original or the 1687 reprint) also appears in many copies of Chaucer editions printed prior to the edition in which the engraving first appeared (for example, a New York Public Library copy of the 1561 edition); it even appears in some manuscript versions of Chaucer (for example, the important early manuscript of Chaucer MS Cambridge, Gg.4.27). I suspect that many such stray engravings are lithographic copies as well.

20. David W. J. Gill and Christopher Chippindale, "Material and Intellectual Consequences of Esteem for Cycladic Figures," *American Journal of Archaeology* 97 (1993): 601–59. For the elevation of the forgery to the status of the collectible, see William Voelkle, with Roger S. Wieck, *The Spanish Forger* (New York: Pierpont Morgan Library, 1978), on forged fifteenth- and sixteenth-century manuscript leaves, now sold as collections of the forger's work. See also the popular and useful Clifford Irving, *Fake!: The Story of Elmyr de Hory, the Greatest Art Forger of Our Time* (New York: McGraw-Hill, 1969).

21. Blades, *Life and Typography of William Caxton.*

22. Letter of Blades to Henry Bradshaw, 30 November 1857, quoted in Robin Myers, "George Isaac Frederick Tupper, Facsimilist, 'Whose ability in this description of work is beyond praise' (1820?–1911)," *Transactions of the Cambridge Bibliographical Society* 7 (1978): 113.

23. Robin Myers, "William Blades's Debt to Henry Bradshaw and G. I. F. Tupper," *The Library*, ser. 5, 5 (1978): 278; quoted also in her "George Isaac Frederick Tupper, Facsimilist," 114.

Chapter Thirteen   The Ersatz Book II

1. Paul Needham, "Gutenberg Bibles in Electronic Facsimile," *PBSA* 98 (2004): 355–63; Peter L. Shillingsburg, *From Gutenberg to Google: Electronic Representations of Literary Texts* (Cambridge: Cambridge University Press, 2006); Dane, *Myth of Print Culture*, 124–42, for notes on the *Canterbury Tales* Project; and Dane, *Out of Sorts*, 118–40, on the Piers Plowman Archive. See also on the failing support of such projects by publishers, J. Stephen Murphy, "The Death of the Editor," *Essays in Criticism* 18 (2008): 289–310; and Peter Robinson, "Current Issues in Making Digital Editions of Medieval Texts, or Do Electronic Scholarly Texts Have a Future?" *Digital Medievalist* 1 (2005), http://www.digitalmedievalist.org/journal/1.1/robinson.

2. Michael Maittaire, *Annales typographici ab artis inventae origine ad annum MD* (The Hague: Vaillant, 1719); Panzer, *Annales typographici* (1793–1803); Ludwig Hain, *Repertorium Bibliographicum*, 4 vols. (Stuttgart: Cotta, 1826–38). The best history of these catalogues in English is Paul Needham, "Counting Incunables: The IISTC CD-ROM," *Huntington Library Quarterly* 61 (1999): 457–529.

3. An example of such information is the following: "The date in the colophon reads 'secŭdo cal. Septembris,' interpreted by BMC as 2 Sept.; CIBN corrects GW's transcription." There is no reference to what is corrected; the strange "secŭdo . . ." is a transcription of *secundo cal'. septembris.*

4. *The Illustrated ISTC on CD-ROM*, gen. ed. Martin Davies (Reading, UK: Primary Source Media, 1996; 2nd ed. 1998).

5. A later, but more ambitious, digitization project is from the Bayerische Staatsbibliothek, whose goal is to digitize its entire collection of nearly ten thousand editions—one copy per edition (at present, slightly more than one thousand are available). This would constitute nearly a third of fifteenth-century books. See further Bettina Wagner, "The Present and Future of Incunable Cataloguing," *The Library*, ser. 7, 9 (2008): 197–209.

6. Needham, "Counting Incunables," 489, mischievously notes that it is now possible to search how many books have Christmas-day colophons or colophons with the date of Columbus's first New World landfall.

7. See my *Myth of Print Culture,* chap. 2, "Twenty Million Incunables Can't Be Wrong," 32–56.

8. Mead, *Incunabula in the Huntington Library.*

9. Compare the figures from earlier I-ISTC to the following questions: How many folio editions of Cicero were printed in Germany? 21 (cf. online search: 32). How many folio editions of Cicero were printed in Venice? 98 (online: 107).

10. "Dates printed in colophons in German style by saints' days or according to the Roman system of Kalends, Nones and Ides are uniformly reduced to the present-day style of day, month and year. Months are abbreviated to the first three letters of the English name of the month, except 'June' and 'July' in full, and 'Sept.' In printing towns where the year-number commonly changed on a day other than 1 January, such as Venice (1 March), Florence (25 March), and Paris (Easter), year dates from the early part of the year are often expressed in such forms as 1491/92, 1499/1500. Occasionally a printer can be shown to have used both styles of dating, common or local, indifferently, and decision is accordingly uncertain unless documentary or physical evidence (from types or woodcuts) is available. On rare occasions the date as printed is impossible in any system" (ISTC, introd.).

11. This is an objection raised also in the review of ISTC by Needham, "Counting Incunables," 514.

12. For a complex way of working around these problems by converting the database, see Jonathan Green, "Opening the Illustrated Incunable Short Title Catalogue on CD-ROM: An End-User's Approach to an Essential Database," *Digital Medievalist* 1, 1 (2005), http://www.digitalmedievalist.org/journal/1.1/green.

13. Suppose there were only one title in the USA—Caxton's *Canterbury Tales,* and there were two copies, one at HEHL and one at LC. I want to know "how many incunables are there in the USA if we don't count HEHL?" No matter how I conduct this search I get one in USA, excluding those at HEHL = 0.

14. Needham, "Counting Incunables"; Peter W. M. Blayney, "The Numbers Game: Appraising the Revised STC," *PBSA* 88 (1994): 353–407; see also Blayney, "STC Publication Statistics: Some Caveats," *The Library,* ser. 8, 4 (2007): 387–97.

15. English Short Title Catalogue, 1473–1800 (London, British Library), estc.bl.uk; Early English Books Online, eebo.chadwyck.com; Eighteenth Century Collections Online, infotrac.galegroup.com (db = ECCO).

16. Donald Wing, *A Short Title Catalogue of Books Printed in England, Scotland, Ireland, Wales, and British America and of English Books Printed in Other Countries, 1641–1700),* 3 vols. (1945–51), 2nd ed., 4 vols. (New York: Modern Language Association, 1972–98).

17. See R. C. Alston and M. Jannetta, *Bibliography: Machine Readable Cataloguing and the ESTC (A Summary History of the Eighteenth Century Short Title Catalogue)* (London: British Library, 1978); and the essays in Henry L. Snyder and Michael S. Smith, eds., *The English Short-Title Catalogue: Past, Present, Future* (New York: AMS Press, 2003).

18. Full collations were included in one of the prototypes for STC, by George W. Cole, *Check-list or Brief Catalogue of the Library of Henry E. Huntington (English Literature to 1640)* (New York, 1919).

19. See chapter 2 above. A translation is as follows: The book is numbered in leaves. There are 10 unnumbered leaves, followed by 219 leaves numbered in roman. 3 unnumbered leaves follow. Leaves 220–383 follow, numbered in roman (two consecutive leaves in this series are foliated "CCC").

20. According to the introduction, *Early English Books II* began in 1957 and included books in Wing. This project is still incomplete. These "new units" of microfilm are being digitized and will be added to EEBO. As of 2008, EEBO claimed *Early English Book* units 1–80 (STC1) are available online; as are units 1–129 of *Early English Books II* as well as the Thomason Tracts.

21. Brief histories of the company can be found on ProQuest websites, http://www.proquest.com. G. W. Cooke, "Eugene B. Power: Father of Preservation Microfilming," *Conservation Administration News* 54 (1993): 5. UMI was sold to Xerox in 1962 and to Bell and Howell in 1985.

22. Early English Books Online—Text Creation Partnership, "Project Description/Goals and Strategies," http://eebo.chadwyck.com/. That this accuracy rate is grossly overstated is a point made by William Sherman in "EEBO: The Missing Manual," delivered at the Renaissance Society of America Conference, San Francisco, CA, March 2006.

23. None of the books I know best (sixteenth-century folio editions of Chaucer; the folios of Shakespeare) were among the 25,000 books in the database (at least, I could not find them.)

24. This of course raised another absurd but very real problem, which was keeping the two databases running simultaneously on a home computer.

25. I should note that it is not always possible to reproduce these results; in my second attempt, I could not search "high" fuzziness and received negative results, explained by the cryptic error message (or correction): "failover from medium/high to low." I think I understand this, but I had to check Wikipedia to be sure.

26. Eric Holzenberg, *Lasting Impressions: The Grolier Club Library* (New York: Grolier Club, 2004), 23–24. At the Huntington, according to its Readers Services Department in 2011, the call for STC books has decreased since the availability of EEBO.

SELECTED BIBLIOGRAPHY

Altenberend, Johannes. *Leander van Ess: Bibelübersetzer und Bibelverbreiter zwischen katholischer Aufklärung und evangelikaler Erweckungsbewegung.* Paderborn: Bonafatius, 2001.

Ashley, Frederick W. "The Story of the Vollbehr Collection of Incunabula." Eleventh Annual Conference on Printing Education, Library of Congress, Washington, DC, June 27, 1932.

Bain, Peter, and Paul Shaw, eds. *Blackletter: Type and National Identity.* New York: Cooper Union, 1998.

Barker, Nicolas. *Bibliotheca Lindesiana: The Lives and Collections of Alexander William, 25th Earl of Crawford and 8th Earl of Balcarres, and James Ludovic, 26th Earl of Crawford and 9th Earl of Balcarres.* London: Quaritch, 1977.

————. "The Forgery of Printed Documents." In *Fakes and Frauds: Varieties of Deception in Print and Manuscript,* ed. Robin Myers and Michael Harris. Winchester: St. Paul's Bibliographies, 1989. 109–20.

Barnard, John, and D. F. McKenzie, eds. *The Cambridge History of the Book in Britain.* Vol. 4, *1558–1695.* Cambridge: Cambridge University Press, 2002.

Bayerische Staatsbibliothek Inkunabelkatalog. 7 vols. Wiesbaden: Reichert Verlag, 1988–. http://www.bsb-muenchen.de/inkunabeln.181.0.html.

Bennett, Stuart. *Trade Bookbinding in the British Isles, 1660–1800.* Newcastle, DE: Oak Knoll Press, 2004.

Bibliothèque Nationale. *Catalogue des Incunables.* 2 vols. Paris: Bibliothèque Nationale, 1981–2006.

Bidwell, John. "The Study of Paper as Evidence, Artefact, and Commodity." In *The Book Encompassed: Studies in Twentieth-Century Bibliography,* ed. Peter Davison. Cambridge: Cambridge University Press, 1992. 69–82.

Blades, William. *The Life and Typography of William Caxton, England's First Printer.* 2 vols. London: J. Lilly, 1861–63.

Bland, Mark. *A Guide to Early Printed Books and Manuscripts.* Chichester: Wiley-Blackwell, 2010.

Blayney, Peter W. M. "The Numbers Game: Appraising the Revised STC." *PBSA* 88 (1994): 353–407.

―――. *The Texts of King Lear and Their Origins.* Vol. 1, *Nicholas Okes and the First Quarto.* Cambridge: Cambridge University Press, 1982.

Boghardt, Martin. "Partial Duplicate Setting: Means of Rationalization or Complicating Factor in Textual Transmission." *The Library,* ser. 6, 15 (1993): 306–31.

Bowers, Fredson. *Principles of Bibliographical Description.* Princeton: Princeton University Press, 1949.

―――. "The Problem of the Variant Forme in a Facsimile Edition." *The Library,* ser. 5, 7 (1952): 262–72.

―――. "The Yale Folio Facsimile and Scholarship." *Modern Philology* 53 (1955): 50–57.

Bradshaw, Henry. *Collected Papers of Henry Bradshaw.* Cambridge: Cambridge University Press, 1889.

Briquet, C. M. *Les Filigranes.* Ed. Allan Stevenson. 4 vols. Amsterdam: Paper Publications Society, 1968. Originally published 1907.

Burger, Konrad. *Monumenta Germaniae et Italiae Typographica: Deutsche und italienische Inkunabeln in getreuen Nachbildungen.* 10 vols. Berlin, 1892–1913.

Carter, John. *ABC for Book Collectors.* 8th ed. Ed. Nicolas Barker. Newcastle, DE: Oak Knoll, 2004. Originally published 1951.

―――, and Graham Pollard. *An Enquiry into the Nature of Certain Nineteenth Century Pamphlets.* 2nd ed. Ed. Nicolas Barker and John Collins. London: Scolar Press, 1983. Originally published 1934.

Catalogue of Books Printed in the XVth Century Now in the British Museum. 13 vols. 1908; London: British Museum, 1963–.

Chappell, Warren. *A Short History of the Printed Word.* New York: Knopf, 1970.

Coates, Alan et al., eds. *A Catalogue of Books Printed in the Fifteenth Century Now in the Bodleian Library.* Oxford: Oxford University Press, 2005.

Collins, John. *The Two Forgers: A Biography of Harry Buxton Forman and Thomas James Wise.* New Castle, DE: Oak Knoll, 1992.

Corsten, Severin. "Ulrich Zells früheste Produktion." *Gutenberg Jahrbuch* (2007): 68–76.

Dane, Joseph A. *Abstractions of Evidence in the Study of Manuscripts and Early Printed Books.* Aldershot: Ashgate, 2009.

―――. *The Myth of Print Culture: Essays on Evidence, Textuality, and Bibliographical Method.* Toronto: University of Toronto Press, 2003.

―――. "On Metrical Confusion and Consensus in Early Editions of Terence." *Humanistica Lovaniensia* 48 (1999): 103–31.

―――. *Out of Sorts: On Typography and Print Culture.* Philadelphia: University of Pennsylvania Press, 2010.

―――. "Perfect Order and Perfected Order: The Evidence from Press Variants of Early Seventeenth-Century Quartos." *PBSA* 90 (1996): 272–320.

————. *Who Is Buried in Chaucer's Tomb: Studies in the Reception of Chaucer's Book.* East Lansing: Michigan State University Press, 1998.

————, and Alexandra Gillespie. "The Myth of the Cheap Quarto. In *Tudor Books and Readers,* ed. John King. Cambridge: Cambridge University Press, 2009. 25–45.

De Hamel, Christopher. *A History of Illuminated Manuscripts.* 2nd ed. London: Phaidon, 1994.

————, and Joel Silver. *Disbound and Dispersed: The Leaf Book Considered.* Chicago: Caxton Club, 2005.

De Ricci, Seymour. *English Collectors of Books and Manuscripts (1530–1930) and Their Marks of Ownership.* Cambridge: Cambridge University Press, 1930.

Derolez, Albert. *Codicologie des manuscrits en écriture humanistique sur parchemin.* 2 vols. Turnhout: Brepols, 1984.

————. *The Palaeography of Gothic Manuscript Books, from the Twelfth to the Early Sixteenth Century.* Cambridge: Cambridge University Press, 2003.

Dibdin, Thomas Frognall. *Typographical Antiquities: or The History of Printing in England, Scotland, and Ireland.* 4 vols. London, 1810–19.

Diehl, Edith. *Bookbinding: Its Background and Technique.* 1946. Reprint, New York: Dover, 1980.

Eliot, Simon, Andrew Nash, and Ian Willison, eds. *Literary Cultures and the Material Book.* London: British Library, 2007.

Essick, Robert N. *William Blake at the Huntington: An Introduction to the William Blake Collection in the Henry E. Huntington Library.* San Marino, CA: Huntington Library, 1994.

Febvre, Lucien, and Henri-Jean Martin. *The Coming of the Book: The Impact of Printing 1460–1800.* Trans. David Gerard. London: Verso, 1976. Originally published 1958 as *L'apparition du livre.*

Foot, Mirjam M. *History of Book Binding as Mirror of Society.* London: British Library, 1999.

Freeman, Arthur. "*Everyman* and Others, Part I: Some Fragments of Early English Printing, and Their Preservers." *The Library,* ser. 7, 9 (2008): 267–305.

Fry, Francis. *A Description of the Great Bible, 1539 and the six editions of Cranmer's Bible; also of the editions, in large folio, of the Authorized Version of the Holy Scriptures, printed in the years 1611, 1613, 1617, 1634, 1640 . . .* London: Willis and Sotheran, 1865.

Gascoigne, Bamber. *How to Identify Prints: A Complete Guide to Manual and Mechanical Processes from Woodcut to Ink-Jet.* New York: Thames and Hudson, 1986.

Gaskell, Philip. *A New Introduction to Bibliography.* New York: Oxford University Press, 1972.

Gatch, Milton McC. *The Library of Leander van Ess and the Earliest American Collections of Reformation Pamphlets.* New York: Bibliographical Society of America, 2007.

————, ed. *"So precious a foundation": The Library of Leander van Ess at the Burke Library of Union Theological Seminary in the City of New York.* New York: Grolier Club, 1996.

Gesamtkatalog der Wiegendrucke, 10 vols. Stuttgart: Hiersemann, 1928–. http://www.gesamtkatalogderwiegendrucke.de/.

Gibson, Strickland. *Early Oxford Bindings.* Oxford: Oxford University Press, 1903.

Gillespie, Alexandra. "Caxton's Chaucer and Lydgate Quartos: Miscellanies from Manuscript to Print." *Transactions of the Cambridge Bibliographical Society* 12 (2000): 1–25.

————, ed. *Manuscript, Print, and Early Tudor Literature.* Special issue, *Huntington Library Quarterly* 67 (2004).

Goff, Frederick R. *Incunabula in American Libraries: A Third Census of Fifteenth-Century Books Recorded in North American Collections.* New York: Bibliographical Society of America, 1964.

Goldschmidt, E. P. *Gothic and Renaissance Bookbindings.* 2 vols. London: Benn, 1928.

Greg, W. W. *A Bibliography of the English Printed Drama to the Restoration.* 4 vols. London: Bibliographical Society, 1939–59.

————. "The Rationale of Copy-Text." *Studies in Bibliography* 3 (1950–51): 19–36. Reprint, *Collected Papers.* Ed. J. C. Maxwell. Oxford: Clarendon Press, 1966. 374–91.

————. *The Variants in the First Quarto of "King Lear": A Bibliographical and Critical Inquiry.* Oxford: University Press, 1940.

Haebler, Konrad. *German Incunabula: 111 Original Leaves.* Trans. André Barbey. 2 vols. Munich: Weiss & Co., 1927.

————. *Italian Incunabula: 110 Original Leaves.* Trans. André Barbey Munich: Weiss & Co., 1927.

————. *West-European Incunabula: 60 Original Leaves from the Presses of the Netherlands, France, Iberia, and Great Britain.* Trans. André Barbey. Munich: Weiss & Co., 1928.

————. *Typenrepertorium der Wiegendrucke.* 5 vols. Leipzig, 1905–24.

Hain, Ludwig. *Repertorium Bibliographicum.* 4 vols. Stuttgart: Cotta, 1826–38.

Hazlitt, W. Carew. *A Roll of Honour: A Calendar of the names of over 17,000 men and women who throughout the British Isles and in our Early Colonies have collected MSS. and printed books from the xivth to the xix century.* New York, 1908.

Hellinga, Lotte, and J. B. Trapp, eds. *Cambridge History of the Book.* Vol. 3, *1400–1557.* Cambridge: Cambridge University Press, 1999.

Hellinga, Wytze, and Lotte Hellinga. *The Fifteenth-Century Printing Types of the Low Countries.* Trans. D. A. S. Reid. 2 vols. Amsterdam: Hertzberger, 1966.

Hind, Arthur M. *A History of Engraving and Etching from the 15th Century to the Year 1914.* 1923. Reprint, New York: Dover, 1963.

———. *An Introduction to a History of Woodcut.* 2 vols. 1935. Reprint, New York: Dover, 1963.

Hinman, Charlton. *The First Folio of Shakespeare: The Norton Facsimile.* New York: W. W. Norton, 1968.

———. "The Halliwell-Phillipps Facsimile of the First Folio of Shakespeare." *Shakespeare Quarterly* 5 (1954): 395–401.

Hirsch, Rudolf. "The Size of Editions of Books Produced by Sweynheim and Pannartz between 1465 and 1471." *Gutenberg Jahrbuch* (1957): 46–47.

Hobson, G. D. *English Binding before 1500.* Cambridge: Cambridge University Press, 1929.

Hodnett, Edward. *English Woodcuts, 1480–1532.* 2nd ed. Oxford: University Press, 1973. Originally published 1935.

Hunter, Dard. *Papermaking: The History and Technique of an Ancient Craft.* 2nd ed. New York: Dover, 1978. Originally published 1947.

Husby, Scott. Bookbindings on Incunables in American Library Collections, http://www.bibsocamer.org/BibSite/Husby/.

The Illustrated ISTC on CD-ROM. Gen. ed. Martin Davies. Reading, UK: Primary Source Media, 1996; 2nd ed. 1998.

Indice generale degli incunaboli delle bibliotheche d'Italia. 6 vols. Rome: Libreria dello Stato, 1943–81.

Isaac, Frank. *English and Scottish Printing Types, 1501–58, 1508–58.* 2 vols. Oxford: Bibliographical Society, 1930–32.

Jenkinson, Francis. "Ulrich Zell's Early Quartos." *The Library,* ser. 4, 7 (1926): 46–66.

Johnson, A. J. *Type Designs: Their History and Development.* 3rd ed. Norwich: Andre Deutsch, 1966. Originally published 1934.

Kyriss, Ernst. *Verzierte gotische Einbände im alten deutschen Sprachgebiet.* Stuttgart: Hettler, 1951–58.

Laird Michael, and Paul Needham. "Unofficial Index to Ilse Schunke's *Die Schwenke-Sammlung.*" BibSite. http://www.bibsocamer.org/BibSite/Laird-Needham/schwenke.html.

Lerer, Seth. "Medieval Literature and Early Modern Readers: Cambridge University Library Sel. 5.51–5.63." *PBSA* 97 (2003): 311–32.

Maittaire, Michael. *Annales typographici ab artis inventae origine ad annum MD.* The Hague: Vaillant, 1719.

Marks, P. J. M. *The British Library Guide to Bookbinding: History and Techniques.* London: British Library, 1998.

McGann, Jerome J. *A Critique of Modern Textual Criticism.* Chicago: University of Chicago Press, 1983.

McKenzie, D. F. "Printers of the Mind: Some Notes on Bibliographical Theories and Printing-House Practices." *Studies in Bibliography* 22 (1969): 1–75.

Reprint, *Making Meaning: Printers of the Mind and Other Essays*. Ed. Peter D. McDonald and Michael F. Suarez. Amherst: University of Massachusetts Press, 2002. 13–85.

McKerrow, Ronald B. *An Introduction to Bibliography for Literary Students*. Oxford: Clarendon Press, 1927.

McKitterick, David. "'Not in STC': Opportunities and Challenges in the ESTC." *The Library*, ser. 6, 2 (2005): 178–94.

———. "Old Faces and New Acquaintances: Typography and the Association of Ideas." *PBSA* 87 (1993): 163–86.

McLaverty, James. *Pope, Print, and Meaning*. Oxford: Oxford University Press, 2001.

McLeod, Randall. "Un-Editing Shakespeare." *Sub-stance* 33 (1982): 26–55.

Mead, Herman Ralph. *Incunabula in the Huntington Library*. San Marino, CA: Huntington Library Press, 1937.

Mores, Edward Rowe. *A Dissertation upon English Typographical Founders and Founderies (1778)*. Ed. Harry Carter and Christopher Ricks. Oxford: Bibliographical Society, 1961.

Mosley, James. *Typefoundry: Documents for the History of Type and Letterforms* (blog). http://typefoundry.blogspot.com/.

Moxon, Joseph. *Mechanick Exercises on the Whole Art of Printing (1683–4)*. Ed. Herbert Davis and Harry Carter. 2nd ed. New York: Oxford University Press, 1962.

Myers, Robin. "George Isaac Frederick Tupper, Facsimilist, 'Whose ability in this description of work is beyond praise' (1820?–1911)." *Transactions of the Cambridge Bibliographical Society* 7 (1978): 113–34.

———. "William Blades's Debt to Henry Bradshaw and G. I. F. Tupper." *The Library*, ser. 5, 5 (1978): 265–83.

Needham, Paul. *The Bradshaw Method: Henry Bradshaw's Contribution to Bibliography*. Chapel Hill, NC: Hanes Foundation, 1998.

———. "Counting Incunables: The IISTC CD-ROM." *Huntington Library Quarterly* 61 (1999): 457–529.

———. "Division of Copy in the Gutenberg Bible: Three Glosses on the Ink Evidence." *PBSA* 79 (1985): 411–26.

———. "Gutenberg Bibles in Electronic Facsimile." *PBSA* 98 (2004): 355–63.

———. *Incunabula from the Court Library at Donaueschingen. Sale LN4389*. London: Sotheby's, 1994.

———. *The Printer and the Pardoner*. Washington, DC: Library of Congress, 1986.

———, and Blaise Agüera y Arcas. "Temporary Matrices and Elemental Punches in Gutenberg's DK Type." In *Incunabula and Their Readers: Printing, Selling and Using Books in the Fifteenth Century*, ed. Kristian Jensen. London: British Library, 2003. 1–12.

Nickell, Joe. *Pen, Ink, and Evidence: A Study of Writing and Writing Materials for the Penman, Collector, and Document Detective.* 1990. Reprint, New Castle, DE: Oak Knoll, 2000.

A Noble Fragment: Being a Leaf of the Gutenberg Bible (1453–1455), with a Bibliographical Essay by A. Edward Newton. New York: Gabriel Wells, 1921.

Oldham, J. Basil. *English Blind-Stamped Bindings.* Cambridge: Cambridge University Press, 1952.

Painter, George. *William Caxton: A Quincentenary Biography of England's First Printer.* London: Chatto & Windus, 1976.

Palmer, Nigel F. "Blockbooks, Woodcut and Metalcut Single Sheets." In *A Catalogue of Books Printed in the Fifteenth Century Now in the Bodleian Library,* ed. Alan Coates et al. Oxford: Oxford University Press, 2005. 1–50.

Panzer, Georg Wolfgang. *Annales typographici ab artis inventae origine ad annum MD; Annales typographici ab anno MDI ad annum MDXXXVI continuati.* 11 vols. Nuremberg: J. E. Zeh, 1793–1803.

Parshall, Peter W., Rainer Schoch et al., eds. *Origins of European Printmaking.* New Haven: Yale University Press, 2005.

Pearson, David. *English Bookbinding Styles, 1450–1800.* New Castle, DE: Oak Knoll, 1995.

———. *Provenance Research in Book History.* New Castle, DE: Oak Knoll, 1998.

Peterson, William S. *The Kelmscott Press: A History of William Morris's Typographical Adventure.* Berkeley: University of California Press, 1991.

Piccard, Gerhard. *Wasserzeichen: Findbücher.* 17 vols. Stuttgart: Kohlhammer, 1961–96. http://www.piccard-online.de/.

Pickwoad, Nicholas. "The Interpretation of Bookbinding Structure: An Examination of the Sixteenth-Century Bindings in the Ramey Collection in the Pierpont Morgan Library." *The Library,* ser. 17, 3 (1995): 209–49.

Pollard, A. W., and G. R. Redgrave. *A Short-Title Catalogue of Books Printed in England, Scotland, and Ireland, and of English Books Printed Abroad (1475–1640).* 1926. 2nd ed. 3 vols. Revised and enlarged by W. A. Jackson, F. S. Ferguson, Katharine F. Pantzer. London: Bibliographical Society, 1976–91.

Proctor, Robert. *Index to Early Printed Books in the British Museum . . . to the Year 1500.* London: Kegan Paul, 1898.

Prothero, G. W. *A Memoir of Henry Bradshaw.* London: Kegan, Paul, 1888.

Purpus, Elke, ed. *Blockbücher des Mittelalters: Bilderfolgen als Lektüre.* Mainz: Gutenberg Gesellschaft, 1991.

Reed, Talbot Baines. *A History of the Old English Letter Founderies.* 1887. Ed. A. F. Johnson. London: Faber & Faber, 1952.

Rummonds, Richard-Gabriel. *Nineteenth-Century Printing Practices and the Iron Handpress.* 2 vols. New Castle, DE: Oak Knoll, 2004.

Sack, Vera. *Die Inkunabeln der Universitätsbibliothek und anderer öffentlicher Sammlungen in Freiberg und Umgebung.* 3 vols. Freiburg im Breisgau: Harrassowitz, 1985.

Savage, William. *A Dictionary of the Art of Printing*. 1841. Reprint, London: Longman, 1941.

Die Schwenke-Sammlung gotischer Stempel- und Einbanddurchreibungen, nach Motiven geordnet und nach Werkstatten bestimmt und beschrieben von Ilse Schunke. Beiträge zur Inkunabelkunde, 3, 7. Berlin: Akademie Berlag, 1979; Beiträge zur Inkunabelkunde, 3, 10. Berlin: Akademie Berlag, 1996.

Simpson, Percy. *Proof-Reading in the Sixteenth, Seventeenth, and Eighteenth Centuries*. London: Oxford University Press, 1935.

Snyder, Henry L., and Michael S. Smith, eds. *The English Short-Title Catalogue: Past, Present, Future*. New York: AMS Press, 2003.

Steinberg, S. H. *Five Hundred Years of Printing*. New ed. Ed. John Trevitt. New Castle, DE: Oak Knoll, 1996. Originally published 1955.

Stevenson, Allan. "Paper as Bibliographical Evidence." *The Library*, ser. 5, 17 (1962): 197–202.

———. "The Problem of the Blockbooks." In *Blockbücher des Mittelalters: Bilderfolgen als Lektüre*, ed. Elke Purpus. Mainz: Gutenberg Gesellschaft, 1991. 229–62.

———. *The Problem of the Missale Speciale*. London: Bibliographical Society, 1967.

———. "Watermarks Are Twins." *Studies in Bibliography* 4 (1951): 57–91.

Stoddard, Roger E. *Marks in Books*. Cambridge: Harvard University Press, 1985.

Szirmai, J. A. *The Archaeology of Medieval Bookbinding*. Aldershot: Ashgate, 1999.

Tanselle, G. Thomas. *Bibliographical Analysis: A Historical Introduction*. Cambridge: Cambridge University Press, 2009.

Taylor, Gary, and Michael Warren, eds. *The Division of the Kingdoms: Shakespeare's Two Versions of King Lear*. Oxford: Clarendon Press, 1983.

Twyman, Michael. *Early Lithographed Books: A Study of the Design and Production of Improper Books in the Age of the Hand Press*. London: Farrand Press, 1990.

Updike, Daniel Berkeley. *Printing Types: Their History, Forms, and Use: A Study in Survivals*. 2nd ed. 2 vols. Cambridge: Harvard University Press, 1937.

Vander Meulen, David. "The Identification of Paper without Watermarks: The Example of Pope's *Dunciad*." *Studies in Bibliography* 37 (1984): 58–81.

Veröffentlichungen der Gesellschaft für Typenkunde des XV. Jahrhunderts. 32 vols. Berlin, 1907–39.

Vervliet, Hendrik D. L. *The Palaeo-typography of the French Renaissance: Selected Papers on Sixteenth-Century Typefaces*. 2 vols. Leiden: Brill, 2008.

Wagner, Bettina. "The Bodleian Incunables from Bavarian Monasteries." *Bodleian Library Record* 15 (1995): 90–107.

———. "The Present and Future of Incunable Cataloguing." *The Library*, ser. 7, 9 (2008): 197–209.

Warren, Michael. *The Complete King Lear (1608–1623)*. Berkeley: University of California Press, 1989.

————, and Gary Taylor, eds. *The Division of the Kingdoms: Shakespeare's Two Versions of King Lear.* Oxford: Clarendon Press, 1983.

Williams, William Proctor, and Craig S. Abbot. *Introduction to Bibliographical and Textual Studies.* 4th rev. ed. New York: Modern Language Association, 2009.

Wing, Donald. *A Short Title Catalogue of Books Printed in England, Scotland, Ireland, Wales, and British America and of English Books Printed in Other Countries, 1641–1700).* 3 vols. 1945–51. 2nd ed. 4 vols. New York: Modern Language Association, 1972–98.

Zedler, Gottfried. *Von Coster zu Gutenberg: Der holländische Frühdruck und die Erfindung des Buchdrucks.* Leipsiz: Hiersemann, 1921.

INDEX

registration, defined, 68

relief cut, defined, 127. *See also* woodcut

restoration and repair, 48, 64–65, 72, 156, 164–65

Rhodes, Dennis, 199

Rolewinck, Werner, 172, 173

Rosenbach, A. W., 166, 167

Rosenwald, Lessing J., 167

rotunda. *See* type classifications

Rowe, Nicholas, 41

Roxburghe, John Ker, 3rd Duke, 156, 158, 159, 160

rules, in page format, 18, 73

running heads, 18, 22, 69, 73

Sammelband, 169, 171–78; defined, 168, 171; types, 172–78

Savaronola, 176

Scheide Library, 163

schooltexts, 95. *See also* Donatus

Schunke-Schwenke catalogue, 154–55, 173

seriatim printing, 70

Shakespeare, 39, 66, 78, 80, 94, 190–91, 228; 1623 Folio, 1, 2, 6, 8, 9, 10, 18, 34, 63, 86, 96–98, 188–89; facsimiles of 1623 Folio, 204–7; *King Lear,* 1, 2, 96–99, 193–94, 204; metrics, 97–98; Norton facsimile of First Folio, 2, 205, 221; variant texts, 80–83; Yale facsimile, 205

sheet (paper): defined, 28; relation to format, 51–52

Shore, Jane, subject of pamphlet collection, 173–74

signatures, 18; defined, 31–32; inferred, 33; unsigned books, 35–36

Sotheby, Samuel L., 53–54

Speculum humanae salvationis, 138

squash, defined, 127

standing type, 12

state (bibliographical), 193–95; defined, 73, 195; variant states, 74–77

Staunton, Howard, 205, 207

stereotyping, 12, 70, 255n9

Sterne, Laurence, *Tristram Shandy,* marbled page, 25

Stevenson, Allan, 56, 140

stop-press correction, 73–77, 195

Stow, John, 198. *See also* Chaucer, early folio editions

Tate, John, 50

Terence, 44, 160; Ambergau edition, 199–200, 202; Giunta edition, 95, 100; Grüninger edition, 129; Mentelin edition, 95; representation of verse, 94–95

Text Creation Partnership (TCP), 222–24. *See also* Early English Books Online (EEBO)

textual criticism, 204–5. *See also* variants

Theobald, Lewis, 1, 2

title page, 22; importance in cataloguing, 184, 196, 201–2

Tonson, Jacob, 35

Towneley MS (Huntington Manuscript HM 1), 92

tract volume. See *Sammelband*

tranchefile, defined, 48

Tupper, G. I. F., 209–10

type: blind impressions, 72; distribution and redistribution, 69; identification, 111–15; meaning, 123; measurement, 22, 111–14; relation to page format, 18, 101; sizes, 119; "typographical value," 185; variant letterforms in early type, 115–16

typecase, defined, 67–68, 103–5

Joseph A. Dane

is professor of English

at the University of Southern California in Los Angeles.

He is the author of a number of books, including

The Long and the Short of It: A Practical Guide to European

Versification Systems (University of Notre Dame Press, 2010)

and *Out of Sorts: On Typography and Print Culture.*